THE HUMANE SOCIETY OF THE UNITED STATES

Complete Guide to

CAT CARE

THE HUMANE SOCIETY OF THE UNITED STATES

Complete Guide to
CAT CARE

Wendy Christensen

and the Staff of The Humane Society
of the United States

 ST. MARTIN'S GRIFFIN ✠ NEW YORK

THE HUMANE SOCIETY OF THE UNITED STATES COMPLETE GUIDE TO CAT CARE. Copyright © 2002 by The Humane Society of the United States. All rights reserved. Printed in the United States of America. No part of this book may be used or reproduced in any manner whatsoever without written permission except in the case of brief quotations embodied in critical articles or reviews. For information, address St. Martin's Press, 175 Fifth Avenue, New York, N.Y. 10010.

www.stmartins.com

Design by Kathryn Parise

LIBRARY OF CONGRESS CATALOGING-IN-PUBLICATION DATA

Christensen, Wendy.
    The Humane Society of the United States complete guide to cat care / Wendy Christensen.—1st ed.
        p. cm.
    ISBN 0-312-26929-3 (hc)
    ISBN 0-312-32608-4 (pbk)
    EAN 978-0312-32608-1
    1. Cats—Handbooks, manuals, etc. 2. Cats—Health—Handbooks, manuals, etc. I. Title: Complete guide to cat care. II. Humane Society of the United States. III. Title.

SF447 .C48 2002
636.8—dc21   2001057892

10   9   8   7   6   5   4

CONTENTS

NOTE

THIS BOOK IS INTENDED to provide useful information regarding the care of cats. However, a word of warning is in order.

Cats sometimes behave unpredictably, especially when they are under stress. Caring for a cat inevitably involves some risk of injury to the cat, to other animals, to persons, or to property. Cats sometimes have hidden physical or psychological problems that may cause them to react unfavorably to treatment that would otherwise be considered proper. Laws regarding the treatment and disposition of animals vary from place to place, and lobbying and other forms of activism are regulated or may otherwise result in legal consequences.

The information provided in this book is not intended to substitute for veterinary, legal, or other professional advice. The information in this book should be used with caution, and you must either rely on your own judgment in using this book or else seek professional advice. Your use of this book expressly indicates your assumption of risk of injury or other consequences resulting from interacting with animals or using any products or procedures mentioned in this book. Neither the coauthor nor The Humane Society of the United States assumes any liability for any injury to persons or property that may result from the use of this book.

ACKNOWLEDGMENTS

- -

THE HUMANE SOCIETY OF THE UNITED STATES COMPLETE GUIDE TO CAT CARE truly has been a collaborative effort. The contributors from The Humane Society of the United States, Deborah J. Salem, Nancy Peterson, Randall Lockwood, Ph.D., Frantz Dantzler (who took many of the photographs), Martha Armstrong, Geoffrey Handy, Kathy Milani, and Emily Richburg, wish to thank Paul G. Irwin, HSUS president and CEO, for his commitment to the project.

They join coauthor Wendy Christensen in thanking Michael Denneny and Christina Prestia of St. Martin's Press for their care in shepherding the book through to publication and in acknowledging the important role cats have played in their lives.

FOREWORD

A QUIET REVOLUTION took place sometime in the 1980s. Stealthily and without fanfare, the cat became the most popular pet in America. Dogs are still found in more homes, but cats lead in absolute numbers (not counting aquarium fish!), with more than 70 million cats sharing their lives with us.

Unlike many other species, the cat has remained largely unchanged by the process of domestication. Through generations of selective breeding, *we* chose the sizes, shapes, and behaviors of many animals, including dogs and many species of farm animals. In contrast, cats chose *us*. Those wild ancestors of our modern feline companions who tolerated or enjoyed the proximity of humans and other cats stayed in our homes, temples, marketplaces, and alleyways while their less enterprising cat colleagues scurried back to the wild. The fact that we humans have had comparatively little impact on the biology of cats makes them particularly endearing and challenging companion animals. They retain many of the skills and behaviors of a wild beast, yet—as this book clearly shows—they need us. Whether they choose us by simply showing up on our doorstep or by giving us that special look or friendly head rub when we choose them at a shelter, we have a commitment to honor that choice.

The cats in our lives seem to work hard at understanding us. We must be truly puzzling creatures to them. We are giants who can be as friendly and playful as a small kitten, or who can provide the same gentle grooming as a mother's touch. We magically fill darkened rooms with light and cause marvelous food to appear from inside little metal cans. We can open windows that let in the sounds and scents of the outside world, and we can control the ferocious roaring monster that lives in the closet—the vacuum cleaner!

Historically, the relationship between people and cats has gone through dramatic changes. Cats have been worshipped as gods, reviled as demons, treated as furry little children, and respected as unique creatures with distinctive needs. Even though we know more about cats than ever before, many cats still do not have the benefit of committed, compassionate caregivers who are prepared to make the small investment of time, money, and understanding to meet those needs. That is the goal of this book: to give the reader the resources to make this relationship work.

Sharing our lives with a cat, and building a lifelong, loving relationship, can be a challenging task. Such a lifelong bond requires patience, empathy, understanding, and tolerance. Fortunately, many of the problems that can arise in sharing our lives with feline companions are easily prevented or solved by looking at ourselves and the world through the deep, mysterious eyes of the cat himself. The guiding principle behind *The Humane Society of the United States Complete Guide to Cat Care* has been our desire to bring a strong sense of respect, wonder, and understanding to the relationships we have with cats. We hope that this approach will enhance the unique relationship you have, or hope to have, with the feline members of your family. The Humane Society of the United States, the nation's largest animal-protection organization, is committed to providing the best possible resources to help people enjoy, enhance, and preserve the relationships with the animals for which we care so deeply. On behalf of The HSUS, I encourage you to join with us in all our efforts to create a truly humane society.

Paul G. Irwin, president
The Humane Society of the United States

THE HUMANE SOCIETY OF THE UNITED STATES

Complete Guide to

CAT CARE

CHAPTER 1

Why the Cat?

Quite simply, cats chose us.

Cat lovers have long appreciated the honor, privilege, and joy of being chosen by a cat. "He will be your friend if he deems you worthy of friendship, but not your slave," reflected cat-loving French writer Théophile Gautier. Living with a cat is a priceless opportunity. If you let him, your cat will take you on a daily voyage of discovery, gently revealing the world through his wise, mysterious, glowing eyes. You'll enjoy—right in your own living room—a precious glimpse of wild nature.

Like any treasured relationship, living with a cat brings costs and trade-offs, cares and worries, heartache and heartbreak. You'll be concerned about whether he's getting adequate nutrition, whether he's happy and satisfied in his life with you, whether he needs medical attention, exercise, a diet, a treat, a feline companion, some serious cuddling—or just a new toy.

Your cat is your companion for life, eager and willing to give you trust, love, and friendship. He's counting on you. Accept his gift. You'll share a lifetime of quiet companionship, lively, joyous play, and steadfast loyalty. In times of trouble, you'll rely on

his comfort, counsel, and ever-listening ear. Cherish the delights of kittenhood, the pleasures of middle age, the sweet wisdom of old age.

LOVE IS NOT ENOUGH

If you're reading this book, you probably love cats. Perhaps you grew up with a beloved furry friend. Maybe you're a recent convert to the mysterious, undeniable allure of cats. That you're reading this book means you realize there's more to cat ownership than falling in love with a winsome kitten and living happily ever after. You know that love is not enough.

Learn all you can about that remarkable creature curled up in your lap or snoozing on your laundry. In this book, you'll meet your cat's ancestors, discover his history and origins, and learn some secrets of decoding his moods, quirks, and behavior. And you'll learn lots of easy, inexpensive, everyday strategies to help you provide the cat you love with a long, safe, satisfying, healthy life.

A CAT IN YOUR LIFE—IS IT THE RIGHT DECISION?

Many people happen into cat ownership without considering why they want a cat—or any pet. Some families adopt a pet because it's the thing to do, because they want to please their children, or because their friends have one. Too often, adopters settle for a cat because they don't have the time or energy to walk and exercise a dog. A cat, they think, is the no-muss, no-fuss pet—a cheap, easy alternative to a dog. Nothing could be further from the truth.

You can't ignore a cat because you're too tired, busy, or stressed to feed and care for him. That tiny kitten you adopt on a whim today will require food, supplies, care, training, socialization, exercise, toys, and medical care for his entire life. Too many cats are relinquished to shelters because their owners never realized that cats require regular veterinary care, including vaccinations, as well as plenty of daily care and attention. Before you fall for that pet-store kitten or succumb to a neighbor's pleas to take one of his latest litter, think hard—and do your homework.

What Are You Looking For in a Cat?

As cats have moved indoors and overtaken dogs as America's most-popular pet, the media—and pet-supply merchants—have developed a heightened interest in cats and their owners. Psychologists, essayists, and other observers are fascinated by the depth and power of the human-cat bond.

Although many dog owners enjoy a **master-subject relationship** with their pets, this is unusual among cat owners—because the cats won't stand for it! Novice cat owners who think cats should come when called, perform tricks on cue, or pull a lost skier through the snow are usually quickly disabused of these quaint notions. Cats *can* be trained to do these things (well, maybe not pulling a skier from the snow), but not because they recognize anyone as master.

There are probably cat owners who maintain an **owner-property relationship** with their cats, seeing them as personal property or livestock—but we hope there aren't many of them! Writer Ellen Perry Berkeley notes, "As every cat owner knows, nobody owns a cat." But it's important to acknowledge ownership of your cat for legal and ethical purposes, and to accept full responsibility for his care and for making decisions that affect his well-being and life.

Many cat owners maintain a **parent-child relationship,** treasuring their cats as if they were their own children. Domestic cats nestle easily into this role. Owners of a "feline child" go the extra mile to consider his unique needs and concerns when making decisions that may affect his life, health, or happiness—just as they would with a human child.

Whatever relationship you and your cat forge, it will be a mutual decision! Ideally, you'll be **partners** in the grand adventure of life. It's no coincidence that our growing awareness of the vital importance of the natural world and the web of all life has blossomed along with our renewed esteem for domestic cats. Living with your cat lets you thrill to a precious bit of natural wildness right in your own home, every day.

Why People Get Cats: Not-So-Good Reasons

"Just like Fluffy"

Did you grow up with a beloved cat? Do you long to relive that experience? Have you lost a cherished cat? Some people adopt a cat or kitten in the mistaken belief, or hope, that they can somehow re-create the friendship they shared with a previous animal companion. This is neither realistic nor fair. Childhood pets, and beloved pets you have lost, have likely attained near perfection in your memory. Can a real cat live up to that? Are you being fair?

Status Value

Knowledgeable animal lovers cringe whenever a distinctive breed or type of cat or dog appears in a popular movie or TV show. They've seen it all before: the rush by status seekers to adopt the pet of the moment, whether a dalmatian pup like the ones in a movie or a sphynx cat from another film. Most status-seeking adopters have no idea of the special needs of the animals they take into their lives and often tire of them as soon as the fad fades. Sadly, status pets, whether domestic or wild, are often surrendered to shelters, turned over to sanctuaries, or abandoned when they become too expensive, large, dangerous, or inconvenient—or when a newer fad animal beckons.

For the Children

Living with a cat can help a child learn about responsibility, commitment, and love. Memories of childhood pets are among our fondest. But a family cat obtained at the wrong time or for the wrong reasons can teach a child all the wrong lessons about pet ownership—and about cats. Never get a cat just because you think the children ought to have a pet and you don't want to bother with a dog, or because your unruly toddler needs to be "taught some responsibility." In chapter 11, you'll learn how to introduce cats and kids so that the resulting relationship is healthy, beneficial, and pleasant for everyone. If your child isn't ready for a pet, surprising him with a cat will neither make him ready nor magically turn him into a responsible pet caretaker. Don't adopt a cat impulsively or casually, and never in an attempt to cure a child's behavior or disciplinary problems.

Why People Get Cats: Good Reasons

Companionship

There's nothing like the company of a cat. Your cat is a loyal friend, a warm sleeping-buddy, a playmate, a confidant, a *presence*. Countless writers and poets have expressed delight, pleasure, and wonder at the everyday miracles of feline life and behavior. French writer Fernand Mery gloried in his cats' "cleanliness, discretion, affection, patience, dignity, and courage." Another Frenchman, Henri Poincaré, noted, "The cat is witty, he has nerve, he knows how to do precisely the right thing at the right moment. . . . He extricates himself from the most difficult situations by a little pirouette." Cats bring joy and delight to everyday life. Stroking a cat can even lower your blood pressure.

Admiration of Feline Traits

If you're able and ready to adopt, there's no finer reason than your admiration for the grace, beauty, and elegance of the domestic cat. Many happy cat owners attracted by the splendid aesthetic qualities of cats have been further delighted by the depth and richness of the bonds they've forged with their feline companions.

Perhaps you admire cats but aren't able right now to responsibly care for one. Hold out until the time is right. Until then, educate yourself about cats. And volunteer at your local animal shelter! Shelter cats always love extra cuddling and attention, and affectionate socialization and gentle handling will make them happier, healthier pets.

Think It Through: How Well Does a Cat
Suit Your Lifestyle?

Think and plan carefully before making a lifelong commitment to a cat. Are you and your family ready for a cat or kitten? (See chapter 3 to learn why the old myth that a cat is a low-maintenance/low-cost alternative to a dog is so untrue!) Can you afford a cat or kitten? Every cat needs regular veterinary attention, vaccinations, surgeries, and emergency medical care when necessary, as well as high-quality food, litter-box filler, and other supplies. You'll need to hire a cat-sitter or pay a boarding facility to look after your cat when your family is away on business or vacation. This can be a considerable expense.

Consider possible health and safety consequences. Has any family member ever experienced allergies to cats or other animals? Do you have a family member with a compromised immune system or serious chronic illness? Does your household include frail elderly persons, infants, or small children? If so, it might be a mistake to add a cat to your family right now.

How stable is your living situation? If you live in rental quarters, how does your landlord feel about pets? Have you checked the language in your lease? Might you be moving soon? Is there a major life change looming for you, such as a divorce, hospitalization, or job change, that may necessitate a lot more time away from home or a move to another city? Any of these situations might mean that this is not the right time for you to consider adopting a cat.

Do you have enough time to devote to a cat? To be happy, satisfied, and fulfilled, cats need plenty of interaction and attention from the people in their lives. Do you live alone and work seventy hours a week? Cats are sociable and intelligent, and loneliness and boredom can cause stress and misbehavior. Or is your household a mad hive of activity, with people coming and going, grabbing quick snacks, and dashing off again? A cat might feel confused and left out in such a busy, chaotic environment where no one has any time just for him.

Consider also the needs and rights of your already-resident pets. Do you have a frail elderly cat who might find newcomers distressing? Do you have a poorly socialized dog who might chase or even attack a cat? Do you already have a large number of pets? Has your home reached its cat-carrying capacity? Are you adopting this cat or kitten because of sympathy or guilt?

A Family Decision

Every member of your family should agree that a cat is a welcome addition to the home you all share. True, cats have a way of winning over even the most dedicated feline-skeptics, but if your household includes someone who genuinely hates or fears cats, it's not fair to a cat, or to that person, to force cohabitation.

Although caring for a cat can be a rewarding educational experience for youngsters, never delegate all cat-care tasks to young children. Make plans to insure that cat supplies are on hand; that the cat is properly fed, groomed, and cared for; and that necessary litter-box maintenance is done every day. And never, ever surprise your family or child with a cat or kitten. Make the decision *together,* plan for the new family member *together*—and select your new feline companion *together.*

Why All the Fuss?

Why, you might ask, is it so important to be careful in deciding whether to adopt a cat or kitten? People adopt cats every day!

Selecting a cat is often a matter of life and death—for the cat. Adopting a cat at the wrong time, or for the wrong reasons, or selecting the wrong cat for your family, situation, or lifestyle, almost certainly means problems later. Intolerance of certain behaviors; lack of attention or proper care; misunderstanding of the cat's needs; financial disputes because the cat's needs weren't taken seriously; changing life circumstances when no accommodation for the cat's welfare can be devised—these problems send too many cats to shelters, where many are euthanized (humanely destroyed) despite heroic efforts to find them good homes.

As a responsible cat owner, one of your tasks is protecting your cat in times of crisis and change. In chapter 17, you'll learn how to plan ahead to keep your cat safe and healthy in the face of a variety of disasters and how to handle a range of feline emergencies with a clear head and steady hand. In chapter 18, we'll look at some of life's inevitable transitions and changes that can affect your cat and your relationship with him. In the same chapter, we'll also explore how to insure that your cat will remain safe, healthy, and cared for if you die or become unable to care for him.

Cats Pay the Price

It's so easy. You bundle the cat—so recently a cute fluffy kitten, but now large, hungry, and a bit rude—into the shelter. You're handed a form: "Reason for Surrender?"

Hmmmm . . . "Moving—can't take cat." Sounds good. You hand over the cat, and you're out of there. Whew!

It happens hundreds of times a day. Are all "surrendering owners" really moving? Perhaps. Or perhaps a new girlfriend doesn't care for cats. Maybe a boyfriend came home with a big dog, or the landlord found out about the cat and threatened eviction. Maybe a parent took a dislike to the cat's mess or smell. Maybe it was a dorm cat—cherished by a houseful of students all year but inconvenient now that everyone is going home for the summer. Maybe a summer-cottage family had no room for the cat in its city apartment when fall came.

Maybe there's no reason at all—people tire of pets every day. This cat, this magnificent descendent of those wild felines who long ago chose to keep company with humans, may face death because of an irresponsible choice by a thoughtless human—a choice made in haste, in capriciousness, in ignorance, in selfishness.

HAVE YOU BEEN CHOSEN?

Cats chose us. In the next chapter, you'll learn how and why. Cats chose us—and they're *still* choosing us. According to a 2000 survey by the APPMA (American Pet Products Manufacturers Association), strays—wandering, previously owned cats who showed up on the doorstep or wandered into the yard and made themselves at home—account for 29 percent of cats in single-cat households. Among owners with multiple cats, 43 percent were chosen by their cats. Many multiple cat owners joke that their homes must be marked with a "Felines Welcome! Cat Lovers Dwell Within!" sign, visible only to cats. Have *you* been chosen?

A SACRED TRUST

The domestic cat has claimed our friendship, our trust, and our hearts. We and our cats share a close, inextricable relationship. There's no going back. Cats chose us; we accepted their gift. This is the *Feline Covenant*, and it's a sacred trust. In chapter 4, we'll explore the Feline Covenant, how it came to be, and what it means to us, to our cats, and to our ever-evolving relationship.

CHAPTER 2

How Did Our Domestic Cats Originate?

The complex, checkered relationship of humans and cats is only a few thousand years old—the blink of an eye in evolutionary terms. And it's only in the last 150 years that we've begun to intervene in feline evolution through deliberate selective breeding. But the feline tribe is ancient. Our domestic cats are the products of millions of years of evolutionary refinement. All cats, wild and domestic, are exquisitely designed, magnificently built, and superbly equipped predators—the ultimate hunters.

YOUR CAT'S WILD ANCESTORS

Let's go back 60 million years to the Paleocene epoch, when the first distant ancestor of that furry bundle cozily curled up in your lap appeared on Earth. The Miacids, founders of the mighty tribe of Tiger, were also the ancestors of all modern mammalian carnivores, including bears and canines.

The Eocene epoch, about 54 million years ago, saw the first true felids. Then, about 50 million years ago, according to fossil evidence, the cat's direct precursor, *Dinictis,* appeared. This lynx-sized carnivore with uncannily catlike teeth was a powerful predator, well adapted to numerous ecological niches. *Dinictis* spread widely and rapidly.

The Oligocene epoch, about 25-to-35 million years ago, witnessed the morning yawns of the fearsome saber-tooth felines, equipped with extraordinarily long, wickedly effective upper-canine fangs.

The first true cat, *Proailurus,* a small, leopardlike feline that likely spent much of his time in trees, appeared during the Oligocene era. In ancient North America, a cheetahlike cat called *Miracinonyx* pursued prey and brought it down by hooking it with huge, strong dewclaws. *Miracinonyx* eventually became extinct. But recent studies show that the modern cheetah, like the long-ago *Miracinonyx,* also uses his dewclaws to snag prey.

Oh, What Big Teeth You Have!

Around 20 million years ago, in the Miocene epoch, the first "modern" felines, ancestors of domestic cats, prowled. Their coming heralded a new era, though the great saber-tooth cats were long in snarling their last. It was 2 million years ago that terrible *Smilodon,* last of the saber-tooth cats, disappeared from much of the world. But old *Smilodon* hung on in at least one place—southern California.

As recently as thirteen thousand years ago, *Smilodon californicus* still terrorized the denizens of what is now Los Angeles. Huge numbers of fossils unearthed from the Rancho La Brea tar pits tell eloquent tales of prey animals great and small who ventured into the cool, inviting waters to drink, and of predators, including *Smilodon,* who pursued them there, confident of an easy meal. Predator and prey alike were doomed, trapped and sucked into the tarry subsurface muck to sink and drown, inadvertently bequeathing their bones, and their stories, to twentieth-century science.

There is some evidence that humans and primitive canines—ancestors of America's second-most-popular pet—lived in close company for many millennia before the dawn of civilization. And by 10,000 B.C. according to fossil evidence, domestic canines were already clearly different from their wild ancestors—and the domestication of the dog was already well established. But the cat still walked alone.

A BRIEF HISTORY OF THE
FELINE-HUMAN RELATIONSHIP

Sometime between 7000 and 5000 B.C. somewhere in northern Africa, a few small, tabby-striped wild felines, natives of the scrub plains and deserts, wandered into human settlements. Adaptable individuals among these African wildcats (*Felis silvestris libyca*, also known as *Felis libyca*) found the hunting good and the company to their liking. With tentative paws, they patted at the notion of domestication.

The Best of Times—Ancient Egypt

Not long afterwards, *Felis libyca* found his way into the narrow Nile River valley in northeastern Africa. The Nile's predictable yearly flood lavishes life-giving organic silts on surrounding farmland, and the river's bounty had given rise to one of Earth's greatest early flowerings of human civilization—ancient Egypt. An artful, ingenious people, the Egyptians mastered observational astronomy to predict the Nile's annual inundation and pioneered the arts of surveying and geometry to locate property boundaries, even under water. Several thousand years before the Christian era, a mighty, long-lasting empire had developed around the agricultural riches delivered so faithfully by the Nile's bounty. Harvests from this rich, well-managed land were stored against need in huge granaries.

The Egyptians vanquished most of their military enemies and enslaved the rest. But against one small, persistent enemy they were virtually helpless: rodents.

The ancient bane of farmers, rodents not only consume huge quantities of grain but foul many times more. In the abundant environment of the Egyptians' granaries, rodents multiplied prolifically and rapidly. The lavish harvest, wrested with so much ingenuity and labor from the land, vanished before the Egyptians' eyes. Pest control became a matter of life and death.

For a time, the Egyptians employed weasels for rodent control. But they found these small mustelids, while efficient rat killers, untamable, disagreeable, smelly, hard to handle, and highly unsuited to living among humans. Worse, weasels are indiscriminate killers, dispatching with equal relish domestic fowl, eggs, hares, birds, and many other kinds of animals. The Egyptians and their weasels muddled along. The rodents grew fat and prospered.

Felis Libyca Makes His Choice

No one knows exactly when or by what means the first cat found himself in the Nile valley. Highly intelligent, adaptable, curious, and opportunistic, like all the feline tribe, he must have thought he'd arrived in cat heaven. For here was the easy life: an abundant, seemingly endless, conveniently concentrated supply of his preferred prey—small rodents. It probably didn't take long for the small cat's splendid hunting prowess to become the talk of the valley.

As more cats arrived and bred, the Egyptians were doubtless delighted to notice that these newcomers were much more agreeable company than weasels. It's likely that the cats who first walked among humans were among the tamest and most outgoing of their kind. They passed along to their kittens, both as genetic endowment and socialization, elements of that tameness and adaptability that allowed them to live in close association with other cats and with people. And so the process of domestication of *Felis silvestris libyca* began.

The Egyptians, as witnessed by their exquisite art, admired beauty, grace, and elegance. What a blessing the cat must have seemed! The cat was not just a protector of their vital stores but the very epitome of the traits they most valued. This wondrous creature in their midst possessed mesmerizing eyes, an uncanny sense of balance, the ability to navigate faultlessly in dim starlight, and a mysterious sixth sense that attuned them to the moods of their human companions.

As early as 3000 B.C., the Egyptians were painting and sculpting cats. A 1450 B.C. tomb painting at Thebes shows that feline domestication was well underway: a ginger domestic cat wears a collar, and his lead is tied to the leg of a chair beneath which he frolics. The cat was now a household companion, in addition to his working role as rat catcher. Another tomb painting shows the tomb's owner with two kittens: one is on his lap; the other, sporting a silver earring, poses prettily beneath his wife's chair.

In Ancient Egypt, Cats Were Worshipped. Cats Have Never Forgotten This!

In 950 B.C., the Nile delta city of Bubastis (meaning, the House of Bast) was made the national capital of Egypt, reflecting the popularity of the cult of Bast, the cat-headed goddess. (She was also called Bastet or Pasht, from which the word *puss* is thought to be derived.) Wife or daughter of the sun god, Bast oversaw happiness, music, dancing, and feminine concerns such as fertility and childbirth. She represented sensual pleasure, happiness, and warmth, and was also honored as a goddess of the moon.

From Egypt to the World

The Egyptians were deeply fond of these elegant, companionable saviors of their agricultural riches yet unwilling to share the gift with the rest of the civilized world. Exporting cats was strictly illegal. By 900 B.C., however, smugglers were transporting domestic cats from Egypt to Italy, Greece, and beyond. Prized wherever agriculture was practiced and food stocks threatened by rodents (nearly everywhere), cats were soon spreading rapidly throughout Europe and Asia.

In ancient Egypt, cats were worshipped: cats have never forgotten this! (TWO CATS AND A BASTET, COURTESY, MUSEUM OF FINE ARTS, BOSTON. REPRODUCED WITH PERMISSION. © 2000 MUSEUM OF FINE ARTS, BOSTON. ALL RIGHTS RESERVED.)

The Greeks and Romans kept cats for utilitarian purposes but never seemed to warm up to the cat's aesthetic or mystical appeal as the Egyptians did. The Romans esteemed cats as symbols of liberty but never elevated them to divine status. The Greeks were familiar with domestic cats—probably smuggled from Egypt—as early as the fifth century B.C.

By A.D. 900, descendants of *Felis silvestris libyca* arrived in the British Isles, where they soon met up with the native wildcat, *Felis silvestris silvestris,* a much-fiercer small feline less amenable to taming and not at all inclined to keep human company. Inevitably, though, crossbreeding occurred.

The value of the domestic cat as a protector of agricultural society was recognized early in Britain. In A.D. 936, a Welsh prince, Hywel Dda, beloved as Hywel the Good, enacted laws to protect cats—a remarkably enlightened act, especially considering what was to come. Monetary values were established for cats and kittens and hefty penalties assessed for killing or stealing domestic felines. A kitten was worth "a legal penny," while a cat who'd proven his worth as a rodent catcher was worth "four legal pence."

Cats arrived in China by 500 B.C. and were known in India by about 100 B.C. They found their way to Persia by the fifth or sixth century A.D. The prophet Muhammad (A.D. 570–632), founder of Islam, was said to cherish his pet cat, Muezza, and adherents of Islam have since held cats in high regard. Feeding the cats of the mosque, where they were traditionally honored guests, was seen as an act of piety.

Domestic cats reached Japan much later. In A.D. 884, a cat from China was presented to the emperor Koko as a royal gift. The Japanese so treasured their cats that they deemed utilitarian rat catching beneath their dignity. Instead, they filled their cities, granaries, and silkworm farms with statues and paintings of cats. Unfortunately, these images weren't much help against rodents. The Japanese endured heavy losses in their economically important silkworm industry until A.D. 1620, when they finally allowed some cats to hunt freely.

The Worst of Times—the Medieval Era in Europe

Just as cats were enjoying pampering and respect in the Orient, they faced big trouble in Europe. By A.D. 1200, cats had fallen into a deep disfavor with the powerful Catholic Church, which deemed them representative of paganism and accomplices of the devil. By the mid–fifteenth century, under the influence of the powerful Church and in fear of the Inquisition, many people came to believe that cats were evil, dangerous, and uncannily powerful. Heretical sects were widely accused of performing secret rituals involving cats. Superstition, fear, and prejudice ran rampant. Hundreds of thousands of innocent people lost their lives, as well as uncounted millions of cats.

As the Roman Empire had crumbled, domestic cats had been cherished in major trading towns throughout Europe. Merchants and traders recognized cats as vital protectors of the great warehouses upon which their prosperity depended. In some of these towns, a cult of Freya became wildly popular. An ancient pagan goddess who drove a chariot drawn by cats, and whose worship and image became mixed up with some of the old residual cults of Bastet, Freya, along with her cult, attracted numerous devotees.

Church fathers preached with vigor and ferocity against this pagan cat worship. In 1484—a low point for both felinity and humanity—Pope Innocent VIII empowered the Inquisition to seek out and destroy Freya cultists and cat worshippers and to burn them as witches. Frightened by the relentless preaching and threats, many people had come to believe that a witch's familiar (her personal emissary to the devil) often assumed the form of a cat—generally a black cat. But any cat became suspect.

The facts that cats are active by night, that they resist human subjugation, that they seem intelligent (which was equated, in an animal, with diabolical powers), even that their eyes glow in the dark—all were claimed as evidence of cats' inherent evil. These unfortunate attitudes, and the tragedy, slaughter, and suffering that resulted, persisted for hundreds of years. Vestiges of these old superstitions still remain today—as the myths and misconceptions we'll look at in the next chapter sadly attest.

Cat's Revenge? The Great Plague

No one knows how many cats were slaughtered in that long, tragic era. Domestic cats are prolific, but the forces arrayed against them were vast and powerful, and the hatred and slaughter went on for centuries. Cats are survivors, though, and they survived. And then came the Plague.

It came out of the East carried by black rats and ravaged Europe in several great waves of death starting in the twelfth century A.D. The Great Plague—both bubonic and pneumonic plague—took a greater proportion of human life than any known war, epidemic, or disaster up to that time. Huge waves of the disease, called the Black Death, swept through Europe for centuries, killing an estimated 25 million Europeans.

Plague is transmitted to humans by arthropods—in this case, fleas carried by rodents. At this low point in human-feline history, when cats were denounced from pulpits and burned as witches' familiars, they might have been of inestimable service to humanity. And no doubt, many *were* unsung heroes, dispatching rats with their usual efficiency and verve—but largely unappreciated by their suffering beneficiaries. In mid-seventeenth-century London, thousands of cats were slaughtered in the belief that *they* were carriers of plague.

The massive social changes throughout Europe in the wake of the Plague's devastation set the stage for a feline comeback of sorts. The Church lost some of its monopoly on salvation as its adherents saw its helplessness in the face of the Plague; bishops had perished as readily as peasants. The loss of huge numbers of laborers who had tended the fields sent survivors flocking to towns, where they became increasingly mobile and independent. They even started to think for themselves. They became more receptive to the charms of the cat.

Make no mistake, though. The cat was far from protected or safe, much less revered. Rituals and festivals that included horrendous abuse of cats, some of them holdovers from the bad old days of religious persecution, continued for hundreds of years.

No doubt, throughout this long, dark era, many individual cats were cherished and protected, and provided joy and comfort—as well as rodent control—for their companions. But legions of homeless felines also roamed fields and towns, prey to whatever cruelty and viciousness humans could devise in the name of entertainment or superstition.

Restoration and Renewal—the Victorian Age

It was a long way back, and the cat's reversion to a favored place in human circles came only gradually—with the painfully slow recession of ignorance and superstition, the advance of scientific knowledge, and the advent of a more equitable, widespread prosperity. With prosperity came, at least for a favored few, leisure that allowed the pursuit of art and literature, music and philosophy, science and learning. Artists, writers, and philosophers—comfortable with paradox, intrigued by ambiguity, and inclined towards independence of thought—have always been the cat's natural champions. By the eighteenth century, poets, writers, and painters incorporated domestic cats into their works in a sympathetic, naturalistic manner.

It was in the nineteenth century, and particularly in the Victorian era, that the domestic cat was finally restored to something like his old position of esteem. Queen Victoria herself was an ardent cat lover, cherishing her pet cats as well as her dogs. She was a tremendous force in reestablishing the domestic cat's good reputation. Victorian Britons, under the tutelage of their queen, cherished home, family, the domestic arts, and, increasingly, cats.

British artist Louis Wain brought cats to children, portraying them as intelligent, friendly companions. His art was a tremendously influential form of humane education. It's said that as the nineteenth century gave way to the twentieth, there was hardly a nursery wall in Britain or America that did not display at least one Louis Wain cat print. Our cats today owe Louis Wain a great debt of gratitude.

THE DOMESTIC CAT TODAY

For domestic cats, the good times have returned—at least in the United States. Nineteen-eighty-five, according to the Pet Food Institute, saw the domestic cat surpass the dog as America's most popular pet. (There are still more "dog households" than "cat households" in the United States, but cat owners frequently own multiple cats.) By 2001, according to a survey by the American Pet Products Manufacturers Association, cats outnumbered dogs 73 million to 68 million. America is going to the cats.

The twentieth century saw numerous advances in the care, welfare, longevity, and reputation of domestic cats. Medical breakthroughs; improvements in our understanding of feline physiology, psychology, and behavior; and numerous innovative products now make cats' lives healthier, longer, safer, and more satisfying.

When it came to bringing cats happily indoors, nothing equaled the powerful, immediate influence of Edward Lowe's 1947 brainstorm: packaged cat litter. His first product was pelletized clay that absorbed liquids and odors, and his bright idea spawned an industry worth almost a billion dollars a year. Prepackaged cat litter made cats more welcome indoors and removed one of the greatest impediments to a safe, indoors-only lifestyle for millions of cats.

Longer, Healthier Lives

Veterinary researchers continue to study diseases that have tragically cut short the lives of cats. Clinicians, scientists, and veterinarians continue to make stunning progress in feline diagnosis, treatment, care, disease prevention, surgery, and emergency intervention. From specialized diets to an astonishing array of feline toilet options, the domestic cat of the new millennium enjoys more comforts, options, and perks than ever before.

The 1920s and 1930s saw the first canned foods formulated especially for cats—a breakthrough that acknowledged that cats were not just smaller dogs. A study conducted by Eileen Karsh, Ph.D., showed that kittens handled between the ages of three and fourteen weeks grow up much better socialized and more attached to humans than kittens not held until seven weeks of age or not held at all. The discovery of this vital "window of socialization" revolutionized thinking about kittens and their care.

In 1944, researcher Mildred Moelk took the first scientific look at "cat talk," discovering that domestic cats command a versatile, expressive vocal repertoire. Cat owners started listening a bit more closely to their cats.

In the latter part of the twentieth century, progress accelerated. The Winn Feline Foundation, founded in 1968, funded extensive research into pediatric (early-age) sterilization; blood-type incompatibilities; feline infectious peritonitis (FIP); skin-disease treatments; feline hyperthyroidism; toxoplasmosis; feline heart disease; feline kidney disease; feline asthma; feline lower-urinary-tract disease (FLUTD); and other medical problems of the cat. Thanks to their efforts, millions of cats are living longer, healthier lives.

In 1972, veterinarians got a reliable test for feline leukemia (FeLV); and, in 1985, they got the first effective vaccine to protect cats from this dreaded disease. In 1978, researchers discovered the critical importance of the amino acid taurine in the feline diet. Adding taurine to commercial cat food has saved the lives of millions of cats. As cats become more valued, precious, and central to the lives of millions of households, advances in medical care, behavioral understanding, and nutrition will continue to improve and extend the lives of our domestic cats.

CHAPTER 3

What Is a Cat?
Myths Versus Facts

Compared to animals like dogs and cattle, cats share a relatively brief history with humans. But what a roller-coaster ride it's been! From worship in ancient Egypt, to condemnation and mass slaughter in medieval Europe, to their status as America's most-popular household pet at the end of the twentieth century, cats have shared a tumultuous relationship with humans.

It's not surprising that domestic cats have been the subject of myths and misconceptions over the centuries. Happily, debunking these untruths is easy.

Myth: Cats aren't really domesticated; they're actually wild animals.

Fact: An enormous amount of irresponsibility, selfishness, heedlessness, and inhumane behavior hides behind this pervasive, harmful myth.

If a cat is just another wild animal, we aren't responsible for its well-being, its medical bills, or even its life. Calling our domesticated cats wild animals makes them someone else's problem—the government's, the scientists', the shelters', the animal-welfare activists'. This common, all-too-convenient abdication of responsibility reflects a misunderstanding of the evolution of the domestic cat and of its unique place in human society.

It was the cat who took the first paw step towards domestication. In taking this step, the cat entered upon an inexorable process of change. This wild animal voluntarily joined human circles and was welcomed and even cherished instead of hunted or banished. The cat graced us with the gifts of his presence and rodent-control talents. We accepted those gifts, a signal milestone in both human and feline history.

In living among humans, the cat changed. To maintain his advantage and favored place, he gradually smoothed out his wild behavior patterns to blend more harmoniously into his chosen new world. Humans prized tame, agreeable, friendly kittens, so, over time, tamer, friendlier kittens appeared. Over the centuries, *Felis silvestris libyca* spawned another species—*Felis catus,* the domestic cat.

By accepting the cat's gifts, humans changed, too. For the first time, humans joined with another species in a relationship that was neither hunter-prey nor master-slave, but more of a coequal partnership. In chapter 4, you'll learn how the Feline Covenant—this ancient agreement of partnership between human and cat—was born. Cats and people were cooperators in a common enterprise—agriculture— though with different agendas. The cat was no longer a wild animal, and he is not a wild animal today. He's still built on a wild blueprint, similar in appearance and behavior to his wild predecessors, but different from them, too. Domestication of the cat is a work in progress, a joint human-feline enterprise. There's no going back.

Myth: Cats are naturally aloof, unfriendly, and solitary.

Fact: In the wild, cats, large or small, survive by stalking and killing their own food. Each cat must exploit and defend as much territory as he needs to obtain an adequate, continuing food supply. Allowing interlopers to take, or even threaten, one's resources is courting starvation. A cat's primary motivation is to obtain enough food to survive. But he must also protect his resource base—his territory—from potential competitors. So wildcats are necessarily secretive, solitary hunters. Over time, people came to believe that *all* cats are aloof, solitary, unfriendly animals.

With the exception of lions on the prey-rich African plains, who live happily in extended family groups called prides, a solitary lifestyle is the rule for most of the world's wild felines. But a look around any large city makes it plain that domestic cats can and do live more-or-less harmoniously in groups—sometimes rather large groups—in "feral colonies." Feral cats are unsocialized cats who may be one or more generations removed from a home environment, and who may subsist in a colony of similar cats living on the fringes of human existence. How is this possible?

Unlike wild cats who hunt and kill whatever game roams their territories, most members of *Felis catus* who live in feral colonies subsist on handouts and garbage, supplemented by occasional meals of small rodents, insects, and birds. The existence of a feral colony is evidence of a stable, reliable food source. When it comes to living situations, the preferences of *Felis catus* are based on the availability of resources, and, to some extent, on individual temperament. Most important are the resources the cats need to survive, such as food, water, and shelter. But resources also include extras— those amenities cats so love, such as comfort, sunshine, and—yes—companionship.

Cats living in groups, assured of plenty of resources (and some extras for insurance), often develop sociable, affectionate personalities. *Felis catus* is a high-contact animal. Cats living together touch noses in greeting, rub cheeks and foreheads, brush gently while passing side by side, and groom one another. These tiny, graceful rituals, repeated dozens of times daily, assist in the mingling and refreshing of a familiar "group scent." By extending these scent-oriented touching behaviors to human friends, cats acknowledge their acceptance of those favored creatures into their social sphere.

Myth: Domestic cats can survive on their own.

Fact: Here, the mistaken belief that cats are really wild animals turns into action—and tragedy. Domestic cats dumped into "nature," in the belief (or hope) that they'll make it on their own, are destined—unless they're extremely lucky—for a short, painful life.

Accustomed to dependence on humans for food, and untrained in the hunt if vital aspects of hunting behavior have not been learned from Momcat during kittenhood, abandoned cats usually starve. If the cat locates a food source, whether garbage or prey, he'll probably have to defend it from whoever is exploiting it. Woefully unprepared for life on their own, abandoned cats are killed in the thousands by predators and vehicles, succumb to disease, or—at best—manage to join a feral colony. If unsterilized (as is common), they father or bear litter after litter of kittens whose prospects may be even worse than their own.

Myth: Cats can't possibly be happy unless they have the freedom to hunt and roam outdoors.

Fact: As you'll discover in chapters 7, 8, and 9, your cat can enjoy a happy, fully satisfying life—and a much longer, healthier one—strictly indoors. True, it takes a bit more time, patience, and commitment from you. But the benefits, for both you and your cat, are incalculable. Your cat is a hunter at heart, but he doesn't need to kill live prey to satisfy his hunting urge. Some creative modifications to your indoor environment, plus time and attention from his human family, will allow your cat to safely gratify his inner wildcat.

Myth: Cats are sneaky, underhanded, or even evil.

Fact: This myth, a relic from the bad old days when cats were thought to be in league with the devil, reflects the deep discomfort some people have with animals who exhibit independence and intelligence.

Unlike the obedient dog, the cat has always "walked by himself." Independence in an animal makes some people uncomfortable, so they attribute to the cat some evil tendencies: savagery, selfishness, sneakiness, vindictiveness, cruelty. But these are human-centered interpretations of feline behavior. Cats do what they do for perfectly valid feline—not human—reasons. Looking at feline behavior strictly through the clouded lens of human imperfection is a poor route to understanding the feline mind.

"Cats are not 'fur people.'" This myth is charmingly promulgated in art and children's books, but unfair to both cats and humans. (RENOIR'S CATS © BY WENDY CHRISTENSEN)

Myth: Cats are "fur people."

Fact: This myth reverses the "devil-cat" myth. Usually well-meaning and genuinely fond of cats, people who profess this odd belief deny themselves, and their cats, a fully realized interspecies friendship. Attributing human motives, whether positive or negative, to cats is unfair to both cats and humans. Cats are cats, not little humans in fur coats or poor imitations of dogs.

Take time to learn about your cat's nature and needs, motivations and behaviors, unique traits and talents, and quirks and moods. Chapter 10 will get you started. The mindful observation of cats, on their own terms, is a rich, rewarding study—and a lifelong project.

Myth: Cats misbehave out of spite, or to get revenge on people they don't like.

Fact: Cats can't talk, so they communicate through body language, which too often goes unnoticed by their human companions. Cats also communicate through behavior, and especially through so-called misbehavior, which has, at least, the advantage of being noticed. What a frustrated cat owner sees as willful misbehavior may be his cat's desperate attempt to communicate that he's deeply distressed, ill, or in pain. When your cat "misbehaves," try to discover what he's trying to say.

Myth: Cats are low-maintenance alternatives to dogs.

Fact: If you have your heart set on a dog, but don't yet have the money, time, or space you feel you need for a dog, getting a cat as a temporary substitute is foolhardy—and unfair. Although you don't have to walk him after dinner, a cat is a sensitive, complex creature who expects, demands, and deserves time, care, and attention. Nor is a family cat necessarily any cheaper to maintain than other animals. In addition to plenty of attention and daily interaction, your cat needs high-quality food and supplies and regular veterinary care throughout his life.

Myth: Cats can't be trained, so don't bother trying.

Fact: Cats are intelligent, adaptable animals. They do what they want, when they want—it's part of their charm. But you *can* train a cat by persuading him that what *you* want is also what *he* wants. (Chapter 10 will get you started.) Training doesn't mean ordering your cat to jump through hoops, sit up and beg, or fetch sticks, though cats can be trained to do these things. It's a pleasant, loving, cat-oriented interaction that depends on two-way communication, a relationship of mutual respect and trust, and a deep understanding of what motivates your cat.

Myth: You can train a cat not to hunt.

Fact: No, you can't. The feline motto might well be "I hunt, therefore I am." A pet cat who's allowed outdoors can be discouraged from presenting evidence of his kills to his owners if they express sufficiently dramatic revulsion. But that doesn't mean he's embraced nonviolence.

Your cat needs to hunt. He's optimized by millions of years of evolution to be a predator. His familiar stalking-and-pouncing behavior is truly instinctual. But both the procedure for administering the "killing bite," and the recognition that prey is food, are learned in early kittenhood from Momcat. A kitten raised away from his mother, or a kitten with a nonhunting mother, will not learn these lessons.

Happily, you can channel your cat's predatory urges into harmless, healthful play. Daily vigorous, interactive play—mock hunting—can satisfy your cat's irrepressible compulsion to hunt. A cat denied the opportunity to stalk, chase, and pounce, or who's continually punished for his predatory behavior, will be a frustrated, confused, unhappy animal.

You risk an unnecessary loss of trust if you constantly berate and punish your cat because his hunting targets are baby rabbits or the songbirds you attract to your garden bird feeders. (What? Those aren't for me?) Do you love your cat *and* your neighborhood wildlife? Do them both a favor. Read chapter 8, and give your cat a safe, satisfying, enriched indoors-only lifestyle.

Myth: If you spay or neuter your cat, he or she will get fat and lazy.

Fact: There is some biological justification for this myth. Estrogen and testosterone appear to inhibit food intake, so sterilized animals may consume more calories than needed. Adjust your cat's diet and portion sizes to reflect his reduced caloric needs after sterilization. Read chapter 16 if you have any doubts about getting your cat sterilized.

A happy, active cat who enjoys daily, vigorous play, and whose diet is tailored to his age and energy needs will be neither fat nor lazy. Read chapter 14 for tips on feeding your cat right, and chapters 7 and 9 to learn how to keep him healthy, lean, and toned for life.

Myth: Cats always land on their feet.

Fact: Cats possess a remarkable self-righting reflex. When a cat falls, his brain transmits real-time messages describing his orientation in space and the positions of his head, body, and limbs to his eyes and to the vestibular (balance) organs in his inner ears. Based on this critical information, the cat turns his head and front limbs towards the ground. With some balancing assistance from his tail, he rapidly aligns his flexible spine with the rest of his body and spreads his limbs out in a "parachute" in preparation for landing. The shock of his touchdown is partially absorbed by his soft paw pads, his flexible leg and shoulder joints, and his floating collarbones. Under ideal conditions, this entire complex maneuver can take place in as little as two vertical feet of fall.

Despite the elegance and utility of the self-righting reflex, many cats are killed or badly injured in falls. A fall from more than six stories is almost always fatal. Even in relatively short falls, cats suffer severe internal injuries, broken jaws, skull fractures, and smashed teeth. Sometimes, a very short fall can be more dangerous than a longer fall, as the self-righting reflex doesn't have time to fully protect the cat during the distance of the fall.

The simplistic formulation of this marvelous adaptation—"Cats always land on their feet"—has resulted in many injured and traumatized cats. People want to test it, so they pick up a cat, flip him over, and drop him. If the result isn't a broken bone or worse, it's a seriously disgruntled cat who'll think twice before trusting another human.

Myth: A ball of yarn is an ideal cat toy.

Fact: Despite the charming Victorian images of kittens in yarn baskets, linear materials such as yarn, string, and thread are dangerous cat toys. Your cat's tongue is covered with sharp, rearward-facing barbs (called *filiform papillae*) to help him self-groom and tear meat from bone. Once something's in his mouth, it's extremely difficult for him to spit it out. He just keeps swallowing and swallowing. This can lead to internal blockage or severe injuries to his intestinal tract. Sewing thread with a needle attached is particularly dangerous.

Myth: Cats suck the breath from babies.

Fact: Cats are often fascinated by babies. This new creature in the house, bringing new sounds, odors, and routines to daily life, naturally arouses feline curiosity. Some observers think cats are attracted to the scent of milk on a baby's breath. It's more likely that cats are attracted to the infant's warmth and fascinated by the attention it gets.

In ages past, it's likely that cats snuggled with infants for warmth or just out of curiosity. Some of these babies died—as most babies did before modern medicine—from some malady unrelated to the cat contact. But it might have been a natural reaction for the grieving parents to blame the death on the cat.

This myth does contain a seed of wisdom. It *is* dangerous to leave a cat unattended with an infant—but not because the cat will suck the breath from the baby. A cat who's suddenly startled by a noise or a light turned on unexpectedly can seriously injure a young child with his claws. It's also possible that a very large cat could fall asleep on a baby's face and inadvertently smother it.

Myth: Cats and babies don't mix—if you're pregnant, get rid of your cat.

Fact: This fear does have a medical basis, but it also reflects misunderstanding. Toxoplasmosis, an infection caused by the parasite *toxoplasma gondii,* can, under certain conditions, harm a developing fetus. While this disease is often blamed on cats, most cases are caused by eating undercooked meats, particularly lamb and pork. Unpasteurized dairy products and raw, unwashed vegetables are other potential sources of infection. In rare instances, infection can occur through the ingestion of soil contaminated with the parasite's oocysts. There's a small, but real, risk to cat-owning pregnant women. If you're pregnant, have someone else handle litter-box chores. Always wear gloves while gardening, wash hands thoroughly after handling garden soil or cat litter, and scrub and peel all root vegetables. Read more about cats, babies, and pregnancy in chapters 11 and 18.

Myth: Cats don't really need to wear a collar or tags—they're for dogs.

Fact: Can you guarantee that your cat will never get out of your house on his own? During an earthquake? A house fire? A burglary? Do your children ever leave doors open? A collar with visible identification, along with other backup ID such as a microchip, is your cat's ticket home. Cats found wandering without obvious IDs have a tragically poor record for being reunited with their owners. Many perish, unknown and unclaimed in shelters, while their owners frantically search for them.

Myth: There's no need to look for a cat who has disappeared, even for days or weeks. He'll find his way back home when he's ready.

Fact: When a pet cat vanishes, it's comforting, and guilt reducing, to imagine him roaming city streets or country meadows, living off the land, enjoying grand adventures. The reality is likely neither glamorous nor pleasant. The dangers to a wandering cat are many, varied, and often horrifying, whether in the city or the country. Read chapter 8 to discover some of them. A cat who disappears for days or weeks and returns, especially more than once, is lucky indeed.

Myth: Cats are cheap, disposable convenience pets.

Fact: Shelters and rescuers in resort areas and near college campuses attest to the annual tragedy of summer-vacation kittens, dorm cats, and campus cats. In early summer, vacationers flock to beaches, resorts, and country towns. How nice, they think, for the kids to have a kitten for the summer! A kitten is easily acquired. Everyone delights in his antics.

Fall approaches. Cars are packed, good-byes said. "What about Fluffy?" ask the kids. "Oh, he'll look after himself," come the reassuring explanations. "He'll catch mice, play in the woods, probably move in with that nice local family . . ." The cabin is locked and shuttered, bowls of dry food and water left on the porch. Chapter 8 reveals some of the perils abandoned Fluffy faces.

Myth: A purring cat is a happy cat.

Fact: This is partly true. But purring can indicate other feelings besides contentment. Purring is an outlet for overflowing feelings of any kind. A cat experiencing *any* overwhelming emotion, from happiness and contentment to anger, fear, or pain, purrs. Badly injured and dying cats often purr loudly. Read chapter 10 to learn more about how your cat communicates.

Myth: Cats have nine lives.

Fact: It is unlikely that many people believe that cats actually have extra lives. But, in modern American society, and even more so around the world, the individual lives of members of *Felis catus* are still too often seen as worth little or nothing. The repetition, even in jest, of this myth helps keep feline life cheap, reinforcing the common belief that cats are a cheap alternative to dogs, who are valued more highly. It keeps cats interchangeable and replaceable. It delays the day when each and every feline life will be valued as the precious gift it is.

Cats, though superbly designed, are small, vulnerable creatures in a world that too often places little value on them. While cats are prolific and resilient as a species, individual cats are remarkably fragile. They face a multitude of risks both natural and man-made. Evolution did not prepare cats for automobiles, for humans with malicious intent, or for many other perils they face daily.

Myth: A cat is just a cat—cats are pretty much interchangeable and easily and cheaply replaceable.

"Your cat was hit by a car? Get another one."

Fact: Many a cat lover who has lost a dear feline companion has had his grief compounded by such heartless comments. To many people, feline life is cheap and cats interchangeable. But cat lovers know that each cat is a unique, precious individual—a life like no other. Look closer: see the irreplaceable, quirky spirit that trots across your kitchen or lounges draped over your foot. Peer into those mesmerizing eyes, and you might just see the universe gaze back.

Peer into those mesmerizing eyes and you might just see the universe gaze back.
(HSUS/DIANE ENSIGN)

CHAPTER 4

The Feline Covenant

DOMESTIC CATS AND THEIR WILD RELATIVES— ALIKE, YET DIFFERENT

Stretching languorously, the sleek young feline sleepily completes his washing-up ritual and slips into wild cat dreams. In the distance, bellows of wildebeest echo as crowned cranes chatter and strut. Sunlight sparkles through the branches of the overhanging acacia tree, dappling the cat's fur with multicolored prisms. Or is that just suburban sunshine, filtered through a lace curtain? And is that twittering and chattering just the afternoon radio talk show?

Within each of our domestic cats beats the heart of the wild. Unlike dogs, who've kept company with humans for untold millennia, cats joined our society relatively recently. Only a species removed from their small wild cousins of the genus *Felis*, virtually all members of *Felis catus* share startling similarities in appearance and behavior with their wild relatives.

Dogs Versus Cats

Domestic dogs vary greatly in size, strength, body conformation, coat type, abilities, predilections, and temperament. These variations reflect the roles—retriever, herder, tracker, protector, pet, hunting scout—they've assumed, or been assigned, over the long course of their association with humans. No two representatives of *Felis catus,* regardless of breed or origin, differ by anywhere near as much as the tiny, delicate papillon and the mighty Irish wolfhound.

Already Perfect

Domestic cats entered human society exquisitely designed and superbly evolved for a specific task—killing small rodents. Because the vital service they provided comes so naturally to them, and because it was so universally valuable, there was no need for humans to tinker with feline genetics. As *Felis libyca* cats spread throughout the world, they adapted slightly in response to differing climates, conditions, and prey populations. But for the most part, the cat came to us already perfect and complete.

Though breeds of domestic cats differ in appearance, and some behavioral characteristics seem to be typical of certain breeds, each cat is a unique individual in personality and temperament. But virtually all domestic cats are built on the same physical and behavioral blueprint—one that is, in many ways, a mere whisker's breadth from the wild. Because cats are such a familiar presence in our environments, homes, and lives, it's easy to forget that these animals who walk so calmly among us have only recently come in from the wild. And in their behavior, our cats still heed some of the wild's imperatives.

The Essential Wild Cat

The basic behavioral blueprint of every cat rests on a blend of two fundamental principles: cats are intelligent, adaptable, independent spirits; and they are predators. The elegant Japanese bobtail in her penthouse apartment and the bobcat prowling the New England woods; that pampered hairless sphynx reclining on a heated pad and nibbling from a crystal bowl; and the thick-furred lynx patrolling the snowy wastes and stalking a snowshoe hare—their similarities of heritage, genetics, behavior, and essential nature are much more significant than the differences in their looks and lifestyles.

"In wildness," said naturalist and cat lover Henry David Thoreau, "is the preservation of the world." Our feline companions represent a precious, irreplaceable reservoir of accessible wildness. Some of the most seductive features of domestic cats are those that evoke most dramatically what we so admire in wild felines: heartbreaking beauty, sinuous grace, uncanny intelligence, that superb aura of self-possession. But we're also powerfully drawn to the wild cats' speed, power, unpredictability, danger, and elusiveness—to their very wildness and otherness. We crave a taste of the wild—but just a taste.

You'll share with your cat a precious glimpse of wild nature.
(*"WHISKERS"* © BY WENDY CHRISTENSEN)

The Power of Neoteny

Domestic cats "selected" themselves as much as we "selected" them. The tamest, most adaptable animals thrived in human society and bred with similarly tame cats. Over time, through the process called *neotenization,* a new creature—the one we know as the domestic cat—emerged.

Neoteny is the retention into adulthood of juvenile features and behaviors—sociability; gentleness; willingness to mingle in groups and be petted and groomed; love of play; and care-seeking and food-begging behavior. Unlike wild cats, even human-raised ones, neotenized domestic cats see humans as companions—honorary cats—rather than as enemies, competitors, or prey. Wild felines are sensitive, territorial, solitary, and hyperalert to potential opportunities, threats, and competition. In neotenized domestic cats, these traits are still present, but smoothed out and calmed by the overriding effects of a lifelong juvenile mind-set. Our domestic cats let us, in writer Fernand Mery's words, "caress the tiger."

THE FELINE COVENANT

In the enigma of a wild heart wrapped in tame, refined packaging lies the domestic cat's greatest charm, mystery, and allure. Cats prize their independence and dignity. But we and our domestic cats have changed one another over the course of our association, and there's no going back. Cats chose us; we accepted their gift. The *Feline Covenant* is a promise for life.

Adoption: A Promise for Life

Neglected and abused cats are, tragically, an evil that our society still does not take seriously enough.
(HSUS/JUDITH HALDEN)

Your commitment to adoption means your life will change, in some ways as it would change if you adopted a child. You'll need to take this cat's needs and nature into consideration in a multitude of decisions, from mundane everyday matters to major life changes. Living with any fellow creature calls for tolerance of individual differences,

preferences, moods, and temperaments. Just like a marriage or other close relationship, it calls for creativity, sensitivity, and a healthy sense of humor. Every cat differs in his need for companionship, play, sleep, personal space, solitude, and affection. Every cat is an individual, a creature like no other. He accepts your gift of adoption, your proffered friendship, as a solemn lifetime commitment.

What Happens When the Promise Is Broken

Sadly, we too often break the promises we make to cats, leaving behind devastated lives, shattered trust, heartbreak, pain, tragedy, and needless death. Here are some of the ways we've failed, and are continuing to fail, our domestic cats:

Feline overpopulation

By allowing, condoning, or even promoting irresponsible, uncontrolled breeding of domestic cats, humans sentence millions of healthy cats and kittens to death each year in the United States. There are simply not enough homes for all the cats that are born.

Breeding for looks alone

In a misguided quest for the newest, most extreme, or showiest cats, irresponsible breeders of certain pedigreed cats not only allow but encourage breeding that produces cats whose look causes them to suffer discomfort, perennial health problems, illness, and even death. Backyard breeders, suppliers of kittens to pet stores, and even ordinary cat owners, observing these fashions in cats, inevitably try to imitate them.

The desire to breed for appearance leads some cat owners to believe that their pet cat can produce kittens that look just like her. They're mistaken—feline genetics don't work that way. These cat owners are also contributing to the tragedy of feline overpopulation.

Neglected cats

There's little sadder than a domestic cat who's slipped into invisibility and neglect in his own home. Such cats, perhaps pampered and cherished as playful kittens, are increasingly ignored as they grow up. Soon, they get no more attention than an old piece of furniture or a potted plant. The lucky ones see a veterinarian occasionally for vaccinations or when they're badly injured. Many spend much of their time outdoors, and are owned only nominally. Some are turned outdoors in the hope they won't return, having become an inconvenience or unwanted expense. Many are never steril-ized. If they're male, their "owners" never deal with, or even know about, the resulting litters of unwanted kittens.

Abused cats

Abuse of cats—and other animals—is, tragically, an evil that our society still doesn't take seriously enough. Although this is very slowly changing, the law doesn't recognize the heinousness of animal abuse. Domestic cats—small, trusting, vulnera-ble—too often become targets of abuse. Threats of harm to family cats and other pets help keep abused spouses and other family members silent and terrorized. Evil in itself, animal abuse is often a precursor to other violent crimes. Many of the most notorious serial murderers and violent criminals were animal abusers as youngsters. "Boys will be boys," say the apologists. Animal abuse is a crime for which society must have zero tolerance. We aren't there yet. Tragically, we aren't even close.

Animal "hoarders"

This all-too-common tragedy is often born of good intentions sabotaged by insufficient means and, frequently, mental instability. The "hoarder" may genuinely love cats—or think she does. She takes in more and more. They breed. She convinces herself that she's the best, or even the only, person capable of caring for them. No mat-ter how good her intentions, sooner or later her financial means and the sheer amount of time, energy, and resources necessary to care for her growing menagerie fail her.

Perhaps she becomes ill, or mentally unstable, or both. The animals—not steril-ized, vaccinated, or provided with any veterinary care—multiply as conditions decline, often precipitously. The vicious downward spiral progresses; the animals continue to suffer. The hoarder may refuse sincere offers of help. Eventually, she dies, or the sheer horror of the situation forces intervention. On the news that night, viewers see the sad results of "another crazy cat lady."

KEEP WILD CATS WILD

Wild felines are notoriously poor pets. Cautionary anecdotes and horror stories abound of hopeful but misguided people who ignored this basic fact. The Humane Society of the United States opposes private ownership of wild cats, large and small, and other wild and/or exotic animals as pets—for good reason. All species of wild cats, particularly large felines such as lions, tigers, cougars (also called pumas or mountain lions), and leopards, are dangerous animals. Small wild felines, such as bobcats, lynx, ocelots, servals, and caracals are potentially just as dangerous. Wild cats are extremely unsuitable pets and unsafe in most situations in which they have direct contact with the public. Because of these cats' speed, strength, and other abilities, removal of their teeth and/or claws doesn't lessen the danger they pose.

It's impossible for most pet owners to meet the complex physical, nutritional, and behavioral needs of such wild animals. Finding competent veterinary care for wild cats can be difficult. Ignorance dooms most wild feline pets to inhumane and possibly abusive lives. Even if hand-raised and bottle-fed, wild kittens and cubs grow up to be unpredictable, potentially dangerous wild adults. An appealing bobcat kitten or cougar cub often grows into an uncontrollable, expensive, destructive liability. He may attack and seriously harm other pets, children, and adults—including his owner. It's extremely difficult to find new homes for these cats. Many of these unfortunate animals are killed for their pelts and meat, or are simply turned loose—a dangerous, inhumane, and irresponsible strategy.

Only qualified, trained professionals should keep wild cats. Help spread the word: keep wild cats wild!

WHAT ABOUT THE "WILD LOOK"?

Cat lovers who crave the "wild look" often turn to breeders who promise to deliver ocelot spots or leopard look-alikes in small, safe, domestic packages. A number of breeds have been pushed, over time, in the direction of a wild coat and body type in a thoroughly domestic package, and a few breeds have even been deliberately created in hopes of achieving this. In some cases, small wild cats have been employed as genetic donors for such efforts—in hopes that they'll bequeath their wild looks, while long-domesticated breeds contribute tameness, predictability, and neotenized, domestic behavior patterns.

Such breeding is a tricky art at best. Responsible breeders must go far beyond the encouragement of a particular look or body type, temperament, and coat length or eye color to perform the finest of balancing acts—the preservation of a wild look in a cat who'll not only be a suitable companion for humans but a well-adjusted, happy, healthy, satisfied animal on his own terms. This can take many generations of careful, controlled breeding, and requires much reflection, study, and soul-searching on the part of the breeder. For cat lovers who might otherwise make an unfortunate decision to adopt an ocelot, bobcat, or cougar cub, though, a cat from such a responsible breeding program can save much heartache.

Beware of "hybrid" felines—cats descended from the mating of domestic cats with small wild cats. Supporting hybridization of domestic cats with small wild cats can encourage capture of wild cats—already endangered in many areas. Hybrid cats are potentially subject to a number of new diseases and health problems. Their behavior may be unpredictable. Vaccinations developed for domestic cats may not work effectively in hybrids. For a safe, ethical, responsible, and humane taste of the wild, adopt a domestic cat—not a wild cat or hybrid.

REPAIRING THE COVENANT: WHAT CAN *YOU* DO?

"If you're not part of the solution, you're part of the problem." Every cat owner is part of the solution—or part of the problem. Be part of the solution—one day, one person, one cat at a time. Here are some ways you can spread the word and honor and promote the Feline Covenant:

Educate yourself.

Learn all you can about cats. Reading this book is a good start! The more you know about all cats—where they come from, how they think, what they need—the better owner and companion you'll be for your cat. And you'll be better prepared to help other cat owners and their cats.

Spread the word.

Become a cheerful, helpful walking cat reference. Know someone who's just adopted a cat or kitten or is thinking about it? Ask if he or she has questions or concerns. Recommend, or even introduce, your veterinarian to this friend or acquaintance. Suggest helpful books, like this one. (When you've finished reading this book, you'll know much more about cats and their care than most cat owners ever will!) Share your knowledge. Is a friend thinking about a birthday-surprise kitten for his toddler? Explain to him (gently) why it's not a good idea. Suggest a picture book about cats and a cuddly stuffed cat instead. Does a coworker complain about litter-box problems? Suggest solutions. Remind her to schedule a veterinarian appointment to rule out illness. If her cat doesn't have a regular veterinarian, recommend yours. You may save her cat's life.

The most common reason cats are surrendered to shelters is supposedly intractable behavior problems. For too many cats, this is a death sentence. Faced with inappropriate elimination or destructive scratching, many cat owners don't know what to do or where to turn. They feel frustrated and helpless, and sometimes fall back on those old myths, deciding their cats are being spiteful or even evil.

Be a lifeline for them, and you'll also be extending a lifeline to their cats. In many cases, a few changes—moving or adding a litter box, changing litter type or box location, installing a scratching post—make all the difference. A visit to the veterinarian to diagnose and treat an underlying illness sometimes solves what was thought to be a behavior problem. Offer your help, but be sensitive. Listen. Share your knowledge, your experiences, your love of cats.

Be a role model for responsible cat ownership.

Sterilize your cat. Treat him to a safe, stimulating, enriched indoors-only lifestyle. Demonstrate through your daily words and actions that your cat is a valued, precious member of your family, no more disposable or replaceable than a child.

Help stop feline overpopulation.

Take every opportunity to promote this message far and wide in your community: "Neuter and spay, it's the kindest way." Be creative. Be polite. But be relentless.

GIFTS OF THE CAT

As the wise, cat-loving French writer Colette noted, "By associating with the cat, one only risks becoming richer." Take that risk! Share those riches the Feline Covenant promises to cat owners and their splendid feline companions.

CHAPTER 5

You Choose Your Cat,
Your Cat Chooses You

SELECTING YOUR CAT

Finding a cat or kitten is simple. Selecting the *right* one for you, your family, and your lifestyle is more challenging. Living with a cat is a lifelong conversation, a privileged relationship with a companion who embodies both wildness and refinement. Entering into this lifelong relationship requires and deserves much planning, reflection, and care. Before you take a cat into your home, life, bed, and heart, do your homework.

Where should you get your cat? Do you crave a pedigreed cat, or prefer a shelter graduate? Should you get one cat? Two? Kitten or adult? Male or female? Longhair or shorthair? Should you adopt a sick cat and care for him? How can you tell if a cat is sick or well? Should you adopt a cat who's been neglected? What's important to you? What's not?

Where Not to Get a Cat: Pet Stores

Pet stores cater to consumers seeking convenient transactions. They usually ask no questions of prospective buyers to insure responsible, lifelong homes for the pets they sell, and they may be staffed by employees with limited knowledge about pets and pet care.

Irresponsible pet stores may not have the slightest idea where the kittens they sell come from. "Backyard breeders," usually irresponsible cat owners who've failed to sterilize their female cats in hopes of making a few dollars, may be the source of many such pet stores' kittens.

Irresponsible pet stores seldom if ever attempt to insure that kitten buyers are able, or even planning, to provide lifelong, safe homes. The Humane Society of the United States urges consumers to avoid patronizing pet stores that sell any live animals except freshwater fish.

Some responsible pet stores work in collaboration with animal shelters to find safe, permanent adoptive homes for shelter animals from the pet-store premises. Adoptable cats, young and old, may be brought to these locations for a period of time to give a new group of potential adopters a chance to see the terrific cats that are available through their local shelter. This arrangement should be clearly identified so you can be sure which humane organization is participating. These adoption programs are usually staffed by employees or volunteers from the local organization, and have the same screening requirements for both the cats and their prospective human families that you'd find at the shelter. The fees are generally the same. Encourage responsible businesses who offer such programs, and reward them with your patronage.

If you're considering a pedigreed kitten, find a responsible breeder who registers his cats with one of the recognized cat registries.

Where Not to Get a Cat: "Free to Good Home" Ads

By obtaining your kitten through a "Free to Good Home" advertisement, you're encouraging an outdated and possibly dangerous practice. By taking the free kitten, you're helping reinforce that old myth that cats are of inherently little or no value. Irresponsible cat owners who can so easily get rid of unwanted kittens will have little or no motivation to sterilize their cats. By adopting their kittens, you're actually rewarding their irresponsibility.

"Backyard breeders," who usually sell kittens cheaply to pet stores, sometimes use "Free Kitten" ads to dump litters they can't sell because they are ill or don't look purebred enough. And unfortunately, individuals seeking cats or other animals for illegal or inhumane purposes often pose as adopters to obtain animals through "Free" ads. Encouraging and patronizing free-kitten dumpers can lead, indirectly, to animal abuse.

There simply are not enough homes for all of the cats being born.
(FRANTZ DANTZLER)

Sometimes Your Cat Finds You

Many cats find their own homes, wandering in off the street as strays. As new strategies such as pediatric sterilization start to show results, and as society starts to value cats more, we hope this will be a declining trend and that fewer strays will have to wander in search of homes. In the meantime, though, your cat may find you. In chapter 19, you'll learn how to determine if the cat you think may be a stray (an unowned cat) actually is one, whether you should adopt him, and, if so, how to help him make the big switch to a safe, happy indoors-only lifestyle in your home.

Taking a Friend or Relative's Cat

Surprisingly, this is the most common source of cats and kittens, according to a 2000 survey by the American Pet Product Manufacturers Association (APPMA). Thirty-nine percent of cat owners with one cat got him or her from a friend or relative. The rate for multiple-cat households was 52 percent. Though obtaining a cat in this way is better than buying a pet-store cat, you might want to take a closer look at why, and how often, your friend or relative has kittens available. If it's a one-time "Oops!" litter, go ahead, but discreetly make sure Momcat is scheduled for sterilization.

But if your friend or relative frequently offers adorable feline adoptables, perhaps some friendly humane education is in order. Why hasn't Mother Cat been sterilized? Money problems? Offer information on low-cost sterilization clinics and "Spay Day U.S.A.," sponsored every year in February by the Doris Day Animal Foundation (227 Massachusetts Avenue, NE, Ste. 100, Washington, DC 20002–4963; www.ddaf.org/DDAF/SpayDay). Perhaps your friend or relative isn't aware of the tragedy of cat overpopulation and doesn't realize how many kittens are killed in shelters for want of homes.

Thinking About a Pedigreed Cat?

Are you interested in a particular *breed* of cat—say a Siamese, Abyssinian, or Manx—that encompasses a known look and personality? Take a few moments to reflect upon just why you want a pedigreed cat. Is a particular look extremely important to you? Are you fascinated by a particular breed's history, lineage, and associations? Do you cherish fond memories of a cat of a particular breed? Do you plan to participate in the world of cat shows? Are you head-over-heels in love with a particular breed? All are valid reasons for considering a pedigreed cat.

A *breed* is a group of domestic cats that a particular *cat registry,* such as the CFA (Cat Fanciers' Association), ACFA (American Cat Fanciers' Association), TICA (The International Cat Association), and other such organizations, has agreed to recognize as such. Accepted cats must conform to the registry's *breed standard* for that breed. There are registries that accept numerous breeds of cats, as well as smaller registries that register only cats of one breed. Usually, all cats of a breed have some group of distinguishing features, such as body shape, overall look, and personality, that sets them apart from members of other breeds.

A breed is not a species. *Species* is a taxonomic (classification) term that refers to a group of closely related, physically similar individual animals that interbreed or have the potential to interbreed. All domestic cats, pedigreed or not, belong to the same species, *Felis catus* (also called *Felis domesticus*).

"Pedigreed" Versus "Purebred"

You may see the term *purebred cat* on a pet-store cage. Responsible breeders and cat registries generally avoid this term because it has little meaning—all domestic cats have some variety in their genetic heritage. A "pedigreed" cat has known lineage and is recognized by a cat registry as belonging to a specific breed. The "pedigree" itself is the registered record of the cat's lineage. To register a cat, the cat's breeder or owner must document that the cat is eligible for registration according to the particular registry's standards and rules.

Dozens of recognized breeds offer cats of known (to a point) ancestry, consistent appearance, and behavior as predictable as can be expected from this most-independent creature. If you want a pedigreed cat, obtain him from a responsible breeder who registers cats with one of the well-known cat registries. First, though, do your homework. Visit cat shows, read books, and speak to reputable breeders.

If you have your heart set on a pedigreed cat, you'll need to decide which of the breeds of pedigreed cats (currently numbering thirty-five to forty-four depending on the registry) both appeals to you and will best suit your lifestyle, temperament, and personality. It's very easy to fall in love with a winsome pedigreed kitten at a cat show. But think before whipping out your checkbook and bundling that tiny kitten home. What do you know about the breed? The breeder? The kitten's health history?

Cat shows are great opportunities to meet breeders and find out about a variety of breeds, as well as to see superior examples of each. You'll probably find yourself drawn to a few breeds. Talk to the breeders. Most are glad to answer serious inquiries and to provide breed and cattery literature. Collect up-to-date information at breed-club displays, which are excellent sources of expertise, advice, and literature.

Never forget that every cat, whatever his heritage, is unique. Within a breed—even within a single litter—individual cats can exhibit vast differences in behavior, temperament, demonstrativeness, energy level, territoriality, requirement for affection, and other traits. Although certain characteristics are considered typical of a particular breed—for example, a typical Siamese is much more vocal than a typical Manx—it's unfair to expect a kitten to behave in any predefined way.

Although personality differences among breeds haven't been scientifically researched, anecdotal evidence from breeders, cat owners, and veterinarians tends to correspond with the popular images of breed personality. Taking a close look at your home and family environment will help you select the pedigreed cat that's right for you. Here are some general guidelines:

PEDIGREED CATS
Easygoing and Friendly, Good with Children

American shorthair	Ragdoll
British shorthair	Scottish fold
Maine coon	Snowshoe
Manx	Turkish van
Norwegian forest cat	

Active, People Oriented, Attention Loving, Can Be Demanding

American curl	Javanese
Balinese	Korat
Burmese	Siamese
Colorpoint shorthair	Singapura

| Egyptian mau | Sphynx |
| Japanese bobtail | Tonkinese |

Quiet, Undemanding "Lap Cats"

Birman	Nebelung
Bombay	Russian blue
Chartreux	Scottish fold
Havana brown	Selkirk rex

Active Athletes

Abyssinian	
Bengal	
Ocicat	
Somali	

Grooming-Intensive

| Himalayan |
| Persian |
| Turkish Angora |

These generalizations only scratch the surface of the variety of personality and temperament among pedigreed cats. Many breeds offer a variety of colors, markings, fur length and texture, and eye color. Some breeds are recognized by only one registry, others by several. Some breeds, especially newer ones, are quite controversial and require extra study and reflection before adoption. Keep in mind that all breeds result from genetic divergence away from *Felis catus*. Often, the more a cat deviates from the size and shape of the average tabby cat, the more likely he'll be to have special grooming, medical, and dietary needs.

If, after you've done your homework—and some soul-searching—you still have your heart set on a particular breed, go ahead with confidence. But realize that living with a pedigreed cat brings special responsibilities as well as special joys. As the owner of a pedigreed cat, you'll share with responsible breeders a mission to enhance the image of all domestic cats, whatever their origins, as valuable animals, worthy of society's respect and protection.

Finally, even if you think you're enamored of a particular breed, visit local shelters. Pedigreed cats sometimes turn up there. Or you may meet a cat that looks just like the breed you crave. If the pedigree itself isn't as important to you as the cat's appearance and personality, he might be the cat for you. Contact a local "breed-rescue" group that handles the breed you seek. These groups work tirelessly to find new homes for pedigreed cats who've been given up for adoption or otherwise become homeless.

Shelter Cats Are Special Cats!

"There are no ordinary cats," maintained cat-loving French writer Colette. Cats of all kinds, from fancy to homely, populate our shelters. But most shelter cats are proudly "ordinary," blessed with sturdy constitutions, hybrid vigor, and all the feline grace, predatory skill, and magnificence with which nature and evolution have endowed them.

In fact, for most potential cat owners seeking to add a cat to their lives, the local animal shelter is the best place to obtain one. The sad fact that there are so many homeless cats also means that virtually every shelter offers a selection of cats you simply can't find anywhere else—cats of all ages, personalities, colors, coat lengths, and more. If you've decided on a shelter adoptee, congratulations! Pick a date to visit your local shelter. If you're sure you want a kitten, remember that most kittens are born in springtime. The plethora of kittens available in June is a mixed blessing. You'll likely have your pick of a rainbow of color and pattern, but it's sobering to realize that this exuberant flowering of life represents so much irresponsibility and heedlessness. Too many of the marvelous little beings will never find homes.

Shelter cats—tiny kittens to exuberant adolescents to stately old gentlemen—offer adopters the usual feline charms of delightful unpredictability, plus a uniquely feline

Animal shelters do all they can to ensure that all adopted cats are as healthy and well suited to their new lives as possible.
(FRANTZ DANTZLER)

Shelter cats offer adopters the usual feline charms of delightful unpredictability, plus a uniquely feline brand of affectionate gratitude and the profound satisfaction of saving a life.
(KATHY MILANI)

brand of affectionate gratitude and the profound satisfaction of saving a life. Shelter graduates seem to have a talent for making their owners and families feel particularly honored.

Most shelters take great pains to insure that the cats and kittens they place go to stable, permanent, safe homes. Don't be surprised when shelter workers quiz you closely or have you fill out a form, detailing your home situation, family members, lifestyle, other pets, and other issues that may seem rather personal. They'll be especially interested in cats you've owned before and what happened to them. They're not being nosy; they're simply trying to make sure the cats and kittens they place have the best possible chance for a long, happy life and that you and your family will be happy and satisfied, too.

Many shelters offer additional services such as behavior education and counseling, training classes, veterinary advice and procedures, and retail shops where you can purchase pet supplies. Shelters do all they can to insure that all adopted cats are as healthy and well suited to their new lives as possible. The shelter cat you adopt is likely to have been given basic vaccinations and any treatments needed for fleas, ear mites, and internal and external parasites.

The cat you adopt—even if just a tiny kitten—may have been sterilized. Many shelters have policies calling for pediatric (or early age) spaying and neutering. They've found that sterilizing kittens as young as eight weeks of age, who weigh at least two pounds, is a safe, sensible, and economical way to help stop the uncontrolled breeding of unwanted cats. Don't add to the "litter problem." If your shelter doesn't sterilize animals before you're able to take them home, have your veterinarian perform this important surgery either upon adoption or by six months of age.

One Cat or Two?

Are most or all of your family members away at work or school during the day? Consider adopting a pair of cats or kittens. Cats are inquisitive, intelligent, friendly, curious creatures, susceptible to loneliness and boredom that can bring on behavior problems. Two kittens will amuse and groom each other, play and snooze happily together, and share an irreplaceable intraspecies friendship that will contribute immeasurably to their health and happiness. Don't worry if the two kittens aren't littermates; they'll quickly bond. Caring for two cats will be more expensive over the course of their lives, but the psychological, social, and behavioral benefits of bonding, friendship, and companionship are worth it for them—and for you.

If you have the opportunity to adopt littermates, don't pass it up. Littermates are already friends and will help each other to quickly get used to you and their new home. If you see a litter of three, though, think hard before breaking up the little family group. Perhaps you could take all three? If that's not possible, see if the shelter has a singleton kitten who needs a home.

Kitten or Cat?

If your family already includes cats, an older kitten (age six months to a year) might be a better choice than a grown-up. Adult cats, especially those unaccustomed to animal companions, tend to have more difficulty fitting harmoniously into a new family setting with a social group already established. Kittens are much more adaptable, generally considering other creatures, of whatever size or species, as potential playmates.

Then there's the cuteness factor. Kittens are cute, cute, cute! It's a special joy to watch a kitten bloom from tiny fluff ball to mature cat. But it's also a big responsibility. A kitten alone, especially if he's your only pet, may be homesick for a while for his mom and littermates. With two or more kittens, your job of socialization will be easier, as the kittens will help each other reinforce the lessons they've learned. Plus, they'll each have an understanding playmate nearby eager to help work off all that excess kittenish energy that might otherwise be directed into destructive behavior.

Having kittens in the house is a lot like having rambunctious toddlers—complete with needle-sharp claws and teeth, infant clumsiness, and a zest for adventure that can exhaust the sturdiest owner. Curtains and pants legs are perfect for climbing; electrical cords are great for chewing; feet and ankles are ideal for hunting and biting practice. Not ready for quite that much excitement?

Consider an adolescent cat—one about one-to-three years of age. Past the most tumultuous phase of kittenhood, your adolescent cat is still wide-open to new experiences. He's playful, active, curious, adventurous, adaptable, and ready to make friends with everyone in your family. Even if he hasn't quite finished growing, you have a good idea of how large he's going to get. He's already sterilized. You know his grooming requirements, food and litter preferences, temperament, and unique personality traits. You might even know some of his history.

Adult Cats: What You See Is What You Get

Or imagine a mellow, mature cat—three years of age or older—joining your family circle. He's full-grown. Shelter workers usually know which of their mature cats prefer quiet, peaceable environments, which enjoy lots of activity, which do well with kids or dogs, and which can't abide other cats. With so many unknowns taken care of, you can concentrate on settling in with your new friend and getting to know him at your own pace.

Many people think they have their heart set on a kitten, often in the mistaken belief that adolescent and adult shelter cats have intractable behavior problems or are not adaptable enough to thrive in unfamiliar environments or bond with new owners. But lovely, well-socialized adolescent and mature adult cats sometimes find themselves in shelters because their owners died or were forced by medical conditions or difficult life situations to give them up. These adult cats, and especially the elders among them, are difficult to place into new homes, mainly because of misconceptions.

Adopting a mature cat, one at least three years of age, is a special joy—for both of you. It's a rare privilege to be chosen for friendship by a wise older cat who's decided that you're worthy of his attentions! Your mature adoptee will take his time getting to know you and your family. He'll explore his new home, sniffing out the stories in scents, reveling in sounds and textures. He'll select his favorite hideaways, sleeping spots, laps. Mature cats have precious years left, and plenty of love to fill them.

Adopting a mature adult cat might mean some increased veterinary expenses for special diets, dental care (especially if his teeth have been neglected by previous owners), and treatments for age-related conditions like arthritis, hyperthyroidism, or diabetes. If the cat is older than eight or nine, schedule a veterinary visit to obtain a baseline blood panel to use as a basis for comparison if your new cat starts experiencing health problems later. Treating your adult adoptee to a safe, indoors-only lifestyle will help insure that he enjoys the longest, healthiest possible life with you.

Imagine a mature, mellow shelter cat joining your family circle.
(FRANTZ DANTZLER)

Save Two Lives, Save a Friendship

Sometimes, two or more cats from the same household find themselves in a shelter together. And cats who spend their days in common rooms in many shelters while awaiting adoption often form friendships with compatible feline souls. (Perhaps they compare notes on the foibles of their previous owners.) Accustomed to a relaxed, multiple-cat environment, these mature adult cats have often learned a live-and-let-live attitude and engage in as much or as little social interaction as they prefer.

Adopting a pair of cats who are friends is especially rewarding. Your new friends will be wise and comforting companions, providing each other with priceless psychological support, mutual grooming, and a playmate who won't run them ragged. They share a special bond with a confidante of their own age and species who understands, on a cat level, what they've been through. You'll all appreciate the more graceful integration into your home life their friendship enables. With a familiar face, a familiar scent, and a familiar purr to cuddle up to, your new cats will experience far less stress during the transition to their new life.

Male or Female?

Many people find that domestic cats work out best in mixed-sex groups or pairs. If you're a novice cat owner, or a prospective adopter considering a pair of cats or kittens, a mixed pair might be your best choice.

Longhair or Shorthair?

A fluffy, longhaired cat with a dramatic plumed tail is a glorious sight and can be a source of pride and joy—as long as he's kept clean and well groomed. But without meticulous daily coat care, he can develop painful mats and snags, suffer from frequent hair balls from self-grooming, and pick up alarming amounts of dust and dirt, even indoors. Longhaired cats sometimes need help keeping their "bloomers" clean, and may need an occasional warm washcloth wipe-down, or some clipping of rear-end fur. Your longhaired cat requires a commitment to daily grooming above and beyond the ordinary daily care all cats require. Do you have time for this?

If you don't plan to keep your cat indoors all the time, or if you can't commit yourself to daily grooming, a shorthaired cat is a better choice. A longhaired cat who ventures outdoors will likely pick up difficult-to-remove grime, burrs, weeds, bugs, dirt, and other foreign matter in his coat. With all that fur, it will be harder to tell if he has fleas, ticks, or other external parasites, or whether he's suffered injuries or wounds that may lead to abscesses. (Shorthaired cats can also pick up these unpleasant things outdoors—but they'll be easier to spot.) All cats, and especially longhaired cats, who spend time outdoors will need bathing occasionally. Indoors-only cats, whatever their coat lengths, seldom if ever need bathing if their grooming needs are regularly attended to.

If you're adopting an adult cat, you'll be able to see immediately how much daily coat care he'll require. With a kitten, it's harder to tell. A fluff ball can grow into a sleek, smooth shorthair who requires no more than a quick rubdown with a chamois. Or he can fluff out even further and require daily brushing. Looking at the kitten's mother may not help, as he might not take after her in this regard. If your kitten grows up with more fur than you expected, learn to provide the grooming he needs and schedule enough time for it. Read chapter 15 for tips.

Shedding

It's a fallacy that longhaired cats always shed more than shorthaired cats. All cats shed. There are wide individual differences, irrespective of coat length. Shedding occurs more in winter, when the heat is on indoors. But some cats shed all year round, and risk developing frequent hair balls from ingesting large amounts of hair while self-grooming. Perennial shedders benefit from regular brushing, combined with daily rubdowns with a grooming glove or a slightly dampened washcloth to remove loosened hair.

Choosing a Healthy Cat

Most every kitten is irresistible. But a healthy, well-adjusted cat or kitten is your best choice for a lifelong companion. Beware the strong temptation to adopt a cat or kitten because you feel sorry for him. That sickly, sneezing waif, the kitten shunned by his littermates, or the one who hangs back, shows no interest in play, or seems ratty—these animals can be more costly than you realize, both in dollars and in heartache. (Sometimes, sadly, a kitten is shunned because his littermates realize that he's ill.) If you do choose to adopt such a kitten—a course recommended only to the dedicated and experienced—choose with your eyes open, and with full understanding of the potential costs.

Choosing the right cat is important! Take as much time as you need. If your shelter has a kitten room (equipped with safe toys and climbing furniture, and perhaps comfortable chairs for prospective adopters), take advantage of it. Assure yourself that you're getting the right cat or kitten for you and your lifestyle.

Spend a few moments just observing the kittens interacting with their littermates or other kittens. If possible, observe the kitten's mother. Allowing for the fact that she's been raising an active, hungry family, does she seem generally healthy and content?

How does she interact with her offspring? At least some components of temperament are inherited.

Sizing Up Personality and Health

Watch the kittens together. Look for playfulness, activity, bounce, and that unmistakable zest for life. Ideally, go for the middle-of-the-pack kitten—the one who is neither the most assertive, nor the shyest. These middle kittens are usually more friendly, easygoing, tolerant, and well-adjusted. A properly socialized kitten will neither run right up to an unknown person, nor run away and cower in fear under a chair. Stoop down, or sit on the floor. Extend your hand, and call gently. Watch the kitten who approaches you with curiosity, a bit of reserve, but not excessive fear. Let him sniff your hand. If he accepts it, stroke him gently.

A normal, healthy kitten is playful, inquisitive, and curious. When you pick him up, he should feel relaxed and amiable, not tense, fearful, or defensive. His claws should not be out. He should purr when stroked and respond with enthusiasm to playful overtures. Dangle a string or toss a ball—he should give merry chase! Beware of a lethargic, depressed, or dull-eyed kitten, or one who shows little or no interest in his surroundings. Evidence of lack of self-grooming may indicate illness.

A kitten or cat who continually shakes his head, or paws or scratches at his ears or other areas, may be ill, or may have ear mites or other parasites. A kitten who staggers, stumbles, sways, or falls down frequently, walks in circles, or seems confused or in pain may be seriously ill.

Once you've tentatively settled on a kitten or cat, it's time for an informal health check. (Your veterinarian will do a more complete health survey at his first visit.) Start by just observing. As the kitten or cat becomes more comfortable with your presence, gradually introduce more touching and interaction.

The Nose-to-Toes Once-Over

Nose

Look for a clean nose, with no mucus discharge or runniness, and clear breathing, with no sneezing, wheezing, or sniffling.

Mouth

Teeth should be bright and white; gums a healthy pink. Beware of bad mouth or breath odors and visible inflammation or sores in the mouth, or if he flinches or shows evidence of pain or discomfort as you check his mouth. Find out if he's been getting regular dental care. If so, continue it. If not, give him a chance to settle into his new home before gradually introducing toothbrushing. Your veterinarian can show you how to clean your kitten's teeth, and can recommend appropriate tools and products for a lifetime of dental health. See chapter 15 for tips.

Eyes

Eyes should be bright, clear, lively, and curious, with no discharge, redness, crustiness, clouding, excessive tearing, swelling, or inflammation—all signs of possible illness. If more than the tiniest sliver of the nictitating membrane (the white "third eyelid" in the inner corner) is showing, it might indicate illness. Watch for crossed eyes (a problem with some of the oriental breeds), which can affect visual acuity.

All-white cats with blue eyes are often deaf. All-white cats with one blue eye may be deaf on the side with the blue eye. This is caused by a genetic condition.

Ears

Ears should be sweet smelling; a bad or sour smell may indicate a yeast infection or some other problem. Ears should be free of discharge or brownish, waxy, crusty goo that may indicate the presence of ear mites. A cat with ear mites scratches vigorously and frequently, often digging at his ear with his hind foot. Though terribly annoying, ear mites can be eradicated, so a mite infestation alone should not stop you from adopting the cat.

Under the tail

Check for signs of diarrhea. The anal region and the backs of the rear legs should be clean, well groomed, and free of discoloration. The anus should not look swollen or inflamed, or protrude from the body.

Verify the kitten's sex while you're at it. Veterinarians are often amazed—and amused—by proud new owners of a male kitten they had adopted as a female, and vice versa. Do the "punctuation tests": A male kitten has two dots under his tail, like a colon but side-by-side. A female kitten has a dot with a vertical line beneath, like a semicolon.

Paws and claws

Claws should be neatly clipped. Gently squeeze the kitten's paw to extend the claws to check. If his claws haven't been clipped, do this necessary grooming at home. Your veterinarian can show you how. (Read chapter 15 for tips.) Does your cat have extra toes? Don't worry! This genetic condition, called *polydactyly,* won't cause him any problems—and is extra cute, to boot!

Coiffures and Creepy-Crawlies

Coat

The hair coat should be sweet smelling, fluffy, glossy, clean, and free of parasites (such as fleas), with no mats, sores, scabs, scaling, crustiness, redness, or missing patches of fur. Keep in mind that rambunctious kittens sometimes get minor scratches while playing.

Watch for signs of itching. Ruffle the fur and look for fleas. If you suspect fleas, run a comb through the fur over the cat's back. Shake the comb out over a damp paper towel. Black specks that turn red on the damp towel are flea droppings.

Beware of excessively shedding fur, a ratty or spiky-looking coat, or fur that looks dingy and dirty. A healthy cat spends a lot of time self-grooming; lack of interest in grooming can indicate illness. Bald, patchy spots may indicate ringworm—a zoonotic (transmissible-to-humans) fungal infection.

Shaping Up

Size

A kitten who's unusually small in comparison to his littermates may have an underlying weakness or illness. A larger-than-average kitten is likely to be a more-assertive and forthcoming pet, especially if his activity level and degree of bossiness match his size.

Overall odor

The kitten should smell sweet and fresh. Fecal odors may indicate ongoing diarrhea. Dirty, bad, or "off" odors may indicate infection, stomach upset, dental problems, skin infection, or serious underlying metabolic disorders.

Body conformation and condition

Gently stroke the cat or kitten from head to tail. Feel for lumps, bumps, swellings, and any spots that make him flinch, vocalize, or show pain or annoyance. Beware of a hard-feeling, bulbous-looking, potbellylike tummy in an otherwise normal-sized kitten—it may indicate internal parasites such as roundworms. Your kitten or cat should be sleek and well rounded but not fat. You should be able to feel, and just barely see, his ribs. Limbs should be straight and well proportioned, and he should move easily and gracefully. A healthy cat feels taut and well muscled—neither paunchy nor scrawny.

Gait

Watch him walk, run, and leap. His gait should be graceful, balanced, and assured. Limping or favoring of a limb could indicate an abscess, a hidden injury, a congenital bone or muscle defect, or some other problem or disease. When greeting a familiar cat, or in play, a kitten should hold his tail high, or in the relaxed, half-raised "adult" position.

Hearing check

Check the cat or kitten's hearing by making a sudden loud sound (for example, clap your hands out of view of the cat). He should startle briefly and look towards the sound.

Once you've sized up your chosen cat or kitten and run through this simple health check, it's time for the trip home. Before you leave, though, ask which vaccinations and health treatments he's already had. Schedule a get-acquainted visit with the veterinarian within a few days. Keep your new friend isolated from other cats and animals in your home until his veterinarian has given him a clean bill of health. Your veterinarian has the knowledge and experience to detect underlying health problems and danger signs you may have missed, to administer appropriate tests and vaccinations, and to prescribe any necessary medications or treatments, such as miticides for ear mites.

Ideally, your new feline friend will enjoy an exclusively indoor lifestyle. By understanding your cat's needs for space, exercise, scratching, and interactive play, and by providing for these needs within your own home, you'll be setting the stage for a longer, healthier, safer life for him, and a closer, more-fulfilling interspecies friendship for both of you. You'll be able to observe his activities and development up close, while protecting him from diseases, accidents, becoming lost, and other heartbreaks that are the fate of so many outdoor cats. (Chapter 8 fully explains the advantages of keeping your cat indoors.)

Finally, enjoy your new companion. If you've adopted a kitten, remember that kittenhood is fleeting! Whatever your cat's age, make the most of the get-acquainted phase of your relationship, this magical time of exploration, discovery, and bonding. And keep your camera handy and loaded with film.

Adopting an Adult Cat Who's Been Neglected or Mistreated

Try to find out as much as possible about the history, socialization, and temperament of any cat you're considering adopting. While you should never rule out a cat just because he's had a difficult life, be realistic. A cat who's suffered serious neglect, abuse, or trauma may be psychologically, physically, and behaviorally affected by those experiences for life. Patience, persistence, love, and trust can help rebuild an abused cat's shattered spirit and trust in humans, but it can be a long process with many heartaches, and there is no assurance that he'll ever completely recover. It can be tremendously rewarding and gratifying, but it's not for the faint-of-heart.

If you want a healthy, well-adjusted cat for a family pet, steer clear of cats with difficult backgrounds. Beware of adopting a special-needs cat or a cat with a history of abuse just because you feel sorry for him. If you're unprepared, unable, or just too busy to offer the patience and special care his medical problems, handicaps, serious behavioral problems, or other complications require, you might end up doing him more harm than good. And if his special needs turn out to be too much for you, returning him to the shelter will only compound his pain and confusion.

If, after sober reflection, you want to adopt a special-needs cat, it's vital to insure that everyone in your household will welcome this challenge, and to carefully consider the effects the presence of this cat may have on animals that already live with you. If you feel you're ready and able to offer a very special cat the patience, love, care, and support he needs, go ahead with a joyful heart and open eyes.

WHAT WILL HAPPEN IF THIS KITTEN OR CAT DOESN'T FIT INTO YOUR HOUSEHOLD?

Ideally, you've done your homework, soul-searching, and preparation. The cat or kitten you adopt should share your home for life. But sometimes even the best-intentioned adoption doesn't work out. What do you do then?

Giving up a cat should never be a casual or impulsive decision, made in the heat of anger, frustration, or desperation. Has your life suddenly taken an unexpected turn? Don't just give up your cat! Take a deep breath. Write down alternatives, and imagine scenarios in which it may be possible to keep him. Could a friend or relative keep him for a limited time? Could you board the cat until your crisis has passed?

If none of your options seem promising, and you obtained your cat from a shelter, breeder, or a breed-rescue organization, call them. Many shelter and breeder contracts require that you notify them first if you cannot keep your cat for any reason. Your shelter, breeder, or rescue group will want to know why you need to give up the cat. They'll also want to know as much as possible about your cat's lifestyle, temperament, and health. Although you may feel they're being nosy, they're just trying to insure that your cat gets the best-possible chance for a new permanent home with as little upset as possible.

What if your new cat or kitten is chronically misbehaving (shredding the furniture, urinating all over the house), or is experiencing a serious conflict with another cat or animal in your home? There are numerous behavior-modification and other cat-sensitive techniques you can try. Review chapter 10 and look anew at the situation from the cat's point of view. Consult cat-behavior books, or a professional cat-behavior specialist.

If you adopted your cat from a shelter, seek advice from their cat experts. Many shelters offer training and behavior counseling, or can refer you to providers of those services. Shelter personnel want you and your cat to have a happy, trouble-free life together, and they stand ready to help you resolve behavioral problems and intercat conflicts.

Ask your veterinarian for advice. He can suggest behavioral and training strategies, and also prescribe medications that may calm and steady your cat while he is learning more acceptable behavior patterns. Remember, though, that medication without behavior modification may not be effective in the long run.

Many humane organizations, shelters, and schools of veterinary medicine offer hot lines you can call to discuss your cat's behavior and other problems. You'll speak with an experienced cat-behavior specialist or an upper-level veterinary student with a special interest in, and knowledge about, feline behavior. Many of these services are free.

Prevention is much easier and more effective than dealing with a difficult situation that's gotten out of hand. Ask the hard questions; take a candid look at your life situation, environment, and resources; and do your research and soul-searching *before* you adopt that cat or kitten.

In the next chapter, you'll learn how to get ready for the arrival of a new cat or kitten in your home. Being prepared with the proper supplies, equipment, and furniture, and insuring that your home is a safe, secure, cat-friendly environment, will go a long ways towards heading off any possible problems with your new arrival.

CHAPTER 6

Getting Ready and the First Days Home

SIMPLE GIFTS

Since 1985, when cats overtook dogs as America's most-popular household pets, cat owners have been targeted with increasing zeal by purveyors of cat litter, food, toys, and other supplies. Your local supermarket offers a dizzying array of cat products. Add to this the offerings of pet superstores, specialty retailers, and the Internet. The field of cat boxes (litter boxes), fillers, and related accessories, for example, has become increasingly crowded with ever more complicated, expensive solutions to a straight-forward problem. A novice cat owner might well be daunted by the vast range of choices in box fillers alone.

For successful cat keeping, here's all you really need:

1. this book
2. sufficient resources—money, time, space—to support your cat
3. a safe indoor environment, suitably enriched for feline satisfaction and enjoyment

4. high-quality, nutritionally balanced cat food
5. cat-friendly, human-acceptable indoor feline toilet facilities
6. a veterinarian
7. a sincere commitment to the Feline Covenant

In many ways, we and our cats are alike. We crave a safe, predictable, pleasant, clean, harmonious environment. We crave stimulation and excitement—but in manageable, nonthreatening doses. We savor contact, conversation, and touching—but on our own terms. We resent it when someone invades our personal space without our consent. We're sensitive to stress and change in our daily routines. We love entertainment and play, and thrive on fresh air, warmth, and sunshine.

As responsible, sensitive cat owners, it's our continuing responsibility to provide our cats with a stimulus-rich, entertaining, intriguing environment that satisfies their essential physical, mental, and psychological needs, and we must do this while offering them the safety and security of a protected indoors-only lifestyle. In this way, we not only enhance our cats' well-being, but also immeasurably increase the pleasures and joys of cat keeping for ourselves.

THE SECRETS OF THE CAT REVEALED!

Later on, in chapter 10, you'll discover much more about your cat's nature and behavior—how he communicates through his rich, multimodal vocabulary, how he learns, and how to train him (yes, it can be done!). You'll discover lots of tips for making your life together harmonious, fun, and satisfying. These ten secrets will get you started:

1. Always look to your cat for guidance. Mindful observation of him may teach you more than any one book ever can.
2. Every cat is an individual, unique as a snowflake. As your cat's owner, you're in the best position to observe your cat and know what's normal for him.
3. The two major causes of misbehavior in an otherwise healthy cat are boredom and stress. It's your job to prevent these. Cats don't misbehave out of revenge, spite, or inherent meanness.
4. Much feline behavior is, essentially, communication. What we call misbehavior is actually an attempt to get our attention, to break through our

human preoccupations, and to communicate important information. If we ignore this communication or misinterpret it, it will tend to escalate until we get it.

5. Cats live in the present. This is not to say they don't remember people, places, and events, for they clearly do; but they neither regret the past nor fret about the future.

6. Cats are polite and sensitive, and expect, and respond positively to, politeness and sensitivity from their companions.

7. Cats love routine and ritual, and dislike change. They are happiest in a relatively harmonious, predictable environment.

8. Cats crave stimulation and excitement, but in manageable, cat-controllable doses.

9. Cats are a high-contact species—but expect, and respond best to, contact that's on their own terms.

10. Cat-box maintenance—that most daunting barrier to an indoors-only lifestyle—is really quite straightforward. With an accurate understanding of your cat's needs and wants in this important area, the right tools and supplies, and a positive, can-do attitude, the litter-box blues are a thing of the past. Read chapter 7 to get the real scoop. Ignore the clamor of advertisers, and listen to your cat!

Ready, set, charge! You'll want to stock up on supplies for the new arrival. (Depiction of individual products does not imply endorsement by The Humane Society of the United States)
(FRANTZ DANTZLER)

READY, SET . . .

A trip to the pet-supply store, some thoughtful cat-proofing, and a call to your veterinarian are musts before you bring your new kitten or cat home. (See the supply list in the box on page 84.) Even if your family already includes cats, treat the new arrival to his very own food bowl, water bowl, and toys. He'll need his own litter box at first, too. Take a critical look around your home—from the point of view of an active, curious kitten or an adult cat thoughtfully and thoroughly exploring his new environment.

WHAT IS CAT-PROOFING?

Cat-proofing insures that your home is safe, healthy, and free of any possible dangers to your new cat. Effective cat-proofing encompasses *prevention, awareness, and supervision.*

Prevention

These are the obvious health-and-safety measures like locking away all poisons and toxins and securely screening windows.

Awareness

Encourage every member of your family to adopt attitudes and habits that promote feline safety and health. These habits and attitudes will also make your home a safer, healthier place for you and your family.

Supervision

Especially while your kitten is young, or your cat is getting to know his new home, extra attention and vigilance are required. If your cat is an indoors-only pet, everyone in the family must become familiar with door discipline (see page 70). Keeping your cat safe and healthy is an everyday, family affair—and an important part of the Feline Covenant.

Like human babies at the crawling stage, kittens are intelligent, agile, curious, and apt to put everything in their mouths. With a kitten in the house, it's particularly important to keep poisonous substances, cleaning products, medicines, and sharp objects inside closed cabinets with childproof latches. Now let's take a tour of your home with the three aspects of cat-proofing—prevention, awareness, and supervision—in mind.

All Around the House—A Checklist for Cat-Proofing

If your family includes babies or toddlers, you've likely eliminated many safety hazards and made numerous modifications to insure their health and safety. With a kitten or a cat, though, you need to go even further. Because cats are so agile and mobile—they can leap to great heights, jump long distances, and wiggle into incredibly small spaces—it's vital to approach cat-proofing from a cat's or kitten's point of view. Do a survey of your home on all fours, noticing—from the point of view of an inquisitive feline—any potential hazards and "attractive nuisances."

Cleaning Up

Living with a cat or kitten means cleaning up all spills immediately. Whether food, cleaning product, or some other kind of substance, anything left on the floor will find its way onto your cat's paws or coat and into his mouth. Clean up spills and rinse the areas thoroughly with clean water. If you have even the slightest suspicion that your cat has consumed a poisonous substance, call your veterinarian or emergency veterinary clinic immediately and follow their instructions. If you can't reach either, call the ASPCA's National Animal Poison Control Center (ASPCA/NAPCC—see box on page 83). Keep the phone numbers of your veterinarian, emergency animal clinic, and the NAPCC by your phone.

One strategy for protecting your cat—and your family and the environment— from toxic cleaning substances is to reconsider your approach to housecleaning. Instead of using caustic or poisonous chemicals, clean with steam. A number of appliances are now available that heat ordinary tap water to steam. You can clean and sterilize virtually any surface in your home, from tiles to windows to carpets—all with no chemicals or chemical residue for your cat to walk in or lap up. Citrus-based and other natural or "green" cleaners are both safer and more ecologically sound than the traditional chemical cleaners. Always check the labels carefully, and follow directions— even for products that are advertised as "all-natural" or "safe."

Trash Talkin'

To your kitten or cat, your trash cans and garbage pails are big toy boxes, full of interesting odors and tempting tastes. But because of the dangers that can lurk in your trash—everything from sharp can lids to spoiled food to bacteria-laden tissues—you need to protect your cat from his natural urges to spill, explore, and sample your trash.

1. Use covered trash containers. Find containers with tight-fitting lids that latch rather than just sit on top.
2. Keep your garbage and trash cans inside cabinets fitted with childproof (and cat-proof) latches.
3. Cats love to stand up on their tiptoes to peer into trash cans, often toppling them. Place a heavy weight (such as a six-by-six cinder block, or six common bricks) in the bottom of the trash container. Then put your plastic bag or other liner in the container. Use a container with a lid, too.
4. Trash or garbage that would be dangerous for your cat, should he get at it, should *immediately* be put outside the house into an outdoor receptacle.

Window Safety

No matter what your new cat's age, securely screen all windows. What cat doesn't adore sitting perched in a window, watching birds flutter around the feeder? Make sure bird-watching is a safe hobby for your cat by fitting all windows with securely mounted screens. Avoid nylon or fabric screens; your cat's claws can shred these in seconds. Screen upper casements as well. A motivated cat can jump much higher than you think and slither through surprisingly narrow openings. Sunning cats are sometimes tempted to take off after passing birds, resulting in the tragedy known as feline high-rise syndrome.

Anything that hangs or dangles fascinates cats. Secure curtain pulls and window-shade pulls: if your cat accidentally gets his head tangled up in one, he could hang himself. Kittens are particularly at risk. Cut the looped cords on shades, blinds, and curtains, or wind them securely around hooks mounted next to the window.

Cats and kittens are often attracted to the hanging, dangling fabrics of curtains and drapes—handy climbing ladders to access lofty heights. Besides being tough on the curtains themselves, frolicking felines can get tangled up in the fabric or hung up by their claws, or tumble down from the top if a curtain rod collapses under their weight. Cats have a built-in "righting reflex," but they can still be seriously injured in falls.

Prevent Shocking Developments

Never leave hanging or dangling electrical, telephone, or computer cords where your cat can reach them, and never let him play with cords or electric appliances, even if they're turned off or unplugged. And though they don't conduct electricity, never let your cat play with those attractively coiled telephone cords. Make *all* cords off-limits—they're not toys. If you see your cat playing with a dangerous or inappropriate object, divert his attention with a vigorous interactive-play session or a cat-appropriate toy.

Your cat can suffer a deadly electric shock if he bites or claws through the protective insulation on live cord. Even if he isn't killed, he can suffer painful, slow-to-heal electrical burns to his mouth and paw pads.

Use cord-guide systems or PVC tubes to keep cords out of paw reach. Or tape the cords securely to baseboards. Check the tape frequently to make sure it's not peeling or being clawed off. Another alternative is to spray or coat cords with an aversive or bitter-tasting substance such as "bitter apple," or in a pinch, cat-safe bitters. Cover electrical outlets with childproof plug covers; if your cat sprays an open wall outlet, it could start an electrical fire. Keep electric equipment and appliances unplugged when not in use. This includes irons, hair dryers, toasters, coffeemakers, and other small appliances with switches your cat could inadvertently turn on.

Fireplaces, Wood Stoves, and Candles

A cat curled cozily on the hearth or beside a wood stove—it's a charming image. Cats adore warmth, and they can enjoy wood stoves and fireplaces safely if you exercise care and vigilance. Never leave your cat unsupervised near any open fire. Equip your wood stove or fireplace with a secure screen so that your cat cannot get access to the open flames. Safety equipment and materials (such as chemical fire-extinguisher sticks or a bucket of sand) for quickly extinguishing any fires should be kept handy, safely stored nearby.

Candles and cats just don't mix, period. The possibilities of the cat knocking over a candle and setting the house—or himself—on fire are just too great. If you have a cat, skip the candles.

Keep all household and kitchen matches, and matches used by smokers in your family, safely stored out of reach, in a metal container stored in a cabinet with a childproof latch. (If you, or a member of your family, smokes, adopting a cat or kitten might be the perfect time to consider quitting. You'll enjoy better health, your food will taste better, and you won't be exposing this small creature who shares your home to your secondhand smoke.) Keep cigarettes, cigars, loose tobacco, and other smoking materials—which can poison your cat if eaten—safely and securely stored in locked cabinets, completely inaccessible to curious cats.

Deadly Furniture?

Cats love to hide and snooze beneath chairs, and to crawl into the box springs and understructures of furniture. Many cats have been killed when they were caught or crushed by the unforgiving mechanisms of folding beds, convertible sofas, and reclining or swiveling chairs. If you live with a cat, it's safest to forego potentially dangerous mechanical furniture. If you must keep your recliner, never sit down, get up, or operate the reclining or other mechanism unless you are 100 percent certain no cat is underneath or inside the furniture.

Make sure any piece of furniture that a cat could crawl underneath is balanced and seated securely on its legs or base. A heavy piece of furniture could kill your cat by sliding or falling on him.

In the Kitchen

Train your cat to not jump on the counter and stove while you're cooking or preparing food. But always assume he'll do it anyway! Keep him safe, even while your back is turned, by taking these precautions.

1. Don't leave loose knives, scissors, or heavy objects on countertops or the stove top, especially near the edges. Store all knives in drawers.
2. Don't leave glass or other breakable containers on your countertops. Your cat could knock them on the floor and cut his paw pads badly on the shards.
3. Always look carefully before closing appliances such as the oven, dishwasher, freezer, and refrigerator. It takes only a second for your cat to jump inside.

Laundry Room

Train your cat to always stay away from the washer and dryer.

Never close or start these appliances without a careful kitty check. Your cat can easily hop into the dryer the instant your back is turned. Many cats have been killed in clothes dryers, attracted to the warm, cozy space filled with materials bearing their owners' scents.

Many laundry products are toxic. Keep all containers closed and wipe up all spills promptly.

The Bathroom

Always keep the toilet lid down. Not only are most toilet-bowl cleaners toxic, kittens can be trapped and drown in toilet bowls.

Guard filled bathtubs vigilantly. Never leave a cat, especially a kitten, alone in the bathroom with a full tub. He could easily drown. If your tub or shower is fitted with a door, keep it closed. If it has a shower curtain, consider flipping it up over the rod when it's not in use. Otherwise, your cat may decide to use it as a climbing ladder, and possibly fall and injure himself.

Keep all medications, for both cats and people, securely locked in a latched cabinet. They should be covered and in their original containers. Some medications for cats are flavored to make them more attractive or palatable, but can be toxic if an overdose is taken.

Keep all human grooming and beauty supplies safely stored in drawers or cabinets. Some of these are toxic to cats, and many creams and lotions have attractive fruit or food fragrances. Keep small, swallowable items such as bobby pins, hair clips, and makeup brushes picked up and stowed in a drawer. Keep your hair dryer unplugged, and never leave it near water. Keep your cat away from hot appliances such as curling irons and curling wands.

Many common human medications are toxic to cats. Keep your cat away from any preparation containing benzocaine, hexachlorophene, chlorinated hydrocarbons, phenytoin, aspirin, and acetaminophen (Tylenol (™)). Never give your cat a commercially prepared enema designed for humans—it could kill him.

In the Garage

Many indoors-only cats have access to the family garage, at least occasionally. Since so many dangers lurk in the average garage, it's best to keep your cat out. But if he has access, there's a lot of cat-proofing to do.

Antifreeze, or ethylene glycol, is a deadly poison with a sweet taste that's very attractive to cats. It's a very fast poison, according to veterinarians who see the tragedy of antifreeze poisoning every day. To save a cat who's ingested ethylene glycol, you practically have to see him consuming it and rush him instantly to the veterinarian to begin emergency treatment. Owners who notice the symptoms any later often find it's too late to save their cat. The kidneys have already crystallized, and the damage is extensive and irreversible. A teaspoon of antifreeze—just a few licks—is enough to kill a cat.

There are now pet-safe antifreeze products that use the less toxic propylene glycol instead of the more deadly ethylene glycol. But these are also toxic if your cat ingests enough. Clean up antifreeze leaks and spills immediately, and keep your cat completely away from the area.

In the garage, as elsewhere, it's vital to keep all toxins completely out of reach. Lock garden fertilizers, pesticides, rodenticides, pool chemicals, and auto supplies like oil, antifreeze, and gasoline in adequately ventilated storage areas behind a securely latched door.

Never store dangerous substances in glass jars or bottles, and keep an eye on plastic containers for leakage and deterioration. Many auto, lawn, and garden products and pool chemicals are not meant to be stored for long periods. These caustic and toxic substances can eat through plastic containers, especially when subjected to the temperature swings of an unheated garage or workshop. Even if you store such substances in a locked cabinet, chemicals from deteriorating containers can leak out.

Advanced Cat-Proofing

You'd be amazed at the size of the openings a cat can crawl through. Cover all holes in your walls or baseboards, even if they seem too small for your cat. Look for openings in odd places, such as under loose carpeting on closet floors. You'd never think to explore under there—but your cat will! Many cats have become trapped within walls of homes, and it's often tricky to extricate them.

If you have a furnace or other heating appliance, make sure it's securely enclosed and that all covers are latched in place. Your cat could crawl into a small opening and be severely hurt or burned, or even killed.

Your cat can choke, or suffer serious internal blockages, from small items like rubber bands, elastic hair bands, paper clips, staples, buttons, milk-jug rings, bread tags, balls of foil, and parts from badly made cat toys. Cats love to play with these things. Whenever you see such an item out loose, pick it up immediately and either throw it away in a covered trash can, or stash it in a drawer. If you see your cat playing with an unsafe item, take it away and divert his attention with a cat-safe toy or game.

Look out for loose change, too. U.S. pennies minted after 1982 are made of copper plating around a core of potentially toxic zinc. The *zinc toxicosis* that can result from an ingested penny can damage your cat's red blood cells and even cause kidney failure. To be on the safe side, keep all pennies and other coins away from your cat. Do the wildlife a favor, too, and don't discard pennies where wild animals could get at them.

Chocolate contains a substance called theobromine that's poisonous to cats. Never leave chocolate in any form—candies, chocolate bars, baking chocolate—out where your cat can get at it, even if it's in a closed dish. Chocolate is even more poisonous to dogs than to cats. If you have a multispecies home, be especially careful to put away all chocolate. And, of course, never feed any chocolate to your pet.

Crinkly plastic bags are attractive to cats, but are *not* safe toys. Dispose of plastic bags where your cat can't get them. Dry-cleaning-type soft plastic bags can suffocate your cat.

Never let your cat near sewing, knitting, or craft materials such as hot-glue guns, airbrushes, oil paints and solvents, craft knives, thread, sewing needles, or glues. Never allow your cat unsupervised access to linear materials such as rubber bands, string, yarn, and thread. Because of the structure of your cat's tongue, it's extremely difficult for him to spit out such materials. Swallowed yarn or string can cause internal blockages and severe intestinal injuries.

Soft, seemingly innocent materials such as socks, modeling clay, plastic bags, and plastic bubble wrap can, if ingested, block your cat's digestive tract. These blockages are doubly dangerous because they don't show up on an X ray, making diagnosis tricky and delaying treatment. Fortunately, cats are much less likely than dogs to consume inappropriate nonfood materials.

Finally, *look up.* Cats are much more attuned to the third dimension—height—than we are. They love heights and actively search for ways to get above it all. If you keep breakable items, or possibly dangerous items that may appeal to your cat (such as dried flower arrangements), on high shelves, be sure there's absolutely no way your cat can get up to them. Look for nearby furniture that might serve as a handy launching pad for a determined cat.

Everyday Safety—Proactive Protection

Your cat's natural curiosity is boundless. He'll be especially interested in anything new in your home, from furniture to bags of groceries to tradespeople to visiting relatives.

While modern veterinary medicine can provide your cat with vital protection against a variety of diseases, only you can protect his life, health, and safety in your everyday life at home. Advances in veterinary technology and science can save your cat's life, cure him of numerous diseases, and patch him up after accident or trauma. But prevention of accidents is much cheaper, not to mention much easier on your cat and on you, than any veterinary intervention. Get in the safety habit. The Humane Society of the United States and the American Red Cross jointly have published *Pet First Aid: Cats and Dogs*—a handy first-aid guide for cat and dog owners. It's available from The Humane Society of the United States, 2100 L Street, NW, Washington, D.C. 20037, www.hsus.org.

Don't Tempt Fate

Especially if your new cat is a kitten or "teenager," store fragile objects, breakables, and valuable antiques in a spare bedroom or other area designated as a cat-free zone. High, totally inaccessible shelves can form a part of your cat-free zone.

If your cat inadvertently destroys or breaks something, take a deep breath and reflect before punishing or blaming him. Are you being fair and realistic? Your cat is a small, active, athletic animal who needs to run, romp, and play. You can't realistically expect him to watch out for your priceless Ming vases. And is it fair to leave out Grandma's antique brocade rocker, with its oh-so-tempting, claw-attractive fabric? Do your cat, your nerves, and your antiques a favor by placing such objects where your cat can't get at them and won't be tempted by them every day.

Door Discipline

If you've decided on a safe, indoors-only lifestyle for your cat, it's vital that he not be let outside by a well-meaning visitor, inattentive child, or uninformed tradesperson. It's your responsibility to insure that all members of the household understand feline-access rules. Although it takes some practice, especially for youngsters, everyone in your family must learn to enter and exit your home mindfully—and always looking down!

Since cats are so responsive to ritual phrasing, develop a coming-in ritual and a going-out ritual to be used by each member of your family. For example, when coming inside you could open the door slightly, look down, place your foot in the opening, and call out, "Back, back, kitty cat!" When you are leaving, tossing a treat to the opposite side of the room works wonders. Use a simple phrase like "You're in charge of mice! Be back later!" In addition to distracting the cat long enough for you to get out of the door, this will become a familiar ritual for your cat, offering reassurance and indulging his love of routine.

If you're adopting a cat who's had access to the outdoors and you want to keep him in, or if you've decided to convert your previously indoor-outdoor cat to an indoors-only pet, door discipline is especially important. Keep a spray bottle filled with water near the door. If your cat tries to escape, close the door quickly and immediately give him a gentle spritz. This gets his attention in a harmless way, and clearly communicates your disapproval. Then, divert his attention to a toy or game, and perhaps praise his leaping ability. Although it's been said that one should never try to "outstubborn" a cat, this is precisely what you need to do—at least for a while.

The Kitty Count

Do a kitty count every time you leave the house. With one cat, this is a snap; just make sure you know the cat is where he belongs. But if you have more than one cat, it's especially important to insure that all of them are present and accounted for, and that no cat is locked in somewhere he doesn't belong.

YOUR CAT'S SAFE RETREAT—FOR SERENITY AND SAFETY

Door discipline is especially important when visitors or strangers such as tradespeople are around. For extra safety, every cat's home should have a "cat safe retreat"—a basement, a spare bedroom, even a small bathroom or powder room—equipped with a litter box and other necessities to accommodate the cat at a moment's notice. When a longer incursion of visitors is in the works (such as a party), add some extras to the safe retreat—a bowl of food, some extra toys, perhaps a few hidden treats. In a pinch, your cat's carrier can be his safe retreat—if you've accustomed him to it as a safe place. If things get especially noisy or distressing, cover the carrier with a towel, but allow for air circulation—don't let him get overheated.

A Sign on the Door Can Save a Life

Always place a large, noticeable sign at eye level on the door of the safe retreat whenever the cat is in residence. When the visit, party, or excitement is all over, check all exit doors for proper closed status and make a safety sweep of the house before releasing your cat. Be sure to praise him for his forbearance.

Do you need to bring in twelve cases of cat litter from your car? Is the plumber fixing your kitchen sink? (Plumbers always seem to make twenty trips out to the truck and back!) Install your cat in his safe retreat first. Inform everyone who visits your home that your cat doesn't go outdoors, and tell them about his safe retreat. Ask that they not open any door without reading the sign posted on it first. Insist—make a point of it. Don't worry that they'll think you're a fanatic. You should be! Your cat's life might depend on your attention to these details.

CAT-SAFE GREENERY

Cats love to nibble greenery. You can indulge this predilection without guilt if you keep these basic safety guidelines in mind:

1. Be absolutely sure that any plant to which your cat has access is safe to eat. Make sure all parts of the plant—leaves, flowers, berries, roots, stems—are safe. Check the list of poisonous, toxic, dangerous, or irritating plants in the box, or ask your veterinarian. If in doubt, leave it out. (Page 85 has a list of cat-safe plants.)
2. Know the origin even of safe plants. Plants from nurseries, home centers, and supermarkets often have been sprayed with insecticides, including such toxic-to-cats substances as organophosphates and carbamates. Both of these insecticide ingredients can cause serious neurological damage and even death. Even a bit of leaf-nibbling on such a plant can make your cat violently ill. Symptoms include large amounts of saliva and drooling, freely flowing tears, copious urination and diarrhea, twitching, nervous or frantic behavior, and breathing difficulty. If your cat consumes a large amount, he may simply collapse. If your cat shows these symptoms after being around any plants, he requires swift emergency veterinary intervention.

3. Watch for fallen leaves and water drips from hanging plants. Unless the plant is safe and you've used no chemicals on it, your cat could become ill from eating the leaves or drinking the water.

4. Flower arrangements are lovely, but potentially dangerous. Unless you grew and arranged the flowers yourself, you have no way of knowing exactly which plants are included, where they came from, or what they've been sprayed or preserved with. It's best to prevent your cat from accessing such arrangements. Many popular flowers, such as lilies, are lethal to cats.

5. Dried flower arrangements can also be deadly. Many dried plants are preserved with toxic chemicals or colored with toxic dyes.

6. If you choose to grow plants specifically for your cat's enjoyment, good for you! Grow wheat (not "wheat grass") or oat-grass sprouts for healthy nibbling, or catnip for some feline ecstasy. Always use sterilized potting soil (not garden soil from outdoors) and untreated seed. Don't plant ordinary lawn grass; it has razor-sharp spines that can cut your cat's mouth and digestive tract.

   If you plant catnip, keep it in a room inaccessible to your cat and offer him some fresh leaves occasionally. If you leave your catnip plant accessible, he'll likely soon love it to death! Besides, catnip may lose its delightful effect if indulged in too often.

Eating even perfectly safe plants may cause your cat to vomit greenish liquid with plant fragments. This is perfectly normal, unless it's constant and excessive.

As part of your initial cat-proofing *before* your new cat or kitten comes home for the first time, conduct a houseplant survey and remove any potentially lethal flora. Or move all houseplants to your cat-free zone—which you then can name, in proper Victorian style, "the Conservatory."

THE EXCITEMENT BUILDS!

You've made your room-by-room, cat-proofing sweep. You've installed childproof (and cat-proof) latches on all cabinets where anything remotely dangerous is stored. You've placed Grandma's brocade rocker, your priceless Ming vases, and the model ship your dad built in your cat-free zone.

You've gone on a cat-supplies shopping spree. You're all ready with litter, litter boxes, food and water bowls, a scratching-post-and-climbing-tree combo, a comfy cat bed, kitten (or cat) food, and safe toys. You've set up a room where your new companion will spend his first few days getting used to the sounds, smells, and rhythms of your home. You've started your at-home cat-care library, and your responsible-cat-owner continuing education program, by buying and reading this book. You're almost ready!

Now, notify your veterinarian that you're planning to adopt a cat or kitten.

HOMECOMING DAY AT LAST!

When your new cat arrives at home, he'll be excited and curious, but also wary—and, perhaps, lonely for his littermates or buddies back at the shelter. He must become familiar with a multitude of new sights, sounds, smells, voices, and impressions—a big job even for an adult cat and even more so for a kitten.

When your cat first comes home, let him get comfortable by exploring a single room at first.
(FRANTZ DANTZLER)

Help him adjust by introducing him gradually to his new environment. Keep him isolated from the family hubbub for several days while he becomes attuned to your home and you gracefully manage introductions.

For the first several days, let him get comfortable and explore a single room. You and other family members should share lots of quality time with him, speaking softly and starting to forge loving bonds. If you have other cats, don't let them see the newcomer just yet. They'll need time to adjust, too.

Cats and kittens require virtually no house-training. Simply show your new arrival the facilities. He'll know what to do. Read chapter 7 to learn how to set up and maintain your cat's toilet facilities. Happily, human and feline priorities in this important area mesh nicely.

THE TRIP HOME

A sturdy carrier is a necessity, especially if you're adopting an adult cat. Don't expect to rely for long on a cardboard carrier. While such carriers are fine for transporting a kitten, adult cats, when motivated, can shred them in seconds. If you're adopting a pair of cats who are already good friends, they can share the same carrier—if it's large enough and they aren't crowded or cramped. But be ready with a second carrier in case the stress of the day makes either cat more nervous than expected.

WHAT'S UP, DOC?

Besides you, your veterinarian is the most-important person in your cat's life. Choose a veterinarian who likes and understands cats *and* their owners. Learn her emergency and beeper numbers, and know who covers the practice when she isn't available. Don't neglect or postpone your new cat's essential initial examination, especially if you have other animals at home.

You new friend's first checkup should include a feline leukemia (FeLV) test, examination of ears and eyes, survey for possible parasites, and any necessary vaccinations against feline viral rhinotracheitis (FHV-1) and feline calcivirus (FCV), panleukopenia (feline distemper), feline leukemia virus (FeLV), and rabies (the last, after fourteen weeks of age). Giving your cat all the vaccinations he needs at one time may not be a good idea. See chapter 16, and ask your veterinarian for advice.

The bonding process begins instantly. The initial round of tests can therefore be a nail-biting experience. Though it's unlikely, have you considered what you'll do if your new cat tests positive for feline leukemia (FeLV)? Your veterinarian may suggest you wait a few weeks and then retest the cat, in case the test was a "false positive." You'll need to keep your new cat strictly isolated from any other cats you have until he's retested and—with luck—given a clean bill of health. This can be a stressful experience.

If you obtained your cat from a breeder, check your contract for health guarantees. Shelters will generally take back a cat who is FeLV-positive but not actually ill. However, his prospects for adoption become bleaker. Some cat owners are willing to adopt cats who test positive for FeLV, as many such cats—about 30 percent of infected cats—never become ill, though they can still infect other cats. These caring owners provide homes for many cats who otherwise would be euthanized.

Even if your new cat is healthy and disease-free, be sure to ask your veterinarian how long you should keep him isolated from your other animals, especially other cats. The length of the isolation period will depend on your new cat's age, condition, temperament, and health history. Don't cheat on this important isolation time. It's not worth putting the health of your other pets at risk. When introductions are finally made, you'll know everyone is healthy and ready.

MEETINGS

Getting to Know You: Meeting Other Cats

Cats recognize one another primarily by odor, not sight. In groups, friendly feline acquaintances mix and mingle scents frequently, gently rubbing and grooming one another (allogrooming) and nose-touching to exchange and reinforce a comforting, familiar group scent. A new cat—with an unfamiliar scent—coming into the group can provoke stress or hostility, because the resident cats have no way of knowing whether this newcomer constitutes a threat to their resources: food, water, space, and attention. Therefore, it's to your advantage to initiate the newcomer into the group scent as seamlessly as possible.

To insure that he's healthy and free of external parasites, you'll be keeping your newcomer isolated for several days while he becomes accustomed to the sound, odors, and rhythms of his new home. When he arrives, give him an article of your own clothing, such as an old sweatshirt, to lounge on. After a few days, take this away and put it out where the rest of your cats usually hang out; for example, on a favorite sofa or cat condo. The combination of your familiar scent and the new cat's scent will help to jump-start the familiarization process.

Every few days, exchange bedding and a few cat toys between new and resident cats. Allow cats several days of complete visual isolation, then several more of partial visual isolation. A screen door on the isolation room can let the cats get to know and smell one another in a safe, controlled way.

When the isolation period recommended by your veterinarian at your cat's initial checkup is over, and the cats finally, and gradually, get together, monitor their interactions vigilantly. Be discreet, though. Let your cats lead the way. Expect some initial hissing and posturing. If a serious conflict seems to be brewing, or a fight develops, separate the cats immediately and let everybody cool down. Then try again later.

Much about the introduction and familiarization process depends on the age, gender, and temperament of both the newcomer and the resident cats. Although you can help by maintaining a calm, positive attitude—which the cats will pick up—and by facilitating scent mixing, acceptance of the newcomer is basically up to the cats. Let them take their time and integrate the newcomer into the group at their own speed. Forcing the issue won't help, and may slow things down.

Meeting Nonfeline Pets

If your family already includes a dog, the success of his introduction to your cat will depend on his age, breed, maturity, temperament (especially level of aggressiveness), previous experience with cats, and degree of socialization, and on the level of security he's established within the pack structure of your family. A poorly socialized dog of any size can be a danger to your cat. A large, aggressive dog, even if well socialized, can also be dangerous, especially if he lacks previous experience with cats. He may see your cat as prey. Some dog breeds have been bred and trained for many generations to pursue smaller, running animals like foxes and hares. Know your own dog and his habits and predilections.

Even if you're absolutely confident that your dog will not pose a danger to your cat, be vigilant and make the introductions slowly and gradually. (KATHY MILANI)

"Fluffy, Meet Rover"

Keep your dog confined away from your cat—either in a separate room, or in his crate—for the first several days as your cat explores his new home. When you're ready for the first meeting, trim your cat's claws first. (Read chapter 15 to learn how.) Then, pick a quiet time when you can devote your full attention to this important introduction. Even if you're absolutely confident that your dog will not pose a danger to your cat, be vigilant, and make the introductions slowly and gradually. You want to do the following:

- train your dog not to treat the cat as prey and not to roughhouse with him

- physically control your dog completely until this training is complete
- prevent your cat from becoming frightened or defensively aggressive
- habituate both pets to each other's presence
- allow both pets to enjoy pleasant, rewarding experiences in each other's presence

Make sure the room where you conduct the first meeting includes a high piece of furniture, inaccessible to the dog, to which your cat can retreat to feel safe. Use a secure leash to keep your dog under control. Your cat will likely hiss and puff out his fur. He may lash out with his claws, back off in fear, or even try to run away. Let him—don't try to restrain him. Keep this first meeting short. Afterwards, reward both animals with lavish praise and treats. Repeat several times until both animals are sufficiently desensitized to each other's presence. But remain vigilant. Don't allow your pets to interact unsupervised for at least several weeks. The scent-swapping and scent-habituation techniques described earlier for introducing a new cat are also worth trying in dog-and-cat introductions.

While conducting the first few introductory meetings, keep plenty of distance between the animals. It's essential to minimize any chasing, aggressive, fearful, or defensive behavior in either pet. Maintain a cheerful, positive attitude. Both animals will pick up on your mood and tone of voice. Speak softly and encouragingly. Even once things are going well, never leave them together without supervision, and separate them at the first hint of trouble. One hostile interaction can set the process back to square one, or worse.

If you have a dog with socialization problems or dominance issues or who does not respond instantly to verbal commands, don't adopt a cat until these problems have been solved. By exposing your cat to a dog who's insecure, unpredictable, or aggressive, you may be putting the cat's life in danger. You're also risking making the dog's problems worse by complicating a social situation that's already confusing to him. Address the dog's problems first, and keep the animals completely separated until you're confident that the interaction will be safe and pleasant for everyone.

Finally, never just put the two pets together to see what happens or let them work it out. That's a recipe for disaster.

Friend—or Prey?

If your family includes small animals such as hamsters, gerbils, rats, mice, cage birds, or rabbits, the key advice for introductions is "Don't do them."

To your cat, these are prey animals. Even if your kitten or cat has been socialized in a home with small animals and has always acted friendly towards them, don't take any chances. Keep these other animals strictly away from, and out of the reach of, your cat. Never leave your cat unsupervised with a bird, rabbit, small mammal, or other small pet. Even if the cat knows a particular small animal personally—as an individual—his pursuit instinct is powerful, hardwired, and undeniable. A particular pattern of movements by the prey can instantaneously trigger the cat's instinctual pursuit reaction. The small animal can be hurt or killed extremely quickly.

The resulting anger and blame will only confuse and frighten your cat. After all, he's a predator, doing what predators do. The fact that he knew the victim is immaterial. Don't judge your cat by human standards or expect him to be anything but a cat. It's not fair to tempt your cat's predatory urges with the presence of prey he's not allowed to stalk or kill.

Likewise, it's not fair—and it may be cruel and inhumane—to expect a small prey animal to live his life in fear of your cat. To that small animal, your cat—even if the cat has no realistic access to him—is a lethal threat, every moment of the day and night. Even if the small pet is in a secure cage, it can still hear, see, and smell your cat. The resulting stress and fear can seriously debilitate your small pets. If you want to keep small pets (prey animals) along with your cat, keep them completely separate from each other, ideally in different parts of the house where they cannot see, hear, or smell each other.

Meeting Children

The youngsters in your family are bound to be excited and thrilled about the new cat or kitten. Take it slowly, though. Let your new cat settle into his own room and get used to the sounds and odors of his new home before you introduce him to other members of your family.

If your family includes babies or very young toddlers, wait until the cat is very comfortable in your home before introducing them to your cat. Older children can make the cat's acquaintance as soon as he's well settled in and relaxed. Especially if this is your family's first cat, review with them the basic principles of feline etiquette before they meet the new cat. Always supervise all interactions between the new cat and young children, especially at first.

When it's time for the cat to meet the kids, pick a time when both children and cat are calm and relaxed. Never just pick up the new cat and plunk it into a child's arms. The cat could lash out in confusion or fear. Caution the child against yelling excitedly or running right up to the cat. Here's how kids (or anyone) should approach a new cat:

1. Gently lower yourself to the floor. Speak softly to the cat. Avoid making harsh or sudden noises or any sound that might seem to the cat like a hiss or growl.
2. Move slowly. Keep your hands visible. Whatever you do, don't trap, grab, or corner the cat.
3. Don't hover directly over the cat. Bend down or sit on the ground. Keep speaking softly.
4. When the cat seems comfortable with your presence, slowly extend one hand. Let him approach you at his own pace. He'll probably sniff your hand.
5. Offer a few tasty cat treats. Either place these on the floor in front of you, or, if the cat is acting friendly and curious, lay them in your open palm.

Anyone meeting a new cat for the first time should let the cat set the pace of the relationship. If the cat or kitten does crawl up on your lap, congratulations! You have a new friend. But don't restrain him. Let him move about as he pleases and leave when he wants to. Remember, "The cat goes where he pleases, and pleases where he goes!"

FELINE ETIQUETTE 101

Cats are sensitive, polite creatures who expect and appreciate sensitivity and politeness in their companions. Before your new cat or kitten comes home, review these feline-etiquette tips with every member of your household—especially youngsters.

Your Cat's Space Bubble

Space is important to cats. It's a vital, but often overlooked, aspect of the environment that each cat sees as an important resource. Each cat, like each person, has a personal space bubble within which he does not like being touched or disturbed, except by *very* intimate friends. Depending on your cat's personality and temperament, his personal space bubble may be tiny, or may extend for several feet. Always respect your cat's personal space, except when absolutely necessary, such as for health care, medical or emergency treatment, or essential grooming. It's just as rude to invade a cat's personal space without permission as it is to invade a human's.

Always Ask First!

Speak gently to your cat before picking him up or handling him in any way. Never surprise him from behind, or grab him in such a way that he feels cornered or that he can't escape. Whether you're initiating a petting or grooming session, performing an informal health checkup or routine dental care, or giving a pill or other medication, speak in a gentle, calm, reassuring tone of voice. Even if your cat doesn't understand your words, he'll readily pick up your mood and tone. If you're nervous, for example, about giving him a pill, he'll be nervous too, and tense up—making the whole experience more stressful and difficult for both of you.

Picking Up and Holding Your Cat

Holding your cat can be a warm, close, loving interaction, helping you build trust and enhance your mutual bond. But holding a cat against his will, or picking him up against his will, can make him fearful and wary of you. Some cats intensely dislike being picked up, preferring to show affection on their own terms, not yours. Often, if you sit down quietly next to such a cat, he'll crawl into your lap willingly and make himself comfortable. But it has to be *his* idea!

Even if your cat loves being held and snuggled, always ask first. Never surprise him from behind, or try to pick him up while he's sleeping, eating, washing, or using the litter box. Never tower over a cat and then just scoop him up. If you get into the habit of actually asking the cat if you can pick him up, it will help you remember to consider his feelings. This is an especially useful technique for teaching children respect for the cat.

Lower yourself to the floor, or to the level where the cat is sitting. Maneuver yourself so that he's facing away from you. Gently cup one hand beneath his chest and lift him a short way, but not all the way, off the ground. Then raise his hindquarters with your other hand, while carefully tucking his tail to one side. Tuck the cat into the crook of the arm with which you lifted his hindquarters. Always support the cat with both hands. Let him lean his front legs on your other arm for support and security. Hold him securely, close to your body. Don't let him, or any of his legs, dangle in midair.

When he's properly and securely supported, your cat will relax in your arms and probably purr, too. If he struggles or resists, hisses, growls, or shows any signs of displeasure, gently lower him back to the floor or other surface. If a cat who previously enjoyed being picked up and held suddenly resists, lashes out, or tries to escape when you pick him up, watch him carefully for signs of illness or injury.

Never pick up a cat or kitten by the scruff of his neck. Only Momcat knows how to do this properly and safely. Picking up an adult cat by the scruff can seriously harm him. You might occasionally see your veterinarian holding a cat by the scruff of its neck to partially restrain him while performing a necessary medical procedure. This can be a useful technique, but it requires caution and takes practice. Watch carefully and you'll see that the cat's body is always fully supported, and that the veterinarian is simply grasping the skin at the back of the cat's neck, not picking up the cat.

Common Cat Courtesy

Once you have a cat in your home and your life, get into the habit of regularly greeting him and speaking to him—just as you would any member of your family. Never yell at your cat or startle him—unless he's in imminent physical danger. When he's sleeping, don't try to pet him or wake him up deliberately. And never swoop down and scoop him up unexpectedly. It's not only rude, you may get clawed for your insensitivity.

Respect Is the Key

As far as possible, respect your cat's preferences in the amount and type of interaction he likes. Never trap, grab, manhandle, or harass him, or try to make him into a different cat. Some cats are lap cats; some aren't. Some will sleep on your head, some at your feet, and some in the living room—it's their choice. Appreciate your cat for the unique creature he is. Daily respect for his privacy and feline dignity will help strengthen and deepen your mutual bond, and make it more likely that you'll be rewarded with privileged access to his inner circle. He may even allow you to pet his tummy.

In the next chapter, you'll learn how to easily and inexpensively make your home into a cat paradise, filled with exciting, safe opportunities for play, bird-watching, mock hunting, climbing, exploring, and all kinds of other feline fun. You'll learn how to provide cat- and human-friendly scratching-and-climbing surfaces. You'll discover why playtime is serious business and how to make the most of every second of it. And—most important of all—you'll discover how to banish the litter-box blues—forever!

THE NATIONAL ANIMAL POISON CONTROL CENTER

When you suspect your cat has ingested a poisonous or toxic substance, you need accurate, reliable help, and you don't have a second to lose. First, call your veterinarian or local emergency animal clinic. But if you can't reach them, grab your credit card and dial the ASPCA/NAPCC, the American Society for the Prevention of Cruelty to Animals' National Animal Poison Control Center. (Don't call the human poison-control center! While those centers are experts in cases of human poisoning, they can be worse than useless in veterinary emergencies.) Right now, while you're thinking about it, write down these phone numbers and post them by every phone in your house—right under your veterinarian's numbers.

National Animal Poison Control Center
1-888-4ANIHELP (1-888-426-4435)
(with a major credit card)

1-900-680-0000
(*Charges will appear on your phone bill.*)

Gearing Up: Your Feline Shopping List

NECESSARY SUPPLIES
- sticker with veterinarian's phone number and after-hours or pager number for phone
- selection of age-appropriate interactive toys
- sturdy cat carrier for each cat, preferably not cardboard
- food bowl for each cat (porcelain or stainless steel, shallow or low sided)
- water bowl for each cat (porcelain or stainless steel)
- food (age-appropriate and highest quality possible)
- litter box (ideally, one per cat)
- litter, preferably clumping
- sturdy litter scoop
- small trash can with lid and small plastic trash bags to line trash can *or* gallon-size plastic zipper bags
- paint scraper (your secret weapon!)
- crate or box to keep litter-box-maintenance supplies handy
- flea comb
- nail clipper (for nail-clipping)
- toothpaste or dental rinse made specifically for cats
- toothbrush, or finger toothbrush, made just for cats
- cornstarch or small bar of cat-safe, unscented soap (for nail-clipping errors)
- feline at-home first-aid kit (See chapter 17 for list of contents.)

FOR CAT-PROOFING YOUR HOME
- childproof latches for cabinets
- electrical outlet covers
- wire guides or duct tape for covering electrical wires
- holders for curtain and blind cords
- covered trash cans with latching lids
- large bricks to place in trash cans
- fireplace or wood stove screen
- cat-safe bitters or similar concoction for coating electrical wires, in case your cat's a chewer
- cat-free zone—a room in your home for storing dangerous/fragile items
- door wedges, to keep interior doors from slamming and trapping Kitty in or out

POISONOUS, TOXIC, DANGEROUS, OR IRRITATING PLANTS: ALFALFA TO YEW

alfalfa
almond (pits)
alocasia
aloe vera
amaryllis
Andromeda japonica
apple (seeds)
apple leaf croton
apricot (pits)
arrowgrass
Asian lily
asparagus fern
autumn crocus
avocado (fruit and pit)
azalea
baby's breath
baneberry
bayonet
beargrass
beech
belladonna
bird of paradise
bittersweet
black-eyed Susan
black locust
bleeding heart
bloodroot
bluebonnet
box
boxwood
branching ivy
buckeyes
Buddhist pine
burning bush

buttercup
cactus
caladium
calla lily
castor bean
ceriman
charming diffenbachia
cherry (most wild
    varieties)
cherry (pits, seeds,
    wilting leaves)
cherry, ground
cherry, laurel
chinaberry
Chinese evergreen
Christmas rose
chrysanthemum
cineria
clematis
cordatum
coriaria
cornflower
corn plant
cornstalk plant
corydalis
croton
crown-of-thorns
Cuban laurel
cutleaf philodendron
cycads
cyclamen
daffodil
daphne
datura

deadly nightshade
death camas
delphinium
devil's ivy
dicentra
diffenbachia
dracaena (all types)
dracaena palm
dragon tree
dumbcane
Easter lily
eggplant
Elaine
elderberry
elephant ear
English ivy
euonymus
evergreen
fern
flax
four o'clock
foxglove
geranium
German ivy
gold dust dracaena
golden chain
golden glow
golden pothos
gopher purge
ground cherry
hellebore
hemlock
henbane
holly

(cont'd)

honeysuckle

horsebeans

horsebrush

horse chestnut

hurricane plant

hyacinth

hydrangea

Indian rubber plant

Indian tobacco

iris

ivy, most types

jack-in-the-pulpit

Java beans

Jerusalem cherry

jessamine

jimsonweed

jonquil

jungle trumpet

lantana

larkspur

laurel

lily (especially Easter lily, but also tiger lily, daylily, Asiatic lily, rubrum)

lily-of-the-valley

locoweed

lupine

marigold

marijuana

mescal bean

Mexican breadfruit

mistletoe

mock orange

monkshood

moonseed

morning glory

mountain laurel

mushroom

narcissus

needlepoint ivy

nephytis

nightshade

oleander

onion

oriental lily

peace lily

peach (pits, wilting leaves)

pencil cactus

peony

periwinkle

philodendron (all types)

pimpernel

poinciana

poinsettia (low toxicity; irritating)

poison hemlock

poison ivy

poison oak

pokeweed

poppy

potato

pothos, all types

precatory bean

privet, common

red emerald

red princess

rhododendron

rhubarb

ribbon plant

rosary pea

rubber plant

sago palm

schefflera

Scotch broom

skunk cabbage

snowdrops

spotted dumb cane

snow-on-the-mountain

staggerweed

star of Bethlehem

string of pearls

sweet pea

swiss cheese plant

tansy mustard

taro vine

tiger lily

tobacco

tomato (green fruit, stems, leaves)

tulip

tung tree

Virginia creeper

water hemlock

weeping fig

wisteria

yews (all)

CHAPTER 7

The Cat in Your Life, the Cat in Your Home

LIFESTYLES OF THE FELINE AND FORTUNATE

By choosing a protected, indoors-only lifestyle for your new kitten or cat, you've taken a giant first step in insuring his health and happiness and prolonging his life. (Still undecided? Read chapter 8 now!) Your cat is depending on you. Happily, it's relatively simple to provide him an environment that's not only pleasant, stimulating, and enriching for him, but comfortable, enjoyable, and fun for you. The company of cats has been considered one of the finest and rarest of pleasures by generations of artists, writers, philosophers, and connoisseurs of the good life.

Home, Sweet Home:
A Safe, Stimulating Indoor Environment

Even if you've rescued, or inherited, a determined outdoor cat, you can usually change his mind—with some time, patience, and determination. (Chapter 19 will tell you

how.) A sufficiently satisfying, stimulating indoor environment might entice your cat to make the switch himself. Your goal is to make his indoor world so attractive that the dangerous enticements of the great outdoors lose their charm. As we look at what a safe, enriched indoors-only lifestyle consists of, think about how you could adapt these ideas for your own cat, home, and lifestyle. Don't forget: the most important element in your cat's environment is . . . you!

Companionship

Cats are naturally sociable creatures whose personalities blossom when they enjoy regular opportunities to creatively interact with others. Cats can derive tremendous satisfaction from interactive play, conversation, cuddling, and just being together with favorite human companions. A cat whose human friends are away at work or school much of the time can get bored and lonesome. In zoo animals who don't enjoy enough interaction with fellow creatures, this "confinement stress" can lead to serious behavior and even health problems. A cat left alone too much is similarly at risk for boredom, loneliness, stress, and even illness.

The best companion for a cat, other than his human family, may be another cat. Cats amuse, entertain, and groom one another, play and romp together, snuggle together, or just spend time in pleasant proximity, communing. Keeping two cats requires extra expense and effort for the owner, but the payoffs can be tremendous. The cats will not only be happier and more satisfied, but also more active and energetic and therefore less prone to obesity and related health problems. Owners find that interactive play with multiple cats is particularly thrilling, rewarding, and exhilarating.

Scratching and Climbing

Scratching is a natural, normal, healthy part of your cat's daily life. It is not a sign of spite, boredom, or restlessness. Some cats like to scratch a lot, others just a little. It's an individual preference. A scratching cat is not being deliberately destructive or sharpening his claws. Your cat's claws grow in layers, and he periodically needs to shed them, just as a snake sheds its outgrown skin. When your cat scratches, he's sloughing off the itchy old claw sheaths, conditioning his freshly exposed new claws, and getting essential full-body exercise. A good stretch-and-scratch tones every muscle in his body.

He's also leaving a subtle record of his presence and ownership. Your cat's paw pads contain scent glands that leave a personal signature (undetectable to humans, but clear to cats) on surfaces he strokes. The claws on your cat's hind legs need the same kind of regular maintenance, but your cat generally doesn't groom them by scratching—he chews off those old claws sheaths.

By stroking his pads on a favored surface, your cat is saying to other cats, in scent language, "This is mine." Clawed objects can also be visual cues for other cats. Once your cat has placed his personal scent signature on an inappropriate surface (such as your antique armchair), designating it as his preferred place, it's much harder to get him to switch to a more appropriate surface. His scent signature calls him back.

Protecting the surface of prized furniture with a piece of tabletop glass can make life with your indoor cat more enjoyable for both of you.
(FRANTZ DANTZLER)

Vertical scratching posts must be very sturdy and absolutely tip proof.
(KATHY MILANI)

Start your cat off right—and right away—with an irresistible, safe, stable, cat-pleasing scratching post so attractive that your grandma's antique brocade rocker will seem a laughably poor substitute. Although commercial posts are usually covered with carpeting, many cats prefer a tougher, grippier surface—think "tree bark." Most carpeting is too soft and fuzzy to provide satisfying scratching. (Is it any wonder that nubby upholstery fabric is so often a cat's choice?)

Look for a sturdy post or cat tree with a solid, stable base. Or get a length of heavy wood (at least four-by-four, preferably thicker, and at least four feet tall), mount it securely in a large, heavy baseboard, and cover or wrap it with a variety of fabrics: carpet backing, sisal rope, burlap, nubby fabric, cork panel, even plain wood. Observe which your cat prefers. Enhance the attraction by rubbing on some catnip.

Place the post in an attractive location near a favorite sleeping spot. Many cats savor a vigorous postnap scratching session. Don't stash the post in the basement or garage; you want your cat to feel comfortable scratching while enjoying pleasant surroundings and his family's approving company. With some initial encouragement (scrunch down and scratch the post yourself—make it look like fun!), your cat will likely relish his personal post so much that he'll feel no need to improve your upholstery. If he tends to get hung up on his claws (as some kittens do), read chapter 15 for tips on trimming them. And ask your veterinarian to demonstrate the procedure.

Different Strokes for Different Cats

Many cats prefer to scratch plain wood, and an upright two-by-four nailed to a wall will please them immensely. If your cat uses such a scratching surface, or prefers a horizontal scratching surface, provide a separate climbing structure, like a cat tree. Vertical scratching-posts must be very sturdy and absolutely tip-proof, able to withstand leaps and pounces without toppling. If the post falls on top of your cat while he's scratching, or a flying leap knocks it to the floor—landing him in an undignified pose—he'll be understandably hesitant to return. Don't try to save a few pennies by getting a flimsy, discount-store post. This is a long-term investment.

A floor-to-ceiling spring-tension-mounted cat-tree post with platforms and per-

haps a hideaway cave, placed near a window in a central part of your home, serves many purposes: scratching, climbing, perching, napping, bird-watching, people-watching. Cats love heights where they can watch what's going on without being noticed, plan ambushes (real and imaginary), or just take a catnap above it all. A tall climbing-and-scratching tree will likely become your cat's favorite hangout. To keep things interesting, refresh the scratching surfaces from time to time, rub the post with catnip,

A well-used cat scratching tree and a sisal mouse make indoors a safe, stimulating indoor environment.
(FRANTZ DANTZLER)

or even provide a second post with a different view and scratching material.

Consider treating your cat to a real tree log. Lay it on the floor, or affix it firmly to a wall or some other vertical surface. Be sure to check it for mold, fungus, and insects first. If you treat it with an insecticide, check with your veterinarian to choose a product that's completely safe for your cat. Remember, your cat will be giving this enticing object a lot of attention!

Many cats appreciate a selec-

A cruise through Internet sites and advertisements in cat magazines reveals an astonishing array of climbing trees and play centers.
(KATHY MILANI)

tion of scratching surfaces. Provide a main scratching site like a floor-to-ceiling tree and a few smaller posts or sisal-covered pads hung from doorknobs around the house. If your cats enjoys a horizontal scratching surface (either regularly or as a change of pace), get him an inexpensive corrugated cardboard scratch mat (available at pet-supply centers). Often treated with catnip to enhance their appeal, these mats stand up to lots of vigorous scratching.

Climbing-Trees—Plain and Fancy

A cruise through a few Internet sites and the advertisements in cat magazines reveals an astonishing array of cat condos, climbing trees, scratching posts, play centers, and feline-entertainment environments. Some come complete with color-coordinated fabrics, multiple textures of carpet and fleece, and themes—Southwest, tropical, country, patriotic, rustic—to match your decor. Other extras are fleece hammocks, wooly lined caves, or dangling catnip toys. Match your cat, your home, your hair color, or even your mood!

Height is the neglected third dimension. (FRANTZ DANTZLER)

If you can afford them, and find such clever decorative features appealing, go for it. Remember, though—your cat is looking to stretch, scratch, and exercise. He's likely to be just as happy with a tree trunk.

Height—the Neglected Third Dimension

Natural climbers, cats adore observing the world from a lofty perch. Whatever the actual size of your home, you can make it seem twice as large by including the third dimension—height—in planning your cat's indoor environment. If you have tall bookshelves or cabinets with space overhead, set up some pieces of furniture in a step configuration so that your cat can easily access this "sky box" realm.

Lay shelving boards between tall pieces of furniture, cabinets, or appliances. Make long, continuous runs so that your cat has high bridges to navigate overhead. Span doorways, crisscross rooms from side to side. Place securely braced climbing ramps (carpeted boards) angling up to your overhead catwalks.

Mount a series of cat stairs running up a wall to your skyway, or a sturdily mounted, elevated cat shelf that runs perhaps the length of an entire wall. A floor-to-ceiling scratching post could provide another means of access to your cat's skyway. Does your cat like to play hide-and-seek? Provide plenty of secret hideaways. Include a hideaway box or tunnel along the skyway.

Playtime: Serious Business

Your cat has the soul of a hunter, but he doesn't have to capture and kill live prey to gratify his predatory urges. Regular, vigorous mock hunting, ideally a combination of both solo and interactive play, will keep him physically toned, mentally sharp and satisfied, and psychologically healthy. Leaping, pouncing, swatting—-all those instinctual prey-pursuit activities—are deeply ingrained in him. For a cat of any age, play is serious business. Without a stimulating environment with plenty of opportunity to exercise his body, mind, and imagination, your cat can get bored, depressed, overweight, and listless.

A bored, pudgy, listless, unhappy cat is not only a sad sight—he's also more likely to engage in destructive misbehavior or even become ill as his stress and frustration weaken his immune system. Your cat has a deep craving for excitement, stimulation, play, and activity—on his own terms. If there's too little excitement and adventure in his life, he might create some of his own—and you may not appreciate the results.

Worse—and much sadder—he may simply give up, becoming a pale shadow of the lively, vibrant, engaged animal companion he might have been.

Without regular active play, your cat is also at risk for obesity. In chapter 14, you'll learn how common, and how dangerous, feline obesity is, and how you can prevent it. And if he's already too plump, you'll learn how to slim him down safely.

Solo Play

One of the joys of cat watching is observing how your cat's imagination can turn virtually any object into a fascinating toy. Corks, pen caps, empty thread spools, twisted pipe cleaners, and crumpled balls of paper fished from your office wastebasket can provide your cat with hours of chasing activity. But closely monitor anything your cat selects as a plaything. If you notice any sign that he's trying to chew or eat such objects, or is shredding plastic or other toys into small pieces, restrict his access to them. Some cats are shredders or chewers; others aren't. Some cats can make a milk-jug ring last for weeks; others tear it apart in minutes. Know your cat's play preferences.

Many cats adore chasing and pouncing on tiny fake mice, available at pet stores. (Buy toys with synthetic, not real, fur.) These allow for mock hunting at its finest. Your cat will toss his "mouse" into the air, catch it, pounce on it, carry it around, hide it away, defend his prize from other cats, and sometimes, for reasons known only to cats, "drown" it in his water bowl!

Ping-Pong balls and small hard-rubber balls are good for hours of lively chasing action on hard floors. (This can get really noisy at night!) Other great solo toys include an empty spool, an empty tissue box with a ball inside, an empty paper bag, and newspapers spread out for your cat to hide under. Empty cardboard boxes and bags seem to exert a mysterious fascination for cats. Be sure to remove or cut through any handles on bags so that your cat won't get his neck or some other body part caught or tangled up. Offer a selection of sizes and shapes. A fresh green bean makes a terrific cat toy.

Keep a toy box on the floor near your cat's scratching post. Rotate the toys periodically so they'll seem new and fresh.

Interactive Play

Interactive play is special—a chance for your cat to gratify his inner hunter, and for you to thrill to the magnificence, speed, stealth, and power of his predatory skills. It's fun for both of you, and a great way for both of you to stay toned and in shape. The most important element is your wholehearted involvement. Get a selection of interactive toys—special toys you and your cat can play with together. There are a variety of "kitty fishing-pole"–type toys with dangling "prey" and "flying" toys with feathery bird lures (look for synthetic, not animal-derived, materials) to entice your cat.

Let your cat capture his prey occasionally, but not every time. (In the wild, most hunts are not successful.) Remember that even the most dedicated hunter has a relatively short attention span. Quit when he starts losing interest, preferably before he's had quite enough. And always stop immediately if your cat shows signs of exhaustion, fatigue, or shortness of breath.

There are lots of ways to work interactive play into your everyday life. Grow a tail! This can be a simple, spur-of-the-moment tail (a bathrobe sash tucked into your back pocket) or a more-elaborate, formal tail (braided sisal twine or colorful yarn, perhaps embellished with a pom-pom or tasseled tip). Arrange your new tail proudly and let it trail seductively behind you as you go about your chores. Your cat will quickly catch on, dashing behind you and pouncing upon your new appendage. Keep the novelty in your tail by putting it away afterwards. Bring it out again when he seems bored or to distract him from something you'd rather he not do.

Another great interactive game is blowing bubbles. Haven't touched a bubble wand since fourth grade? Don't worry—the skill comes back quickly. Look for the newest wrinkle in bubbles: edible, fruit-flavored, or catnip-scented cat-safe bubble liquid. (If you use old-fashioned soap bubbles, be sure your cat doesn't lick up the soap.) Your cat will happily leap, pounce on, and chase after the mysteriously disappearing prey! This game can get messy, leaving bubble-sized sticky spots on the floor. So enjoy your play session in the kitchen or in another linoleum or tiled floor area, and quickly damp-mop afterwards. Clean floor, happy cat!

Safety First!—Cat-Toy Safety Considerations

Some toys sold specifically for cats are unsafe or inappropriate for them. Flimsy plastic balls that crack and splinter when mouthed; toys with glued-on eyes, wings, or other decorations that are usually pulled off immediately and eaten; tiny, sharp-edged bells; flimsy elastic string; bright but possibly toxic dyes; toys made with real fur or real feathers—none of these has any business anywhere near your cat. Look for sturdy, safe toys, with no small or removable parts. Decorations should be firmly sewn on, not just glued. Bright-colored toys may contain harmful dyes, and color in a toy means little or nothing to a cat anyway. At playtime, cats focus on shape and movement.

Just Say No to Dangerous Plants

Although cats love greens, not all greens are safe for cats. Many common houseplants are deadly poisons, or can cause stomach upsets and skin and mouth irritation. (See page 85 for a list of poisonous, dangerous, and irritating plants.) If you're especially fond of plants that may be dangerous to your cat, keep them completely inaccessible to even a curious, leaping, climbing cat. Keep them in a room you have designated a cat-free zone, or hang them securely from ceiling hooks. Promptly pick up any fallen foliage and wipe up spilled water. Never let your cat drink from water spilled from hanging plants. Make sure your cat has plenty of safe greenery to divert his attention.

The safest course is to keep only completely cat-safe plants indoors. Fortunately, there are many attractive, feline-friendly houseplants. Check out all the choices in the list on page 110.

Just Say Yes to Catnip

Catnip *(Nepeta cataria)*, a member of the mint family, contains a chemical that exerts a powerful attraction for cats. Although cats will eat the leaves, it's the crushed and broken leaves and stems that release the gloriously compelling odor. Cats who have deeply inhaled catnip roll and tumble, prance and purr, leap and dance in pure feline ecstasy. About two-thirds of cats are catnip responders. It's a genetically determined preference. Catnip is completely safe and nonaddicting for your cat, but if you offer it too often, it may lose its effectiveness over time.

Catnip is extremely easy to grow, indoors or out. It's very invasive, though. Planted outdoors, it spreads widely and rapidly through underground runners. If you don't confine it, it'll take over your yard. (Never treat or spray your catnip plants with chemicals, insecticides, or pesticides.) Indoors, grow a few pots on a sunny windowsill in a location inaccessible to your cat. (If he can get at it, he'll quickly strip the plant bare!) Every week or two, offer a generous handful of the fresh or dried leaves and enjoy the show.

A Bed of His Own

If you allow your cat access to your bedroom at night, he may or may not decide to sleep with you. Each cat is different. Respect his preference; don't try to force the issue either way. Even if your cat loves to share your pillow, though, you should provide him with a snug, cat-friendly bed of his own for those times when he decides to dream solo. An ideal cat bed is cozy but large enough to curl up in comfortably. Some cats enjoy high, padded sides; others prefer lower sides they can drape a paw over. Get a washable bed or one with a removable, washable cover. Cats being the individuals they are, there's no guarantee your cat will actually sleep in a bed purchased just for him, however luxurious, well designed, or costly.

A Place of His Own—"Keep Out! This Means You!"

You can't select your cat's favorite places—his private hideaways—even if you want to. No, this is a purely feline decision. Each cat's choices will be different, determined by personality, need for space or silence, and observational opportunities. One cat will hole up in the depths of a closet behind the vacuum cleaner; another will make his nest on the top shelf of the linen cabinet. One cat will retreat beneath the coffee table; another inside that cardboard box you set down in the kitchen one day and now don't dare move. Some cats maintain multiple hideaways, perhaps preferring a quieter one for snoozing and one with a better view of the household action when feeling friskier.

Respect your cat's preferences in hideaways. Dearly as your cat loves you, your interference in his hideaway is not wanted. If you bother or tease him while he's relaxing in a favorite hideaway, he may surprise you with his reaction! Your cat feels safe, comfortable, in control, and relaxed in his private lair, rather like you feel in your own favorite chair. For both of you, it's the one place you can close your eyes, shut out the world, feel safe and calm, meditate and dream.

Your Cat's Toilet—the Litter Box

The complexities of litter-box siting and maintenance and elimination-related behavior problems have often been overemphasized, leading many cat owners to dread the entire subject. What are a cat's priorities in a litter box?

1. cleanliness
2. appropriate location (easily accessible, yet not too near his eating and sleeping areas), preferred type and depth of litter
3. a sense of peace and unhurried calm, freedom from interruption or surprise
4. easy escapability

What are the cat owner's preferences? Low or no odor, cleanliness, easy maintenance, consistency of use. Fortunately, these priorities are quite compatible. For example, if you stash the litter box behind the washing machine with the lint and dust bunnies, it will be neither easily escapable (important to the cat) nor easily maintainable (important to you).

Types of Litter Boxes

A stroll through any pet center or a glance at the advertisements in cat magazines reveals a staggering assortment of elaborate, complicated, and expensive litter boxes. Many are even called litter systems, and some would do a rocket scientist proud. Are these really necessary?

Well, no. If you love gadgetry and don't mind spending some extra money and dealing with moving parts, motors, electricity, or fancy patented mechanisms for sifting, scooping, and state-of-the-art odor control—go for it. But chances are, your cat would prefer simplicity. Many of those superboxes and litter systems are designed to appeal to cat owners—not cats.

What about covered boxes? Dozens of styles of covered litter boxes are equipped with tiny openings, hidden openings, openings that face a wall, or curtains and screens, or are even disguised as furniture or planters. The idea, clearly, is to disguise the litter box by both concealing its existence and confining associated odors inside the box itself.

Put yourself in your cat's place. Would you feel confident and comfortable squeezing around a corner into a tiny opening, into a dark, tiny, smelly chamber? Where you can't see or hear anyone or anything approaching? Where you might be trapped if a rival appears to block the opening? Wouldn't you prefer the corner of the living-room carpet, too?

Would you feel comfortable squeezing into a dark, tiny, smelly chamber? Although some cats adjust to covered litter boxes, others never do. (FRANTZ DANTZLER)

THE HUMANE SOCIETY OF THE UNITED STATES COMPLETE GUIDE TO CAT CARE

Informal studies by cat owners have shown that many cats dislike covered boxes. In the close confines of a covered box, many cats don't know quite what to do with their tails. It's dark. It's smelly. It's difficult to turn around. It's difficult to perform the vigorous movements necessary to bury waste. And the inside height of most available covered boxes is usually inadequate, especially for a large cat. Watch your cat as he uses a simple, open-pan litter box. He stands up tall, doesn't he? Now, imagine trying that in a cramped, low-ceilinged, stinky, covered box.

Elaborate litter-box designs often incorporate odd-shaped parts, plastic grids, screens, ledges, and other devices that promise to somehow take the effort out of regular cleaning and maintenance. But these complicated surfaces actually make cleaning and maintenance messier and more difficult—all those crevices and grids tend to trap wet, smelly, used litter. And while many designs boast charcoal or other filters, no filter, however well it masks odors, replaces frequent scooping and regular cleaning.

Covered boxes make your job of regular monitoring and cleanup much more inconvenient and troublesome. You have to take apart the box (in some cases, a tricky job) just to see if it needs scooping. You'll be less likely to scoop as often as you should. A thorough weekly cleaning becomes a huge undertaking. Because the cover holds in the smell, the odor won't motivate you to remember your regular cleanup, either. But your cat will have to deal with it every time.

Keep it simple, especially when you and your cat are just starting out. Get a plain, open, rectangular litter pan with smooth, flat sides. These are usually plastic, but you can also find stainless-steel models. You could also use an ordinary dishpan or a plastic storage box, as long as the sides aren't too high for your cat to conveniently hop over. Your box should have smooth interior surfaces without indentations where wet, dirty litter can get trapped. Kittens may need boxes with low sides. Large cats may need large boxes with high sides.

If you become intrigued with one of the fancier litter systems, go ahead and try it out. Perhaps your cat will prefer it. But leave a simple, open litter box available for him, too. Observe his choice, and then respect his preference. The most expensive, well-disguised stealth litter box is worthless if your cat finds it too small, too smelly, or too scary to use.

How Many Boxes? And Where?

Many owners of multiple cats have discovered that, just as the "one room in the house per cat" rule is a good general guide to follow, "one litter box per cat, plus one extra" is a good rule for litter boxes. To enhance each cat's sense of territorial security, think in terms of providing a sense of spaciousness, of extras. This will help enhance all your cats' trust in the continuing abundance of resources in your home. Litter-box placement is crucial—perhaps even more important than cleanliness. A cat who's cornered, harassed, or surprised by another cat (even a friend), a noisy piece of machinery, a loud human, an unusual odor, or other stressor while in or near the litter box will be understandably unwilling to take his business there in the future.

A bathroom is an ideal place for a litter-box setup, if there's enough space. Or consider a spare bedroom, laundry room, enclosed back or front porch, or sunroom. Your basement might be perfect, but be sure that the basement is accessible to your cat at all times, and that the litter boxes are placed in an area that's safe, clean, hygienic, tidy, and adequately lit and ventilated. (Remember, you'll be scooping at least once a day!) Keep the litter-box area well away from the furnace, water heater, and other machinery that might come to life with a frightening roar at a delicate moment.

Never assume you can stash a litter box down in a back corner of the basement and forget about it for weeks. If you do, don't be surprised if your cat finds he prefers the corner of the living-room carpet, the bathtub, or even the kitchen stove. Whenever you place the litter box, think: if you wouldn't want to venture there several times a day, why should your cat?

In a multiple-cat household, provide more than one litter station, each consisting of two or more litter boxes. If you live in a multiple floor home, keep litter stations on different floors—perhaps one in the basement and one in an upstairs bathroom. At each station, keep a complete set of litter-care supplies (described below) for quick and easy routine maintenance. If your home is large, consider an extra station, even if you have only one cat—especially if your cat is elderly.

Types of Cat-Box Fillers (Litter)

For the first-time cat-supply shopper, choosing litter, or filler, is possibly more confusing than choosing the type of box. There are dozens of brands, made of dozens of materials, vying for your cat-litter dollars.

Plain natural clay

This gritty-textured litter consists of fairly large particles. It's usually quite dusty. Most types of clay sold as cat litter absorb fairly well, but urine tends to spread, and the clay rapidly becomes saturated. Some brands include fragrances or deodorizing ingredients, but many cats dislike the odors of these. When the box needs cleaning, the entire contents must be discarded. The particles can also tend to get caught between cats' toes. Plain clay is very inexpensive and widely available. The original Kitty Litter—the first commercial cat-box filler, invented in 1947—was plain clay.

Clumping litter

A fairly recent (introduced in 1984) and wildly popular alternative to plain clay, clumping litters contain a particularly absorbent type of clay, *sodium bentonite,* that concentrates urine in compact clumps so that it doesn't spread and can be easily removed. Most cats love the fine, sandy, easy-on-the-paws texture. Although it's more expensive per pound than plain clay, clumping litter is actually more economical, since only the urine clumps and feces must be removed, and the scooped box is topped off with fresh litter. The economy and convenience of clumping litters have caused them to quickly overtake plain clay in popularity. Dust can be a problem. There are numerous brands, some much dustier than others.

Plant-based litters

There's an ever-growing selection of these, made of corn (kernels or corncob flakes); wheat; kenaf (the core of a fast-growing relative of the hibiscus); cedar chips or flakes; compressed or crumbled wood pellets; hardwood sawdust; or other organic materials. These litters claim to be more earth-friendly than mined and dried clay. They're generally dust-free and are less widely available than clays.

"Crystal" or silica litters

The newest contender in the litter wars is silica, a highly absorptive mineral. The litter consists of silica gel mixed with sand. Tiny beads about one-sixteenth to one-eighth of an inch in diameter absorb and trap odors. Liquid evaporates rapidly and the beads remain dry.

Other litters

There are also litters made from shredded, ground, or pelletized newspaper or other recycled paper.

The best litter for your cat is the one he'll use. Even if you're determined to use only natural products, your cat may just not care for the smell, texture, or feel of any of the natural, organic, or plant-based litters. If you're not sure which type of litter your cat prefers, of if he's shown a distaste for the type you've selected for him, set out two or three litter boxes, "cafeteria style," each filled with a different type of filler. See which he prefers. It's wise to observe your cat's choices and accommodate his preferences in this very important matter.

THE CAT IN YOUR LIFE, THE CAT IN YOUR HOME

Easy, Everyday Maintenance—Experts' Secrets Revealed!

Many cats prefer a plain, uncovered box and clumping litter, with its soft, sandy, paw-friendly texture. Forget about plastic cat-box liners—they're a waste of money. Many cats don't like them and tend to shred them with their customary vigorous clawing and scratching, rendering them messy and worse than useless. They make frequent scooping difficult and messy, trapping used litter beneath the inevitably torn plastic, where it smells and festers. Yuck!

Happily, this basic, simple setup also makes regular cleanup quick and easy. Frequent scooping is a plus for your cat, who loves his facilities clean and tidy. Without fancy covers to remove or lots of complicated parts or torn liners to deal with, you'll be more likely to scoop frequently. It only takes a few moments once you get organized and get the hang of it. Your home won't develop that unpleasant, telltale, "Hmmm, do I smell a cat?" odor, and—best of all—you'll have a happier cat.

Keep a small covered wastebasket, lined with a plastic bag, near the box. (Some clumping litters come in covered pails that can serve this purpose as well.) Scoop out feces and clumps once or twice daily or as often as necessary. Add litter as needed. If you decide to recycle the plastic bags you get at the supermarket for lining the used-litter trash can, fine—but double or even triple them up. They're not designed for reuse with heavy, wet used litter.

Another option is to keep a supply of sturdy, self-sealing plastic bags (usually called freezer bags) or plastic grocery bags near the litter box. The gallon size works best. Scoop the clumps and feces into the bag and zip or tie it shut. When it's full, toss it in the trash. Add fresh litter to the box as needed. This system is simple, neat, fast, and economical.

Disposal Dilemmas

Even if the label on your package of cat litter says it's perfectly safe to flush, don't. Especially don't flush used litter if you have a septic system—unless you're really, really fond of the fellow who drives the septic-tank pumping truck.

Although it seems cleaner to flush used litter down the toilet, pollutants that enter the water-waste stream are much more likely to cause environmental problems than those that stay on dry land. When flushed, pollutants and bacteria spread out freely, and relatively uncontrollably, into the groundwater, lakes, rivers, and ocean. The solid-waste stream, on the other hand, is better controlled. Most solid waste today ends up in modern lined landfills, where it's held inert and prevented from spreading.

Advances in the science of *bioremediation* promise to be able, in the near future, to render harmless most pathogens and toxins sequestered in these landfills.

Your Secret Weapon!

Your secret weapon in easy litter-box care costs less than a dollar and is easy to find—but isn't available at any pet-supply store. Go to your local hardware store or home center and look for an ordinary paint scraper—a metal or plastic tool with a wide, flat blade about 3-to-4 inches wide and a wooden or plastic handle. A metal-bladed scraper will rust if you don't wash and dry it off every time you use it, but it's much stronger and will last longer and do the job better.

The purpose of the scraper is to scrape the clumped litter off the sides, corners, and bottom of the litter box. No matter what the advertisements say, no litter-box scoop does this job half as well as an ordinary paint scraper. Run the scraper's blade down the sides of the box and underneath all the large clumps to separate them from the litter-box sides and bottom. Scooping is then much easier—and you'll be sure to get all of it. A litter scoop alone always leaves some used litter behind, and most brands of used clumping litter soon turn to a substance that rivals heavy-duty concrete in strength and persistence. When you're done scooping and scraping, scrape your two tools against each other to remove as much stuck-on wet litter as possible.

Keep your litter-care tools handy. Pop your scooper and scraper into a small plastic bag between uses to help keep everything neater. Near the litter box, keep a plastic milk-crate basket, filled with spare litter, your tools, a supply of plastic bags, your small trash can (if you decide to use one), and a roll of paper towels. You can even get casters (little wheels) for these crates so they're easy to move around as you clean and scoop.

About once a week, or whenever it starts looking dirty and grubby, do a complete cleaning. (Clean one box at a time, so your cat has a place to go if he needs to!) First, scoop and scrape as usual. Then, pour any unused litter (assuming you're using a clumping litter) into a large plastic bag (a trash bag) to reuse when the box is clean. Scrub out the box thoroughly with hot water. Sanitize it by filling it with a solution of one teaspoon of ordinary household bleach to a gallon of hot water and letting it stand for several minutes (where your cat can't get at it, of course). Then, rinse thoroughly and dry with paper towels (or out in the sun). If you have one, use a steam-cleaning appliance to sterilize the box. Avoid chemical cleaners and *never* use ammonia-based cleaner.

When the box is clean, sterilized, and completely dry, refill it with litter (that still-clean litter you saved in the trash bag, plus fresh litter) to a depth of about 2 inches—and you're back in business! Don't imagine, though, that by adding even more litter you can avoid your daily scooping chores or put off regular cleaning and maintenance! For one thing, those massive litter Saharas are much harder to scoop. And many cats dislike litter more than a few inches deep (it's hard to navigate in). Some cats, especially longhaired felines, prefer even less—just a dusting, or even the smooth surface of the bottom of the box, with a handy pile of litter nearby for covering.

Protect Yourself

Always wash your hands thoroughly immediately after scooping or cleaning your cat's litter box or handling any of your litter-care tools. If you're sensitive or allergic to cat-litter dust, wear a gauze or disposable paper face mask while you scoop—and seek out the least-dusty cat litter you can find. Among the readily available supermarket brands of clumping litter, some produce very little dust if handled carefully.

If you're pregnant or immunocompromised, get someone else to handle litter-box maintenance. There's a small, but real, chance a pregnant woman could contract the zoonotic disease *toxoplasmosis,* a parasitical infection that can harm her developing fetus, from contact with the feces of an infected cat. (However, most cases of toxoplasmosis are caused by eating undercooked meats, particularly lamb and pork. Unpasteurized dairy products and raw unwashed vegetables are other potential sources of infection. In rare instances, infection can occur through the ingestion of soil contaminated with the parasite's oocysts.) Immunocompromised persons should always avoid contact with any pathogens or infectious agents.

"Mistakes Were Made . . ."

No cat is always perfect—not even yours! Occasionally, because of illness, stress, an unpleasant experience in or near his litter box, or unhappiness with its cleanliness, your cat may take his business elsewhere. In addition to decoding what's made your cat communicate in this rather forceful manner, you need to clean up the mess!

Cat feces are usually fairly easy to clean up. On hard surfaces such as wood floors, tile, and linoleum, pick up the mess with paper towels and dispose of it the same way you do when scooping the litter box. Clean the area thoroughly with a cat-safe stain-and-odor remover appropriate for that surface.

On carpeting, the trick is to confine the mess to as small an area as possible. With a paper towel, pick up the pile, being careful not to rub or smear it on the carpet. (If your unhappy cat has had an attack of diarrhea on the carpet, things get a bit more complicated. Remove as much as possible without smearing or rubbing it into the nap of the carpet.) Blot, don't rub, with warm, wet paper towels or rags to remove as much of the stain and material as you can. Don't let the area become soaked or saturated. Alternately blot with wet and dry paper towels until you've removed most or all of the visible stain. (You'll likely use several paper towels.)

After testing your carpet with the product for colorfastness, apply an enzyme-based stain-and-odor remover according to the label directions. You might need to reapply the product several times until the stain is completely gone. If the mess has been there for some time and has partially dried, remove as much as possible, let the area dry, and vacuum thoroughly. Then proceed as for a fresh mess.

The Cat-Urine Wars

Cat urine is a smelly, persistent, invasive, and difficult-to-eradicate substance. Worse, your cat's extremely sensitive nose lets him zero in again and again on a spot he's urinated on or marked—even if you've cleaned it repeatedly and can't smell a thing. Inappropriate urination requires immediate, dedicated attention—both to thoroughly clean and deodorize all spots the cat's used and to discover the root cause of the problem. A visit to the veterinarian should be your first step.

Of all cat "accidents," inappropriate urination causes the most cleanup woes. Help prevent it by providing a clean, well-maintained, accessible litter box (or boxes), monitoring your cat's health, and becoming familiar with his daily habits and behavior so that you immediately notice any changes. For your cat's sake and yours, find the problem and fix it. Don't wait until your home smells like a giant litter box.

Urine Cleanup Secrets

Fresh cat urine is acidic and relatively clean and free of bacteria. It's only once it starts to dry that it's converted to alkaline salts—an environment in which odor-producing bacteria flourish. Since fresh urine is acid, while old, dried urine is alkaline, they call for different cleaning strategies.

Although many books recommend cleaning urine with vinegar, never use vinegar on fresh urine—it makes the situation worse. Vinegar increases the acidity of the urine, providing a friendlier environment for alkaline salts—and more odor-causing bacteria—to form. The alkalinized urine is then primed to absorb moisture out of the ambient air and will "return from the dead" time and time again. That's why you might smell ancient cat urine on very humid days.

Instead, blot, don't rub, with dry paper towels or rags; then, blot with rags or paper towels moistened in warm water. Or use club soda instead of water. Blot with alternating wet and dry towels several times, until you've removed most or all of the actual urine. Then, wash the area with a mild, diluted dish-detergent solution (one teaspoon in a quart of warm water), and rinse and dry thoroughly. (Many products contain both a stain remover and an odor remover; check the product label for instructions.) After testing the surface with the product for colorfastness, apply an enzyme-based stain-and-odor remover according to the label directions. You might need to reapply the product several times until the odor is completely gone.

Dried cat urine calls for a different approach. First, it's hard to find, since cats often deposit it in out-of-the-way corners and closets. Otherwise invisible cat urine shows up clearly under an ordinary black light (sometimes called a Wood's light). You can get a black-light-equipped portable flashlight or other lamp at many pet-supply centers or hardware stores. Use it to hunt down old cat urine patches.

Start with a solution of vinegar and water—an acid solution to offset the bacteria-friendly alkaline salts. This will help bring the urine back down to a neutral pH. Flood the area well with the solution, alternately blotting and drying. Use plenty of rags or paper towels. Wash the entire area with a mild, diluted dish-detergent solution (one teaspoon in a quart of warm water), and rinse and dry thoroughly. (Or check the product label of a stain-and-odor remover.) After testing the surface with the product for colorfastness, apply an enzyme-based stain-and-odor remover according to the label directions. You might need to reapply the product several times until the odor is completely gone.

The Tip of the Iceberg

Unfortunately, if the urine is on your carpet, what you see, and can clean up, on the carpet itself is only the tip of the iceberg. Most of it likely soaked through to the backing, padding, underlayment, and even the underlying floorboards. To eliminate the odor (so that your cat can no longer detect it), these must be treated as well.

Cats seem to have a predilection for corners. If the urine is in a corner, your job is a bit easier. Pull up the corner of the carpet and clean and deodorize the underside of the carpet, any padding, and the floor underneath. Let it all dry thoroughly before putting everything back in place. Re-treat if you have the slightest suspicion that any odor lingers.

To be on the safe side, block your cat's access to all areas in which you've discovered and treated cat urine. Carpet-protector mats—with those hard, nubby points—

work well. Place one, pointy side up, over the area. Or use double-sided sticky tape or aluminum foil, both materials on which cats dislike walking.

What if your cat has urinated extensively in several places on a carpeted floor, or if you move into a house in which a previous resident cat did so (something that occurs more often than some cat owners, or real-estate agents, like to admit)? Your best bet may be to remove and discard the carpet, padding, and (in severe cases) even the underlying floorboards. When deciding on replacement flooring, consider a more cat- and cleaning-friendly surface such as sheet linoleum. Use washable throw rugs for warmth and color.

But Can He Learn to Flush?

Some cat owners report success in teaching their cats to use the facilities provided for humans instead of a litter box. Training techniques, detailed in books and videos, involve a gradual acclimatizing and familiarization process and require special equipment, such as a cat-friendly seat for the toilet. However, it's been claimed that some cats taught themselves, probably by observing their humans. These cats reportedly just perch gracefully right on the regular seat rim. Whether or not your cat chooses this route, keep him safe; make sure he can't drink the water or fall in. Toilet hygiene may also be a consideration.

Window Seats and Cat TV

An indoors-only lifestyle doesn't mean giving up sunshine, fresh air, breezes, and the sights and sounds of nature. It does mean enjoying these safely. Cats love a selection of comfortable window seats placed at securely screened windows. Locate several of these around the house so that your cat can follow the sun throughout the day.

While window perches are especially enticing in nice weather, don't forget that sun and fresh air are important in winter, too. Some cats delight in sitting in a screened open window in freezing weather, sniffing subtle messages in the frigid breezes. And few cats can resist snoozing away a long February afternoon in a patch of golden sunlight on a warm floor, entertained by the drift of snowflakes and inhaling deeply of the exhilarating fresh winter air.

What's cat TV? Some new hi-tech computer gimmick? No, just that old-fashioned garden standby—an outdoor bird feeder, set up in your yard and easily viewable from a cat-perch-equipped, securely screened window. Keep the feeder filled year-round to attract lots of feathery friends for your cat's viewing pleasure.

Advanced Indoor Pampering

Can't do enough for your cat? Here are a few more ideas:

- a securely topped aquarium or fish tank filled with fish (if you enjoy fish yourself)
- videotapes designed to appeal to cats, featuring fluttery birds and other feline favorites (Some cats are entranced by these; others ignore them.)
- soft background music (Many cats seem to adore classical music, but beware: many hate opera, especially soprano arias. Respect your cat's musical tastes.)
- some cat owners leave audiotapes of their own voices that play at intervals throughout the day when they're away. Others call their own phone number and speak to their housebound cats through the answering machine.
- a cat tree improved with extra shelves, securely attached, cat-safe hanging plants, caves and hammocks, and other cat-friendly enhancements
- a small fountain, powered by an electric recirculating pump, for soothing sounds and fresh running water (Keep the fountain sparking clean and never treat the water with chemicals.)

While it's fine to locate feeders outside windows so that your cat can bird-watch, avoid indoor live caged birds. Although your cat may delight in watching them, there's always the chance that they'll get out of their cage, or that he'll break in. (Never underestimate a determined cat!) And it's likely quite stressful on the birds, too.

Amusing, Amazing Mazes

For a combination of intellectual challenge and unique collection of casual hangouts and cozy retreats for your cat, build a one-of-a-kind, three-dimensional maze. Use cardboard packing boxes and crates in various sizes and shapes, taped together with packing tape. Build long tunnels, towers with multiple floors, porches. Use your imagination. Add climbing-posts mounted on wide, stable wood bases and covered with spiral-wound sisal rope for access to the maze's upper levels.

Use a craft knife to cut windows, doors, and skylights in several shapes and sizes.

Leave some windows flapped with cardboard; curtain others with bits of cloth. In an interior compartment, stash a snuggly cat bed or pillow, or an old sweatshirt. Place a corrugated cardboard scratching mat inside or on the "front porch." Occasionally, reconfigure the maze, adding and subtracting elements. To encourage repeated exploration, hide treats, a sprinkling of dried catnip, or a new toy inside the maze. Enhance your maze's appearance and cat appeal by locating it near a sunny window and spotting lush green plants all about.

In chapter 9, you'll learn how to provide your lucky cat with opportunities for fun-filled, exciting, safe, and healthy outdoor adventures—either strolling the neighborhood with a leash and harness—and you in tow—or in his very own cat enclosure. In chapter 8, you'll discover lots of reasons for treating the cat you love to a safe, protected, stimulating indoors-only lifestyle—the lifestyle of the feline and fortunate!

CAT-SAFE GREENERY

This is a partial list of cat-safe plants. For maximum safety, grow houseplants to which your cat will have access yourself, from seed. Use untreated seed only. If you buy plants, make sure they haven't been sprayed or treated with fungicides or insecticides.

African violet
alfalfa sprouts
   (Homegrown is best.)
alyssum
bachelor's buttons
basil
bean sprout
   (Homegrown is best.)
begonia
buddleia (butterfly bush)
calendula
catbrier
catmint
catnip
celosia (cockscomb)
chamomile
chervil
cleome
coleus
columbine
coreflower
coriander
cosmos
cress
dahlia
dianthus (pinks)

dill
fluffy ruffles
forget-me-not
gloxinia
heliotrope
hollyhock
hyssop
impatiens
lavender
lemon balm
lemon verbena
lettuce
lovage
marum (cat thyme)
miniature roses
mint
monarda (bee balm)
nasturium
oat grass sprouts
orchid
oregano
pansy
parsley
pea (not sweet pea, which
   is poisonous)
peperomia

peppermint
petunia
phlox
portulaca
rosemary
roses
sage
scabiosa
shasta daisy
snapdragon
spearmint
spider plants
spinach
strawberry
strawflower
   (helichrysum)
sunflowers
sweet william
tarragon
thyme
torenia
verbascum
violet
wheat (not wheat
   grass)
zinnia

CHAPTER 8

Indoors or Out?
Which Is Best for Your Cat?

A TALE OF THREE KITTIES

It's been a long, hard day at work, and Ben's exhausted. But as he swings his car into the driveway, he can't help grinning as his headlights momentarily illuminate four little pointed ears silhouetted in the front window. Making his way into the house (opening the door slowly and looking downwards, as usual), he's greeted with a chorus of chirrups and meows as Bess and Sammy curl around his ankles. Shrugging off his jacket and slipping out of his shoes, Ben settles into his favorite chair, where the two cats join him: Bess stretched out on his lap, and Sammy perched on the chair back above his head. "Ah, stereo . . . ," he murmurs, as the purrs crank up and his stress starts to melt away. A bit later, refreshed, Ben heads for the kitchen. "Can I interest anyone in a bite of supper?"

Meanwhile, Bonnie's also had a long, stress-filled day. As she pulls into her garage, she makes a quick scan of the porch and yard, but Nick's not home yet. She's not surprised; when the weather's nice, he hardly ever comes home before dark. Collecting the mail, she heads wearily into the house. Alas, it's all bills, as usual, including a hefty one from Nick's last visit to the emergency veterinary clinic. She can't help chuckling as she recalls that, banged up as he was, Nick's swaggering attitude seemed to say, "You shoulda seen the other guy!" Bonnie never did figure out who he'd tangled with.

As she prepares her supper, Bonnie makes several trips to the porch to scan the neighborhood and call for Nick. She fills his bowl with fresh water and dishes up his favorite chow, wondering if he might have gotten locked up in the Smiths' garage again. On her fifth trip outdoors, Bonnie's finally rewarded by the sight of her big tabby bounding across the road. After a quick head scratch and meowed "Hello," Nick makes a beeline for supper. Afterwards, he treats himself to a thorough washup—a process Bonnie adores watching. As she eats her own dinner, Nick dozes nearby, purring happily.

But later in the evening, she sees Nick pacing impatiently by the front door. A bit reluctantly, she opens the door. As Nick trots out, blending into the shadows, she calls, "Be careful out there!" Sure, she worries about him. But when she adopted him from a friend who had developed allergies, Nick was already over a year old and accustomed to come and go as he pleased. She feels it would be unfair to confine him and deny him his treasured freedom.

Bess, Sammy, and Nick have a lot in common. All three are well loved, wanted, sterilized cats and enjoy high-quality diets and regular veterinary attention. But the lives, schedules, and concerns of Bess and Sammy, treated to an exclusively indoors lifestyle from kittenhood, are focused on their owner, Ben. While he's at work, they amuse each other and delight in the safe, comfortable, feline-friendly environment Ben has provided, full of thoughtful, cat-pleasing touches. And when he's home, they want to spend every possible minute with him, enhancing their mutual bond and just enjoying one another's company.

Of course, "indoors-only" certainly doesn't mean Bess and Sammy are denied their fill of sunshine, fresh air, and the tantalizing odors that waft in the leafy breezes. In addition to plenty of safely screened window perches, the two lucky cats enjoy plenty of quality lap time with Ben as he sips tea and scans the weekend papers on his shady back porch. The two cats always wear their harnesses and leashes, though—just in case a passing bird proves a bit too interesting.

Nick, on the other hand, finds his primary focus in life outdoors. While he's quite fond of sharing some of his time with Bonnie, playing, purring, or just relaxing quietly, Nick's primary concerns in life revolve around his territory; the comings and goings of wild animals, dogs, and other cats; and the scents, sounds, and sights of his neighborhood.

Nick's life might seem carefree and pleasant, but patrolling and defending a sizable territory can be a surprisingly stressful task. Even though Nick is neutered, Bonnie might be astonished at how far afield he wanders on some of these moonlit nights. Nick enjoys plenty of secret hideaways in his outdoors realm—underneath a shady bush, tucked high up on a wall, even perched on a comfy tree branch. But the world of the great outdoors also holds many elements that are not particularly feline-friendly.

Puncturing a Few Myths

There are many cat owners, like Bonnie, who adore their cats and enjoy strong, loving bonds with them, yet feel their cats can't really be happy if not allowed freedom to roam, at least some of the time. For hundreds of years, people assumed that cats were essentially wild creatures who simply could not thrive if confined. But in recent years, animal-behavior specialists and other experts have, for the first time, carefully studied the actual daily activities of cats. It turns out that cats are very well suited to a protected indoors-only lifestyle, as long as their environment provides companionship, variety, cat-oriented stimulation, and hunting-like play opportunities.

The cat, of all animals who share close relationships with people, is the only one who retains a mysteriously compelling aura of wildness. Every cat owner has seen his furry friend transformed—in a heartbeat—from dozing fireside pet to slinking, fierce-eyed predator. Many cat owners admire this wild side of their cat's personality and fear that an indoors-only lifestyle would blunt or even destroy it.

A look at what animal experts have discovered about the cat's nature, drives, psychology, and daily activities brings good news: You need not fear that an indoors-only, supervised lifestyle will lessen the delightfully wild aspects of your cat's personality. In fact, by indulging his natural feline zest for joyful, frequent interactive play, you'll be able to participate much more fully in this marvelous aspect of his nature. Rather than perform his magnificent leaps, graceful dances, astonishing balancing acts, and everyday frolics for an audience of strangers, your cat will amaze, entertain, and delight you with these uniquely feline gifts right in your own home. A close, loving relationship with your cat brings irreplaceable opportunities to observe and appreciate a precious bit of living wild nature, up close and personal.

Partly because of the many behavioral similarities between domestic cats and their wild feline relatives, a number of myths, misconceptions, and superstitions have grown up around the domestic cat over the centuries. Many of these myths have roots in distant eras when people knew very little about cat behavior and cat psychology, and may even date to unenlightened times when cats were considered sneaky, threatening, untrustworthy, or even evil by nature. We examined—and demolished—some of these myths in chapter 3.

Other misconceptions surround some aspects of indoor cat care such as litter-box management or reflect a misunderstanding of how cats actually spend their time. Wherever they come from, myths about cats and cat care die hard. Let's examine a few more of these common myths—especially those that involve lifestyle choices—and see how they prevent too many cats from enjoying a safe, stimulating, feline-enriched, indoors-only lifestyle.

Myth: Cats need to roam free to be happy and follow their true natures.

Fact: What is a cat's true nature? Let's look at how your cat spends his time. Even wild cats like lions and cougars sleep up to twenty hours per day. The rest of the time, they groom themselves, hunt for and consume prey, do a bit of patrolling and scent marking, attend to elimination activities, play, and just quietly observe their surroundings. Sleeping—by far the most popular feline activity—is still sleeping whether it takes place under a tree or on your sofa. But while snoozing on your sofa, your cat has a much smaller chance of picking up ticks and fleas, getting rained on, or being attacked by other animals.

Self-grooming, every cat's number-two priority in terms of time spent, can be just as efficiently performed in a nice sunny spot on the living room floor as out on the sidewalk, and on the floor there is less chance of being mowed down by an errant bicycle or chased off by a dog. The same can be said of the characteristically feline activity of just quietly watching, relaxed but alert. Much of the time a free-roaming cat is outdoors, he's sacked out or just lounging around somewhere, most likely in less comfort and safety than he'd enjoy at home.

How about eating and eliminating? Eating is easy—the call of the can opener simply replaces the call of the wild, and your cat has much less chance of consuming poisoned, tainted, or pesticide-laced edibles when his meals come out of a can or box. Cat experts have yet to meet the cat who refuses on principle to eat food he didn't catch himself.

In the elimination department, the fastidious cat's true nature is best accommodated by indoor facilities. Feline requirements in toilet conveniences include cleanliness, privacy, and ease of escape in case of danger—all best met with a thoughtfully placed, meticulously maintained indoor litter-box setup. While such a setup is a bit more work for the owner, it will spare her social embarrassment—for example, complaints when the neighbor's toddler discovers a nasty surprise in his sandbox.

That leaves hunting, patrolling, and playing—to a cat, remarkably similar activities, which, more than anything else, are really indicative of his true nature. Cats require daily, stimulating, vigorous, hunting-like play—play that exercises their bodies, tunes their muscles, challenges their minds, and delights their senses. Whether this play results in a dead mouse, or in a cat treat and lavish words of praise from a loved owner, isn't important to your cat. The mock-hunting activity itself is what gratifies his inner wild cat and satisfies the deepest urgings of his true nature.

Myth: You can't control a cat anyway, so why try?

Fact: Providing a safe, stimulating indoors-only lifestyle doesn't mean controlling your cat. Cat owners who see their cats as loved and valued animal companions have neither the desire nor the need to control them. But they do have a strong motive for controlling their cats' access to negative elements in the environment. These owners, far from controlling their cats or denying them expression of their true natures, allow their cats' real personalities to blossom and develop in a safe, supervised, stimulating, supportive setting.

Myth: Cats are naturally nocturnal—they need to be out and about at night.

Fact: Wild cats like cougars and bobcats do, indeed, pursue much of their hunting around dawn and dusk, when their prey tend to be most active. (Some cat-family exceptions are lions and cheetahs, who hunt mostly during the day.) But your domestic cat is an intelligent, highly adaptable animal—after all, he learned pretty quickly to depend on you, not the local fauna, to provide supper! Your cat will readily and happily adapt to your schedule as long as you maintain a comforting, fairly predictable routine. Cats are creatures of habit and will easily adapt to your lifestyle and schedule. In fact, many cat owners rely on their cats as furry alarm clocks—and some owners even boast that their cats let them sleep in on weekends.

You might notice that your cat tends to be most active and lively in the early morning hours and in the evening. This behavior is a vestige of his wild ancestry, still wired deeply into his brain. You'll likely find that evening—just before suppertime—is an ideal time for a vigorous interactive-play session. Many cat owners find that a few moments of quality interactive playtime with their cats in the morning start their day off on the right paw, lifting their spirits even before that first cup of coffee.

Myth: Litter-box maintenance is just too overwhelming a problem.

Fact: In the days before the invention of commercial litter-box fillers, maintaining an indoor feline-toilet facility could be a challenge. But this hardly is the case today, when the cat owner's chief problem is selecting from the many options and products available. The tips in chapter 7 will help you sort out your options and banish litter-box woes permanently.

Myth: A cat is naturally a predator. He'll be miserable if he can't kill anything.

Fact: Yes, your cat is a predator. And yes, he needs to hunt. But he doesn't need to kill prey. Your cat's drive to hunt—that is, to stalk and pounce on prey and preylike objects—is completely separate from his hunger drive. In fact, a kitten who's not so instructed by his mother cat may not realize that the prey he so gleefully pounces upon is food, let alone know how to kill it efficiently and safely. Stalking and pouncing are instinctual, but the knowledge that prey is food, and the correct technique for killing prey quickly and efficiently, is learned in kittenhood.

Your cat needs to engage in hunting-like play frequently in order to satisfy his powerful instinct to stalk, pounce upon, and capture prey. This urge can be easily gratified in daily interactive play with a human or feline friend, or even in solitary cat-directed play with preylike toys. Cats possess marvelous imaginations and easily conjure up a scurrying mouse from a crumpled piece of paper tossed at him, a dancing lure at the end of a "kitty-fishing pole," or toes wiggling beneath a blanket.

Myth: Cats are too aloof, independent, and unsociable to be happy indoors.

Fact: We addressed this myth in chapter 3. People previously unfamiliar with domestic cats are often astounded to discover how sociable these intelligent, adaptable creatures are. Cats can and do live harmoniously in groups that include people, other cats, and other animals. Among their own kind, cats practice elaborate and often sweetly touching greeting and communication rituals. Often, they treat favored people to these same little touches, bestowing upon them the coveted title of "Honorary Cat."

Many owners of multiple pets are familiar with the sleeping fur pile on the sofa, made up of a happy jumble of cats and dogs dreaming the afternoon away. Cats who require a slightly larger personal space bubble are often spotted within a few feet of one another, calmly enjoying the pleasant, nonthreatening proximity of fellow felines. And even when there's plenty of space in a home to spread themselves out, the resident cats seem to often gravitate to wherever the people and other cats are.

Many cat owners are familiar with a "fur pile," in which the household cats sleep together comfortably and voluntarily. Is there enough space in your household for all of the cats to feel comfortable and unstressed?
(FRANTZ DANTZLER)

Myth: Cats fill an important ecological niche as predators.

Fact: Felis catus (or *Felis domesticus*), the domestic cat with whom we share our homes and lives, is descended from *Felis sylvestris libyca,* a small wildcat native to Africa and extreme southwestern Asia. Transported around the world on board the ships of explorers and traders, our cats' ancestors performed valuable rodent-control services. But in virtually all places where domestic cats live today, they're not part of the native ecosystem.

Cats are extremely efficient predators. But when introduced into an ecosystem in which they have not evolved, and which hasn't evolved to accommodate them, they can be destructive and disruptive. Their consumption of field mice and other rodents, while sometimes beneficial to humans, can deplete the prey supplies needed by native predators such as hawks and owls.

Owned cats enjoy tremendous advantages over native predators. Well-fed, sheltered, and provided with medical and other care by their owners, domestic cats are, if not sterilized, prolific breeders who can quickly dominate an ecosystem, driving out other predators and depleting local populations of small mammals and birds, especially ground feeders and ground nesters. While studies have shown that outdoor cats kill mostly rodents and other small mammals, they also kill an unknown number of birds, possibly in the hundreds of millions per year. Today, bird populations are threatened by numerous environmental pressures, from pollution to habitat fragmentation. The bird your cat kills today, and doesn't even eat (he just had breakfast, after all), is one that won't sing sweetly to both of you tomorrow morning—a needless loss for all.

Even if your cat seldom kills birds, his presence will soon drive away potential prey—squirrels, chipmunks, butterflies, frogs, birds—from your yard and environs. He'll be depriving these creatures of the use of a possibly rich supply of food, cover, and habitat, and depriving you of the sights and sounds of the small wild creatures that would otherwise grace your surroundings. Your indoor cat, though, can share with you his delight in observing—from a safe window perch—the scurryings and flutterings of these little marvels of nature. An active bird feeder can keep a watching cat entertained for hours. A deserted feeder is a glum spectacle for human and feline alike.

Responsible, loving cat owners like you want the very best for their cats and want to enjoy a long, happy relationship with them. Though we've punctured a few more myths, you might still have some doubts: can your cat really have a fulfilling, satisfying life without roaming free?

Yes! Even if your cat has been accustomed to a partially or completely unsupervised lifestyle, you can successfully bring him "in from the cold." He'll come halfway if you agree to meet him there. Still not convinced?

Won't My Cat Be Missing Something?

Veterinarians and animal-shelter professionals doubtless wish they had a nickel for every time a cat owner has asked them, "But won't my cat be missing something if he doesn't go outdoors?"

Well, yes. There are *lots* of things your cat will be missing. Here are a few of them:

- being hit by a car
- being shredded by a car engine
- being poisoned by pesticides, antifreeze, herbicides (The list is endless!)
- encountering and fighting with aggressive or territorial cats
- suffering injuries such as abscesses and broken bones
- contending with aggressive dogs or abusive humans
- becoming disoriented or lost while sick or injured

- being trapped in a basement or garage
- contracting rabies
- being exposed to cats infected with:
  - feline leukemia (FeLV)
  - feline panleukopenia (FPV)
  - feline infectious peritonitis (FIP)
  - feline immunodeficiency virus (FIV)
  - various upper-respiratory diseases
- contracting illnesses caught from prey
- contributing to feline overpopulation (if not sterilized)
- being exposed to parasites (fleas, ear mites, roundworms, hookworms, heartworm, ticks)
- becoming a threat to wildlife, especially to small rodents and ground-nesting birds
- upsetting the local balance of nature by competing with native predators or driving off or killing native predators' prey
- transmitting *zoonoses* (illnesses that can be transmitted between humans and animals) to their owners and families

Then there are the trigger-happy hunters; traps (including cruel leg-hold traps, still legal in many places); wild animals, including predators such as fishers, coyotes, and mountain lions; and grease, toxic chemicals, and road tar cats can ingest in grooming their outdoor-dirtied fur.

But What About Me?

If your cat has free access to the outdoors, or limited supervised access to outdoor toilet facilities, you won't need to clean and maintain your indoor litter box quite so often. But even a cat who's allowed outdoors needs a clean, accessible indoor litter box for use in severe weather or times of illness.

Many cats with free access to the outdoors consider it their duty to provide gifts of killed (or partially killed) prey to their favorite humans. Owners of indoor-outdoor cats can expect surprises—snakes slithering out from under the refrigerator; chipmunks racing through the house, neatly ducking under closed doors; partially eaten prey on the kitchen floor or in the bedroom doorway.

Owners of indoor-outdoor cats sometimes find their daily routines complicated by their wish to shelter their cats from threatening weather or other impending dangers, or by their commendable desire to keep their cats indoors overnight. Wandering the neighborhood or nearby woods and fields calling your cat's name, tense evening flashlight searches, trying to reason with a reluctant cat or one who thinks the chase is just a game—all can take a toll in time, stress, worry, and shoe leather.

Expense Considerations

If your cat has free access to the out-of-doors, you probably won't need to buy and dispose of as much cat litter. But any savings you gain are likely to go to your veterinarian. Cats who roam frequently suffer broken bones and battle wounds, porcupine quills, grease-soiled fur, and worse—unwelcome and expensive problems. Patching up your injured street fighter time after time is not only tough on your wallet, it can be tough on your spirit, not to mention hard on your cat.

Human-Cat Bonding Issues

A cat who spends most of his time wandering freely and patrolling his territory will be, like Bonnie's tabby Nick, primarily focused on those activities, rather than on his relationship with his owner. A cat allowed outdoors unsupervised even some of the time will probably be less likely to develop and share with you the close bond many cat lovers crave.

A cat who comes and goes, or who shares only a casual, if fond, relationship with his human family, or whose human companions don't make a sincere daily effort to interact and communicate with him, will seek the social contacts he needs elsewhere. Or, more sadly, he'll simply suppress the more affectionate and sociable aspects of his personality, simply because he hasn't been encouraged to develop them. With cats, as with people, "To have a friend, you must be a friend."

Owners of a cat allowed outdoors unsupervised must also realize that their cat will probably not live as long and as healthy a life as an indoors-only pet. Cats who enjoy a protected, enriched indoors-only lifestyle can enjoy long, healthy lives—up to fifteen to twenty years and even more. But the average life spans of cats who spend any amount of time outdoors unsupervised are estimated to range from approximately two-to-five years—which may be optimistic. And the lives of most stray (lost or abandoned) and feral (never-owned) cats are typically very short, often averaging less than two years. Of course, there are always a few lucky cats—such as those who live in a relatively safe suburban neighborhood with light traffic and few predators or stray dogs—who beat the odds. But is this a bet you're willing to make on your cat's life?

In addition to the dangers your cat faces outdoors unsupervised, this lifestyle choice means you'll likely miss critical early warning signs of illness. Cats are extremely reluctant to show signs of illness or weakness—especially if their status in the neighborhood hierarchy depends on a reputation for toughness. Giving your cat unsupervised access to the out-of-doors destroys your ability to monitor everything he eats and excretes—vital clues in heading off serious potential health problems.

If your cat spends much of his time away from home, his daily routine—when and how much he sleeps, how much he exercises, how often he snacks on wildlife or garbage, how far he roams, whom he spends time with—will remain a mystery. You may even miss injuries—animal bites and other wounds, hidden beneath thick fur, can become badly infected. You could easily miss a clue—in his behavior, his diet, his elimination habits—that could help you prevent a serious illness or even save his life.

Finally, if you let your cat outdoors unsupervised, you must understand that one day he may fail to return home. He may disappear forever. You may never know what fate befell him. Many cat owners have, in retrospect, found this a heavy burden to bear.

Social Issues

You and your family are not the only ones affected by your decision about your cat's lifestyle. Your cat's lifestyle can affect the environment, local wildlife, other cats and pets, and people in your neighborhood, community, and beyond—and even society at large.

Hazards to Motorists

Cats are superbly evolved, but they didn't evolve alongside automobiles. Unlike wild animals, who tend to freeze in the headlights, domestic cats are temperamentally inclined to make a run for it. Their unnerving habit of dashing into roadways, especially at night where only the glow of their eyes might betray their presence until the last second, doubtless causes much swerving and cursing on the part of even cat-loving drivers.

Cats and cars just don't mix. Even if you live on a lightly traveled road, it only takes one car to kill a cat, or one cat to cause a driver to swerve into a tree. If you allow your cat outdoors unsupervised, he may frequently roam much farther afield than you

assume, possibly far away from your relatively safe neighborhood into more dangerous or heavily traveled areas.

Cost to Taxpayers of Animal Control and Related Services

Every year, millions of tax dollars—in addition to donated funds—are spent on
rounding up stray and feral cats, sheltering these cats, and trying to find suitable
homes for as many as possible. It's been estimated that only about 5 percent of all stray
cats admitted to shelters are ever reunited with their owners. Euthanizing (humanely
destroying) cats for whom no homes can be found, and removing dead cats from
roadways, are jobs no one wants to think about. These unpleasant, demoralizing tasks
cost money (often tax dollars) and can take a severe emotional toll on those who must
perform them.

Rabies epidemics also tax public resources. In many areas of the country, domestic cats, feral and owned, are significant carriers of this deadly virus. Because of their
hunting activities, unsupervised outdoor cats are much more likely to come in contact
with wild animals, such as foxes and raccoons, who also carry rabies, thus bridging the
gap between wild reservoirs of the rabies virus and humans. Every year since 1989, the
reported number of rabid cats has exceeded the reported number of rabid dogs.

Sowing Ill Will

Even the best behaved cat might be powerfully tempted to use your neighbor's freshly
planted vegetable garden as a handy outdoor litter box. Worse, he may decide the
sandbox down the street is perfect, as long as those two toddlers are temporarily elsewhere.

Like dogs and wild animals, domestic cats can cause damage and disturbances
while outdoors unsupervised. Cats sometimes break into garbage cans and bags and
scatter trash around, dig up flower beds, spray in firewood piles, yowl and fight at all
hours (especially if unsterilized), and leave unsanitary waste in inappropriate places.

These common feline behaviors can cause much ill will in your neighborhood.
Worse, the inappropriate behavior of unsupervised cats makes it harder for responsible cat owners to promote cats as desirable companions and pets, and cat owners as
trustworthy neighbors and good citizens. Cat behavior that can be portrayed in a negative light serves to reinforce those old myths and superstitions that cats are sneaky,
untrustworthy, unfriendly, and uncontrollable. And finally, in some cases, it can even
encourage hatred of all cats and motivate attacks on individual cats.

Evaluating the Trade-offs

Your relationship with your cat is as unique as you are and he is. Take the time to thoughtfully consider the trade-offs between an indoors-only lifestyle and unsupervised access to the outdoors for your cat. Think of it as a risk-benefit analysis. Are the perils of the outdoors worth the pleasures? Make a list: write down the risks your cat might face in going outdoors unsupervised in your particular environment, alongside the benefits to him—and you—of a safe, enriched indoors-only lifestyle.

Only you can decide how much each of many factors—convenience, safety, your relationship with your cat and your neighbors, needs of native wildlife, social and environmental costs—will weigh in your decision. Now that you know the facts, you need not let myths, fears, and misconceptions about cats distort your judgment.

Starting Off on the Right Paw—Indoors from Kittenhood

According to surveys by the American Pet Products Manufacturers Association, many cats adopt their owners, rather than the other way around. But whether you selected your cat or he selected you, the best time to choose an indoors-only lifestyle is—right now!

Making the decision before you bring a new kitten home—or when you decide to take responsibility for that cat who just showed up purring on your porch, acting like he already owned the place—will be much easier both on you and your new housemate. A kitten will never miss what he's never experienced. And many owners who adopt strays or walk-ins find their cats seem relieved to be freed from the stresses of street life—and thrilled to survey the great outdoors from a safe, quiet, peaceful indoor perch.

If you're adopting a kitten or cat from a shelter, prepare your home and family to welcome him into a safe, stimulating, fun, rewarding, and satisfying environment, with everything he could want only a romp away. Chapters 6 and 7 tell you how. Chances are, even an adult adoptee won't miss the great outdoors. And remember, many shelters require that their adoptees live indoors.

If you're starting off a new cat as an indoors-only pet, or your cat has always lived indoors—good for you! Review the tips in chapters 7 and 9 to make sure you're doing everything you can to make your home feline-friendly and your cat's life exciting, satisfying, and pleasurable. You're sure to find a hint or two to help you enrich your cat's life and have more fun at the same time.

IT'S UP TO YOU!

Understanding, accepting, and savoring the entire range of your cat's personality, from snoozing purr machine to mighty hunter, require love and admiration and a deep sense of responsibility. As a cat owner, you hold the primary and final responsibility for your cat's health, safety, and psychological well-being as well as for the effects—good or ill—he has on his immediate environment and the community. Being a cat owner calls for enlightened respect for your cat's place in your life, your home, the neighborhood, society, and the web of life.

Love is essential, but it's not enough. Cat ownership is a privilege—an opportunity to forge a deep, profound bond with a fellow creature who shares so much with us, yet who's always just a few whiskers—just a few tantalizing paw lengths—beyond our full understanding. Appreciating the big picture and acknowledging your cat's effects on his environment are the first steps to wisdom for cat owners.

CHAPTER 9

Enriching the Feline Lifestyle

THE BEST OF ALL POSSIBLE WORLDS

Even if you've decided to treat your cat to a safe, enriched indoors-only lifestyle, he deserves to experience the best of all worlds, including access to fresh air, sunshine, and natural sights, sounds, and scents. Direct sunshine is a natural source of vitamin D, which is essential to your cat's health. Fresh breezes and natural pleasures will enhance his mood and psychological well-being. Happily, there are lots of ways your cat can enjoy the pleasures of the natural world without encountering unnecessary dangers.

A selection of window perches by opened and securely screened windows is a terrific start. If you can work in a daily stroll with leash and harness, great. But with some straightforward home additions and modifications, you can provide your cat with a much richer, but still protected, natural environment—one he can enjoy whenever he wishes. Best of all, you and your cat can enjoy these pleasures together, enhancing your mutual bond while getting healthy exercise and having lots of fun.

Quality Outdoor Time: Walking Your Cat on Leash and Harness

Cats don't take naturally to walking with a leash and harness. Many cats never really seem to get the hang of walking with a leash and harness, or just don't like it. But, if your cat is adaptable, adventurous, and trusting, it's worth a try.

Besides considering your cat's temperament, use common sense. Take a look at your own habits, temperament, and neighborhood. Some cat owners aren't fond of walking or live in areas where walking may not be safe or practical. In the right circumstances—which include a willing cat—a daily stroll is a great way for cats and people to keep up on neighborhood doings; enjoy local sights, sounds, and scents; and catch up on gossip around the block. Walking is a terrific stress reliever, too.

Harnesses and Leads

A cat's neck and spinal anatomy differs from a dog's. Never use just a collar for walking a cat—a collar alone

Your cat will actually be walking you.
(KATHY MILANI)

is neither safe nor effective for a leashed cat, offering too much chance of escape or injury. With just a collar, any pressure applied to the leash is applied directly to the cat's trachea, possibly causing pain or injury. A harness distributes any pressure from the leash over a much larger area of his body. Use either an H-shaped or figure-eight harness. An H-shaped harness is more secure and, for most cats, more comfortable. Measure your cat's girth (around the largest part of his rib cage) to get an accurate fit. In deciding upon a harness, look for the following:

- lightweight, but sturdy construction, with minimal possibility of discomfort for the cat (Nylon-cord or braid harnesses work well for cats, as does soft leather.)
- a step-in-style harness (This is easier for most cats to accept than an elastic or other construction that you must stretch or reach over his head.)
- metal fasteners and connectors, rather than plastic (All D-rings should be securely welded metal.)

- adjustable closures for a custom fit (Elastic can be too tight for many cats.)
- top-or side-fastening closures (It'll be much easier to affix the harness, and most cats won't appreciate having their tummies handled as you struggle with buckles or latches underneath them.)
- no exposed metal buckles or latches to catch or pull fur (All buckles and latches should be securely covered or padded where they touch the cat.)
- a leash either integrated into the construction of the harness or attached by a very secure device such as an integrated metal D-ring
- A leash made for cats, not dogs (A dog leash, and the clip with which it's attached to the harness, can be much too heavy for a cat and will put strain on the harness.)

More elaborate harness-lead combinations are available. One model, for example, is designed like a jacket. Made of nylon fabric and mesh, it looks like a mini backpack (without the pack). Though the additional fabric touching the cat's body might make this uncomfortable for some cats, and thus harder for them to learn to accept, it's safer and more secure than a plain harness.

Before buying any harness, test the strength of the construction by vigorously pulling and tugging (as your cat will) at the harness itself and the connectors and fasteners. If the connectors are plastic, test them especially thoroughly. Make sure adjustable parts won't slip or loosen inadvertently. Test how easy (or difficult) it is to fasten and release the connectors, latches, or buckles.

For walking your cat outdoors, use a relatively short lead—six feet or less. You need to be able to instantly pick up your cat to remove him from any dangerous situation. It's also vital that the connection point of the lead and harness is secure and won't slip apart accidentally under strain.

Getting Up to Speed

Harness and leash training is best introduced *very* gradually. Start indoors to get your cat used to the smell and feel of the harness. Let him see it at home, in pleasant circumstances. Keep the experience positive and fun.

Experienced cat trainers have had success using the clicker training method. A clicker is a small, hand-held device that makes a unique, sharp clicking sound. Over time, your cat learns to associate the sound of the click with a tasty treat. Start by simply clicking the clicker, then giving him a treat. Repeat until he clearly associates the sound with the treat. This might take a day, or several weeks. It depends on your cat.

Start associating the click-treat sequence with the presence of the harness and leash, then with your cat touching the harness and leash (but not actually wearing it), and, finally, with him wearing the harness. Once you get to this milestone, walk around indoors, in familiar territory, for several days before venturing out. Cat-behavior specialists suggest making your first indoor walks to your cat's food bowl—and making sure there's a favorite food or treat waiting for him! They also suggest limiting your walks to the indoors for at least three weeks, so that your cat will be completely comfortable with the experience.

When you finally brave the great outdoors for the first time, be especially alert to your cat's mood and feelings. If he's spent little or no time outdoors, he'll likely experience sensory overload at first. Take it slow, and let him set the pace. Do your first few walks in a fenced yard or other very safe location. Return indoors immediately if he seems extremely unhappy, fearful, or stressed. Offer praise and encouragement (and treats), keep a sunny, positive attitude, and try again another day.

Offer lavish praise along with the tasty treats, and never, ever try to force your cat to go faster than he wants. One bad experience can set you back to square one or—worse—convince your cat that the whole leash-harness business isn't for him.

If you're successful in using the click-treat training sequence with your cat, try using it to train him to perform other behaviors, like following your lead as you walk or even performing tricks.

If your cat decides to cooperate—and with luck and a lot of patience and persistence—you'll soon be strolling proudly through the neighborhood, astonishing the neighbors with your exceedingly intelligent, handsome, and well-behaved feline.

Who's Walking Whom?

Cat walking isn't at all like dog walking. Your cat will actually be walking *you*. Unless you're willing to invest a great deal of time and diligence in training him to do otherwise, walking your cat will consist mostly of following him as he moseys and meanders, checking out interesting odors, sounds, and sights along the way. He'll dive under promising bushes and may even try to climb a tree or two. He'll stalk birds and squirrels, or roll in the grass, or he may just decide to sit down and have a snooze halfway through your stroll.

Remember, also, that cat walking is unlike dog walking in another very important respect: cat walking has nothing to do with elimination. Cats are much pickier and more private about elimination than dogs. Expecting them to behave in a canine manner in this area is unfair, unreasonable—and likely doomed to failure. Don't imagine you can toss out your litter box once you train your cat to walk in harness and leash.

You can't. Trying to force your cat to eliminate while on leash may well backfire into difficult-to-solve, elimination-related misbehavior problems.

Keep It Safe

Wherever and whenever you walk with your cat, vigilantly monitor his activities and explorations. Keep an eye out for possible dangers: roaming or barking dogs, loud construction or traffic noises, groups of children, and anything else in the environment that may present danger or cause your cat fear or stress. Be ready to remove your cat from danger in an instant—by keeping close enough to scoop him up into your arms at the first sign of trouble. Some of the better-made-and-designed cat-harness-and-leash combinations include an extralarge D-ring you can grab on to safely to quickly pick up your cat. Whenever you're out with your cat, he needs secure, visible identification, so he should wear his collar along with his harness. No matter how vigilant you are and how secure his harness and leash, accidents can happen.

If you walk outdoors during warm weather, check your cat carefully for fleas and ticks afterwards. Do a thorough comb-out with a narrow-toothed comb right after each walk.

If you'd like to have a little more control over the course of your strolls, try tossing a small treat in the direction you want your cat to proceed. Or use your click-treat training strategy and reward him when he stays on the path or stays close by your side. Most cats respond well to praise—the more lavish the better—in conjunction with treats.

An outdoor enclosure, such as a fully screened porch, can be a cat's dream come true.
(RANDALL LOCKWOOD)

"We'll Have Our Tuna on the Veranda, Dearie": Outdoor Cat Enclosures

An outdoor enclosure can be a cat's dream come true. It's his place to run and sun, to climb and frolic, to sniff the breezes and snooze away balmy afternoons. It's his observation post for keeping track of the neighborhood fauna without disturbing their activities or having to defend his territory, honor, or hunting rights. It's a

ENRICHING THE FELINE LIFESTYLE

safe perch from which to safely spy on that annoying neighbor dog and to check out passersby without fear or concern about whether they're friend or foe.

The features of the enclosure you devise for your cat are limited only by your wallet and your imagination. You can also purchase a range of enclosures in kit form. Some of these can be installed in minutes, even if you barely know which end of a screwdriver to pick up.

Commercially Available Enclosures

If you live in rental property or don't want to make modifications to your home, or if there's no obvious way to construct a cat-safe outdoor domain, consider one of the commercial cat porches available. One may be just right for your home and your cat.

There are several designs of commercially made window enclosures, which extend outwards from a window and provide a small but safe airy retreat for one or two cats. (Depiction of specific product does not imply endorsement by The Humane Society of the United States) (HABICAT.COM)

There are several designs of window enclosures. Specialty vendors offer mini-porches and cat cabanas. These easy-to-install, boxlike structures extend outwards from a window much like a greenhouse window and provide a small, but safe, airy retreat for one or two cats. These usually mount in an existing window, in much the same way as a portable air conditioner. Ranging in price from under $100.00 to over $250.00, these are variously made of steel, wood, or heavy plastic, and are equipped with a combination of transparent Plexiglas panels and screens.

Check advertisements in cat magazines, or visit your favorite pet-supply store to see what's available. Cat-behavior specialists warn that these window enclosures might not be appropriate for very active cats, for highly territorial cats easily disturbed by the presence of other cats in the yard, or for cats who like to spray or urine-mark around windows and doors.

Another option is a large rolling cage. Somewhat like a cat-show cage, these large cat playpens can be up to six feet tall. Some are equipped with perches and climbing-trees and have plenty of room for a litter box. If you have a large outdoor deck or patio, this might be the ideal way for your cat to enjoy fresh air and sunshine. You can roll wheel-mounted cages into the sun or shade as appropriate. Never leave the cage outdoors unsupervised, though.

Many cats enjoy such relatively simple enclosures and require nothing more elaborate. For other cats, the experience merely whets their appetites for more fun in the sun. Look into kits for larger, more elaborate, or expandable cat enclosures. One kit, available for under $300.00, includes everything you need to build an expandable, three-sided, 6×6×6-foot, redwood and galvanized wire enclosure, complete with climbing shelves, access door, and screened roof. It's designed to attach to the side of your house. Start with one of these basic kits—and then get as creative as you want!

If You Build It, They Will Purr

If you already have a fully screened porch or deck, you're in luck. Just check it for security and safety, and furnish it with cat-pleasing accessories. If you have a deck or porch without screening, it's neither difficult nor expensive to enclose it with sturdy screening, chicken wire, or hardware cloth. A small cat door or cat flap can offer your cat easy, twenty-four-hour access to his safe "outdoor" domain, or you can get a locking flap for those times you don't want him out. A simple lean-to or shed structure affixed to the side of your house, with access through a window, can be an ideal kitty getaway.

Another, more expensive, possibility is a free-standing gazebo, built on a slab or deck away from the house, with access via an elevated screened walkway or cat tunnel from the gazebo to a window of your house, or to a lockable cat door or flap.

If you can, devise a way to place a litter box in a corner of the enclosure, easily accessible both for your cat's use and for your regular daily cleaning. Shield it from moisture and rain, and don't expect your cat to use it in stormy or frigid weather. He should have at least one clean, accessible, indoor litter box available at all times.

Even apartment and condo dwellers can offer their cat a sunporch. Perhaps you could completely screen an existing deck or patio. (Check with the building owner or homeowners' association first.) A portable cat-door module that fits in any standard sliding glass door can provide your cat access to his screened porch or deck without any need for major modifications or for leaving the door opened all the time.

Plain or Fancy

You don't need expensive cat furniture to enrich your cat's "outdoors" domain. With a towel or pad in the middle, an old tire also makes a great napping spot. Be sure to provide a cozy hideaway basket, some discarded cardboard packing cartons, a climbing-and-scratching post (ideally with platforms at multiple heights), some big pillows or an old comfy chair for lounging, a selection of safe, lush potted plants, a pot or two of wheat or oat shoots, a bowl of fresh, cool water, and a few favorite toys.

Many cats appreciate sisal mats for lounging and scratching, and lush green grass (planted in the ground or in large flats) for napping and rolling. Make sure any grass in the enclosure is safe—not treated with any chemicals, fertilizers, or pesticides. And make sure your cat has nibble-friendly grass, such as wheat or oats, readily available so that he won't eat the sharper-bladed lawn grass.

To provide filtered sunlight and cooling shade, build part of your enclosure, including the roof, from wooden lattice panels (backed with screen for insect control). Cat-safe climbing plants can beautify the lattice. Be creative—add ramps, beams, shelves, boxes, and other cat-climbing and cat-hiding amenities.

In designing enhancements for your cat's enclosure, keep in mind what he wants most:

- access to the heights, for watching and stalking
- places to hide; cozy, protected spots, to see without being seen
- comfort, warmth (Hint: Cats adore polyester fleece fabrics.)
- cat-directed adventure and play opportunities
- pleasing sensory experiences: sounds, scents, sights
- sunshine and shade, available as he desires
- natural scratching surfaces (logs, sisal mats or posts, tree trunks)
- entertainment: activities (human or wildlife) to watch

Incorporating Natural Features

For an even more stimulating, attractive, exciting, naturalistic play space for your cat, build your enclosure around an existing tree, being careful to prevent escape opportunities. Or include large tree branches or pieces of tree trunk for climbing and scratching.

Running, softly splashing, and falling water is attractive and soothing for cats and people alike. Add a small fountain or waterfall powered by an electric pump. Available in small tabletop models and larger floor models, electric fountains range from simple to expensively elaborate. Keep the water clean, pure, and safely drinkable by your curious cat. Never treat the water with chemicals, and change the water and clean the fountain regularly to prevent growth of potentially harmful bacteria and mold.

The Whole Yard?

In some cases, you might be able to offer your cat access to your entire yard, or as much of it as you're willing to enclose in secure wire mesh. Look into enclosure fencing with overhanging top sections that will keep even the most determined leaping cat from escaping and keep out many predators and other dangers. Even if you don't think there are wild animals or other dangers in your area, it's still wisest and safest to enclose the "roof" as well. If you decide not to enclose the roof, extra vigilance is necessary. Never allow your cat in even a fenced yard unsupervised. If your situation permits, you might even enclose a shed or outbuilding within your cat's safely screened domain so that he has one more place in which to play, explore, or snooze privately.

Safety Considerations for Cat Enclosures

Whether your enclosure is made of screen or wire, be sure the screening can't be torn or removed by your cat, or by passing dogs or cats or other animals. Wire or aluminum screen is much safer than plastic or nylon, which can easily be torn or shredded by curious claws. Attach screens firmly to their frames or supports, leaving no loose corners or edges that could be torn free. Don't underestimate the strength of your cat's claws; a nose-to-nose encounter with a gray squirrel (or a stray cat) can be awfully exciting! Some newer, more expensive types of screening materials incorporate stretchable, tear-proof, claw-proof screen.

Chicken wire is a good material for screening a cat enclosure, as it's sturdy and tear-proof, but it won't keep out insects and small mammals (or the occasional small bird). If you live in an area where heartworm is common in dogs, screen out mosquitoes. Cats can get heartworm, too, and it can be serious and even fatal.

Your cat's enclosure should be completely screened—including the roof. Check for, and eliminate, any possibility your cat could catch a toe or claw, or get hung up while climbing or scrambling. Cats are great leapers and agile climbers. If possible, raise the floor of the enclosure a few feet off the ground to keep dirt, dampness, and many kinds of insects away, as well as to keep passing cats and dogs below the level of your cat's face when he's pressing his nose against the screen. (Some feline diseases can be transmitted by the aerosolized saliva delivered in a hiss.)

Your cat needs an easily accessible escape route into the house from his enclosure—either an open window directly into the enclosure, or a tunnel or elevated walkway between the enclosure and your house. He also needs easy access to shade while in his enclosure, as well as hiding places to which he can instantly retreat if he feels threatened.

While your cat is enjoying his enclosure, watch for passing stray cats who could transmit disease through the screens, and for incursions of small prey animals and spiders, fleas, ticks, bees, wasps, and other insects. Be alert for chemical sprays—perhaps being used on a neighbor's lawn—wafting into the enclosure. Avoid unnecessary chemical use on your own property, and keep your cat indoors if a neighbor or lawn-care technician is applying chemicals, fertilizers, or insecticides.

Decide whether you feel comfortable and confident offering your cat twenty-four-hour access to his enclosure, or prefer to restrict access to those times when you're home to supervise. Your decision will depend on where you live, weather and climate, and your cat's individual temperament. Every cat enclosure should be completely secure and safe, with no possibility that the cat can inadvertently escape or that passing dogs or stray cats can break in. (Stray humans are another problem entirely.)

Watch for Intruders

Once you build your cat enclosure, be especially wary of unknown animals, wild or domestic, entering your yard. A determined or large animal (black bear, moose, deer, large dog) can break into any but the most robust enclosure. Use common sense in excluding such incursions and in discouraging unwanted animals (and people) from visiting your yard. Don't tempt the attention of coyotes and other dangerous and nuisance wildlife by leaving pet-food dishes outdoors. Keep trash and garbage in tightly sealed containers, in a closed shed or garage if possible.

Bird feeders can be a pleasant feature—for both you and your indoor cat—in your yard, but be alert for unwanted consequences. In some areas, feeders can attract a range of wild animals, from bears to raccoons, that you'd probably rather not entertain. If your feeders seem to be attracting unwanted animals, take them down for several weeks. Don't leave food out for the wildlife (such as raccoons, deer, geese, squirrels, or opossums), no matter how sympathetic you might feel towards them.

Unsupervised Outdoor Leads—Feline Death Traps!

Never, ever leave your cat outdoors unsupervised on a lead or overhead chain. A cat so chained is not only subject to the vagaries of weather and at risk for heatstroke or frostbite, but he's also helpless against attacks from dogs, coyotes, and evil-minded humans. Once mainly a creature of the open Western plains, the coyote now ranges widely across the North American continent, living in surprisingly high densities and in unsettlingly close proximity to humans and their domestic animals.

Other Dangers

Another danger, both to unsupervised outdoor cats and chained cats, is packs of roaming domestic dogs. Many suburban and rural pet dogs run free and unsupervised, joining up with other dogs. These packs sometimes stalk and kill unwary cats—cats who may be unafraid of dogs because they live with dogs themselves.

A range of other predators can also threaten an unsupervised outdoor or chained cat. Across the northern United States, the fisher *(Martes pennanti)*, a strong, aggressive, forest-dwelling relative of the mink, is increasing in numbers. Fishers (often erroneously called fisher cats) are opportunistic hunters who frequently kill cats, especially in rural areas. Though naturally nocturnal, fishers have been known to hunt by daylight. They're agile tree climbers and can easily scale trees, walls, and fences to get at a chained cat.

By initiating a fight over food, other small mammals, such as foxes, raccoons, opossums, and skunks, can also threaten a chained cat's life. Unable to escape, the cat is forced to fight, possibly leading to serious injury and infection from rabies or other diseases. In areas where they live, bobcats and cougars can pose a threat to chained cats, though it's unlikely that these wary wild felines will closely approach human habitations. Finally, hawks and large owls, especially great horned owls, have been known to take small cats and kittens, though very infrequently.

A chained cat might also tangle or hang himself in his lead or chain, especially if he's attacked or threatened and is desperately trying to escape. Don't subject your cat to these risks. Never leave him on an unsupervised outdoor lead—even for a moment.

CHAPTER 10

Cat Behavior:
A Primer of the Feline Mind

YOUR CAT'S MIND

"If we find cats mysterious," muses author and anthropologist Elizabeth Marshall Thomas, "it is because we have forgotten much of what our ancestors knew about the wilderness." In getting to know your cat's mind, you'll reclaim some of that long-forgotten knowledge. Gaining and sharing this knowledge—seeing the world through the knowing, glowing eyes of your cat—are part of the Feline Covenant, part of our shared heritage of domestication.

Your cat possesses a sophisticated, complex, versatile mind. His ratio of brain weight to body weight—the classic measure of a species' evolutionary development and potential for intelligence—is greater than in most mammals other than apes and humans. His large, highly convoluted cerebral cortex is characteristic of intelligent, problem-solving creatures. Together with his superb array of sensory subsystems, your cat's mental abilities render him a formidable presence in any environment.

The Hunting Urge

Your cat *needs* to hunt. His urge to stalk and pounce is natural, normal, and instinctual. But the knowledge that prey is food, and the skills to kill prey animals safely and efficiently, are learned in kittenhood. That's why cats with nonhunting mothers seldom learn to properly kill prey, and why your cat continues to stalk and pounce even after a big meal. Happily, your cat doesn't have to kill prey to satisfy his hunting urges—mock-hunting play works just fine! Chapter 7 has lots of tips on playing with your cat.

If your cat ventures outdoors, he *will* stalk and likely kill small rodents, insects, and birds. You can't teach him not to hunt or not to kill birds—another good reason to keep him indoors.

Are you mystified by the predawn "kitty crazies"? Does your ordinarily cool, dignified cat turn into a staircase-bounding, drapery-scaling, knickknack-scattering, sleep-destroying rascal, only to reappear later as his usual unruffled self, calmly demanding breakfast? That's his primeval dawn hunting urge in action. Take advantage of it by engaging him in vigorous interactive play before breakfast (and dinner).

How Your Cat Spends His Time

Most wild cats enjoy the luxury of living at or near the top of the local food chain, able to satisfy their nutritional needs with a relatively small expenditure of energy. Unlike rodents, birds, and other animals who must seek food and eat constantly or die, your cat's ancestors gained, through evolution, the luxury of time and leisure for developing other aspects of their personalities. This evolutionary heritage allows your cat the extravagance of sleeping away a good part of his life—eighteen hours a day or more.

After sleep, self-grooming is the most popular cat activity. Your cat spends a large percentage of his waking hours washing, grooming, and preening his hair coat and manicuring his claws. Then there's play, eating, eliminating—and sitting around watching the world go by.

The Art of the Nap

Feline and human sleep patterns are remarkably similar. Like us, cats have sleep phases. Your cat can be easily and instantly awakened during slow-wave sleep (SWS), in which his muscles relax and his breathing slows but he remains alert to a variety of threats and opportunities. After an initial period of SWS, your cat, if undisturbed, transitions gradually to a much-deeper sleep called active, or rapid-eye-movement (REM), sleep. He alternates between these two sleep phases, spending about a quarter of his sleep time in REM sleep.

When arranging himself for a nap, especially during cold weather, your cat often curls into a circle, nose to tail, chin resting on paws. In this position, his tail may lie across his nose, reducing oxygen intake to invite a quicker entry into the deeper, health-giving REM sleep. REM sleep is the most vital phase of sleep, essential to your cat's health and well-being. During REM sleep, your cat's brain generates the same kind of electrical impulses as you do during similarly deep sleep. While your cat's body is relaxed, his mind is extremely active. During REM sleep, his "third eyelids" (also called nictitating membranes) slide completely over his eyes, beneath his eyelids. During lighter sleep, these remain retracted, and your cat remains ready to return instantly to full alertness.

Awakening from a deep REM sleep often brings a burst of movement. Your cat may flick his tail, strike out with extended claws, shake his head vigorously, or even leap up suddenly. If nothing more interesting beckons, he may stretch, lay back down, rearrange himself into a sleep-friendly position, and enter a light, SWS sleep.

What's Mine Is Mine!

Because of his evolutionary heritage as a self-reliant hunter, your cat is deeply concerned with locating, protecting, and defending the resources he needs to survive. To understand your cat's behavior—especially those behaviors some cat owners see as naughty, perverse, spiteful, or just plain incomprehensible—it helps to look at the situation from your cat's point of view—and from the perspective of resource availability and resource utilization.

Your cat prizes a sufficient food supply, fresh water, warmth, privacy, space, opportunities to exercise his body and mind, and "escapability"—the ability to readily and independently remove himself from situations that displease or frighten him.

Change as a Threat

Any alteration in your cat's safe, familiar, comfortable environment spells, in his mind, potential loss of resources or the possible introduction of competitors for his resources. Cat owners are often mystified when changes that seem pleasant to them—new carpeting or furniture, a new romantic interest, a lovely new home—throw the family cats into a flurry of fighting, spraying, and sulking.

If your normal routine is disrupted by a burst of overtime at work, a hospitalization, or a vacation, your cat's natural reaction—*Is my resource base in danger?*—can lead quickly to increased stress and "misbehavior." Unfortunately, it's those very times when your life is busiest or most disrupted that you're most likely to overlook your cat's desperate need for routine, stability, and reassurance.

R-E-S-P-E-C-T!

Space is a vital, but often overlooked, feline resource. Every cat has a personal space bubble into which only very good friends (feline, human, or other) are welcomed. Some cats are touchier about this intimate, personal space than others.

Your cat needs private spaces to escape and get away from it all. Always respect his privacy and his preference in "lairs." Read chapters 6 and 7 for tips on making the space in your home as safe and cat-friendly as possible.

Reduce Stress and Anxiety

Stress is the greatest enemy of feline health and happiness. Much feline stress is caused by **change** and the resulting **uncertainty.** Keep your cat's needs in mind when planning for any changes in your life, whether a move to a new home, a marriage or divorce, a new baby, new carpeting, or a new kitten. When unexpected changes occur, as they inevitably will, don't forget your cat's needs amidst the pressures of the moment. Behavior problems that could easily be prevented with some thoughtful planning and attention to your cat's needs can be difficult to solve once bad habits are ingrained.

No matter how much you love cats, don't make the mistake of adopting more cats than your space, time, and financial resources allow. Just as each tract of land has a limited biological carrying capacity, your household has a feline-carrying capacity beyond which it's unwise and unhealthy—for humans and cats alike—to go. Analyze your family and household to determine how many cats you should take in. As much as you'd love to adopt every cat who needs a home, think first: Is it fair to your family? To your other cats? To your other pets? Can your financial resources handle it? Do you have enough time to devote daily attention to each cat you adopt? Is there enough space for all the cats to feel comfortable and unstressed? Be particularly wary in subjecting elderly, chronically ill, or other special-needs cats to the stresses of adjusting to a new cat.

The Importance of Routine, Ritual, Repetition

To help lessen daily stress, as well as the effects of change, establish daily rituals you can share with your cat. When you feed or groom him, repeat patterns of words in a soothing tone of voice. Keep his interactive toys in a special drawer and open it with ceremony and anticipation before each play session. Hold your interactive-play sessions in the same part of the house each time. Repeat fond nicknames during playtime and snuggle time.

Does this all sound a bit too silly? It's not. These little daily rituals bind you to your cat. And in times of stress or change, these little rituals will give him enormous reassurance, as well as confidence in your continued presence, trust, and love. Your cat likely doesn't understand your actual words, but he's acutely sensitive to your attitude, mood, and tone of voice. The more closely you and your cat are bonded, and the more daily rituals you establish and share, the more he'll key on your mood and emotions.

Is Your Cat Just Bored?

Intelligent and creative, your cat adores routine but also craves regular mental and physical stimulation. If there's too little excitement and adventure in his life, he may decide to create some action of his own. If he wails at 2 A.M., knocks the books off your shelves, unrolls the paper towels in the kitchen, shreds a screen door trying to escape, torments the dog, or picks fights with his fellow cats—he may be bored.

Rule out pain or illness first with a trip to the veterinarian. Then, review chapters 7 and 9 for tips on enriching your cat's life and environment with cat-friendly furniture and climbing surfaces, interactive and solo toys, and plenty of daily attention from family members.

READING YOUR CAT'S BODY LANGUAGE

Although your cat commands an impressive vocal repertoire, he communicates most eloquently through his versatile body language. Every part of his body—tail, eyes, ears, whiskers, paws and claws, fur and coat—and even his overall posture speak volumes about his mood, intent, and current preoccupation.

Tail talk

Confidence and happiness raise your cat's tail, while fear, doubt, and uncertainty lower it. A waving, rapidly lashing, or thumping tail spells trouble, not friendliness. A twitching tail tip often means concentration or indecision—to pounce, or not to pounce? A tail carried high and proud is a friendly greeting.

Eyes

Half-closed eyes? Your cat is relaxed, confident, or perhaps sleepy. Big, circular pupils appear when the light is dim—and when your cat is feeling frightened or aggressive. Bright, lively, twinkling eyes are the sign of a happy, playful soul.

Ears

Your cat's external ear flaps, or *pinnae,* tilt and swivel with the help of approximately two-dozen muscles. The mobile pinnae are also elastic and expressive mood communicators. Your cat's ears stand erect and rotate forward in alertness, flatten in defense, rotate sideways in aggression, or twitch in frustration. Watching the ever-shifting positions of your cat's ears gives you lots of clues to his emotions and intent.

Whiskers

Like ears, whiskers are full of clues to your cat's mood. When your cat's relaxed, his whiskers extend straight outward from his cheeks. They retract gently when he investigates an intriguing odor, and fan forward, twitching and circling, when he's doing more serious exploration. When he's angry or scared, his whiskers flatten back against his cheeks.

Claws

Extended claws are ready for action—either offense or defense. Beware: a sudden noise, light, or some other unexpected stimulus can cause those potentially formidable weapons to instantly appear, in play or in anger, ready for anything. Never let your kitten claw or bite your bare hand or another part of your body in play. When he grows up, it'll be a hard and painful habit to break.

Fur and coat

When he's scared, angry, or excited, the guard hairs all over your cat's coat—especially along his spine—puff out, making him look larger and more fearsome. If he's really excited, his tail puffs out like a fat brush.

Posture

When he wants to look large, threatening, and formidable, your cat stands sideways, on tiptoe, back arched, tail curved and possibly twitching. But when he's approaching an unknown or dominant cat, he tries to minimize his presence by slinking or crouching low, and lowering his ears, eyes, and tail. When he's feeling happy and confident, he prances tall with his ears up, tail raised, and head held high.

Licking

Although your cat spends lots of his waking time licking and grooming himself anyway, he also uses licking as a displacement behavior. When he's confused, he'll stop and lick a paw or his tail until the confusing situation is resolved, he makes a decision, or he feels more confident.

Rubbing and head bunting

Your cat has scent glands near the base of his tail, on his forehead and cheeks, and around his lips. When he twines around your ankles, rubs his face against your leg, or bunts your face or other body part with his head and face, he's marking you with his scent—claiming you as his territory or property. You can't detect the scent mark, but other cats can. It means you've been accepted into your cat's social circle. Accept this for the gift and honor it is.

Rolling on his back

When your cat rolls over on his back, he may be soliciting a tummy rub, or just displaying trust and friendship. If you choose to initiate a tummy-petting session, be alert for signs of a change in mood. Lying on his back, your cat is vulnerable. Watch his ears, eyes, and whiskers for clues that he's had enough—and stop. If he suddenly claws or bites, *don't* pull your hand away—his instinct is to grab harder. Instead, stop moving and try to distract him long enough to defuse the situation and allow you to remove your hand safely. Let him calm down for a while before resuming contact—and let him make the next move.

Kneading

Your cat jumps up on your lap, settles in, and cranks up the purr. Then, eyes half-closed, he starts slowly and rhythmically kneading your lap or legs, extending and retracting his claws, over and over. He may even drool. He's reliving warm, safe memories of kittenhood, remembering when his "milk tread"—the kneading—stimulated the flow of milk from his mother's nipple. Appreciate this honor from your cat—but keep his claws trimmed, and be prepared with a lap robe or heavy sweatshirt!

FELINE VOCALIZATION

Some cats are chatty by nature; others seldom make a sound. Some of this is genetic. The oriental breeds, such as the Siamese, and cats with similar long, lean body types, are often the most enthusiastic talkers. But there's a great deal of individual variation too. Get to know your cat's usual vocal patterns, and never ignore changes. If your usually silent cat suddenly starts talking up a storm, he may be trying to tell you something:

- He may be ill or in pain.
- He may be lonesome or bored, and seeking extra attention.
- He may be trying to warn you of danger. Cats have saved their families by waking them up, meowing or yowling uncharacteristically in the middle of the night to warn of a fire or other danger.
- He may be grieving for a lost companion, human or feline. Many cats meow and wail constantly after losing a friend.
- He may be upset or confused about a change in his life: a move to a new house, a new member of the family, unfamiliar odors from new carpeting or furniture. Be patient and supportive; give him time to adjust to the changes in his world. Maintain a positive, cheerful attitude. He'll pick up on your mood.

Among their own kind, adult cats communicate chiefly through scent and body language. Cat-to-cat communication is a rich symphony of subtle signals we can only begin to imagine. Our clever domestic cats are bilingual, though.

In human company, cats speak a language that, among cat-kind, is almost exclusively reserved for communication between a mother cat and her kittens—a wide range of meows, chirps, trills, and kittenlike squeaks. In adult cats, such vocalizing is mainly used for communication with humans. Neotenization accounts for this, at least in part. And perhaps, observing that humans are primarily vocal communicators, our cats adjust their natural communication styles to accommodate our preferences.

The Cat's Vocabulary

In 1944, researcher Mildred Moelk discovered that domestic cats are able to make seventeen different sounds of three distinct types (purring and murmurs; vowels, or variations of "meow"; and "strained-intensity" sounds such as hisses and screams).

Growling and Yowling

Some of the loudest, most dramatic feline sounds are the growls, wails, howls, snarls, caterwauls, and screams of angry or seriously competitive cats. These sounds can be terrifying, but they're really just extremely loud, dramatic, and often effective warnings to potential combatants or competitors: "Back off, now! I'm much tougher than you—and prepared to prove it!"

The Hiss

The hiss is a sound of annoyance, perhaps mixed with fear and more than a little bluster, depending on the situation. It can indicate pain or stress, too. It means, "Back off!" If your cat hisses while you're petting, grooming, or examining him, stop immediately. Try to determine the cause. Let him calm down. If he hisses whenever you touch a certain spot, he may be injured or ill.

Chattering

One of the oddest sounds your cat makes is a rapid, click-click chattering as he watches birds. His jaw vibrates rapidly, and he may softly squeak in excitement. Cat experts don't agree on the meaning of this. Some feel it's an overflow of excitement or frustration at being unable to pounce on and kill the prey. Feline chattering is almost always in response to birds. Rodent watching is generally a more silent activity.

The Versatile Meow

Cats employ a surprisingly wide range of variations on the standard "meow." Most of these are requests—from kittenish, coy, and shy to forcefully demanding—for your attention. The better your cat trains you to understand and respond to his meows, the more he'll use them, and the richer his vocabulary will become.

The Silent Meow

Nothing can induce the urge to pamper a cat faster than the sweet, open-mouthed, silent meow. But is it really silent? Not to other cats. Cats detect sounds at much higher frequencies than we can—up to 50-to-65 kilohertz, as opposed to our limit of approximately 18-to-20 kilohertz. The so-called silent meow is just an ordinary meow pitched above your hearing range. If your cat often uses his silent meow in your presence, it may be because he's discovered how effective it is in getting what he wants.

The Greeting Trill

Among both wild and domestic cats, when a mother cat returns to the nest after hunting, or wants her kittens to gather round or follow her, she calls out with a soft trill or chirp. The kittens respond with a chorus of excited chirrups and squeaks. This loving, familiar ritual is usually followed by good things: food, warmth, safety. Because our neotenized cats see their owners as their mothers in so many ways, it's only natural that they transfer these greeting and homecoming rituals to us.

"You Talk Too Much!"

Some cat owners become annoyed with their constantly chatty cats or are frustrated because they can't seem to figure out what they want. If your cat is vocal or chatty enough to be a problem or annoyance for you, first schedule a visit to the veterinarian to rule out illness. Give the cat time to adjust to changes in his life. You should also eliminate stress in his environment that may be upsetting him. Be fair, too. Are you being unreasonable to expect a naturally gregarious, friendly animal to remain as silent as a potted plant? Listen to your cat. He might be trying to tell you something very important (like "I love you!" or "The basement's on fire").

If you've decided to help him cut down on the chatter, start ignoring his vocalizations. Be consistent. This may be very difficult, especially at first. Even by responding negatively—if you yell, for example—you're offering him attention and thus inadvertently rewarding the unwanted behavior. When he's quiet, reward him with treats, attention, cuddling, and play.

Purring

The purr is everybody's favorite cat sound—the quintessential music of the cat. Why do cats purr? Although it's a cliché that a purring cat is a contented cat, the purr indicates an overflow of *any* emotion. A cat who's profoundly *anything*—content, happy, furious, in pain—purrs. Badly injured and dying cats often purr. A cat about to give birth accompanies her labor with continuous, powerful, rhythmic purrs. When her kittens are about two days old, they spontaneously begin to purr themselves, helping orient themselves in the group and as a signal to the mother cat that milk is flowing and all is well. As the kittens grow, the first to a nipple often calls his siblings with the loud, intense "dinner-gong" purr.

Among adult cats, purring is sometimes used as a signal of appeasement by a subordinate cat towards a dominant one. The purr likely reduces the chances of an attack or fight, distracting the aggressor or awakening in his mind peaceful memories of kittenhood. A female cat purrs almost continuously during the stress-filled rituals of courtship and mating.

How does your cat purr? Well, no one is exactly sure! There are several competing theories. However it works, though, it's good for you! Research has demonstrated that stroking a purring cat can lower your blood pressure and pulse rate, as well as increase your subjective sense of peace and well-being. Just about any cat owner will attest to the calming, even hypnotic effect of a kneading, purring cat.

CAT TRAINING 101

Many cats enjoy learning tricks—they see it as an intellectual challenge. Training your cat will help you understand him better and communicate with him more readily, and will deepen your mutual bond. It's fun, too!

Your cat isn't a dog. He's not motivated by a desire to "please his master." He's unlikely to learn something just because *you* want him to. What's in it for him? He'll respond best to *patience, consistency,* and *rewards.*

Select a cue noise—a clicker, buzzer, or whistle—that you'll use only for training your cat. At first, make the cue noise every time you feed him, so that he'll learn to associate the noise with food—rather like his running to you when he hears the can opener or a rattling treat can. Do this for several days—until you're sure he associates the noise with food.

Once you start your cat's training program, always follow the cue noise *immediately* with a tasty treat your cat craves, such as tiny bits of cooked chicken or steak. Associate the cue noise with a spoken command and then with the desired behavior. Speak the command along with the cue noise, then make the cue noise again at the *exact* time your cat performs the desired behavior. For example, if you want him to come when called, stand across the room, make the cue noise, and call him: "Tiger, come over." Use consistent wording, sequence, and tone of voice. As he comes over, make the cue noise again and give him his treat. If you're training him to jump, make the cue noise as he jumps. Give him his treat immediately.

When your cat performs a new behavior for the first time on cue, praise and pet him especially lavishly. And don't forget the treat!

Go slow, and be patient. Work on only one behavior until your cat masters it. Give him plenty of time and opportunity to savor his success with lots of positive reinforcement. Avoid distractions during training sessions, and stop if your cat gets bored. Training should be fun, rewarding, and successful—for both of you.

Training Tips

Always remember that your cat is an individual. He may not be interested in training at all—or he may be an eager pupil. If your cat doesn't seem interested, try again later. He may change his mind.

Always be consistent.

Always precede each spoken command with your cat's name. And *always* follow the cue noise immediately with a treat.

Always keep training sessions short and fun. Ten or fifteen minutes every day are plenty. Especially at first, do your training sessions just before mealtimes, when your cat is hungry. This will focus his attention.

Never "starve" your cat, hoping he'll learn faster or be more eager to perform. This is cruel and ineffective (it'll likely just make him mad and uncooperative) and can cause health or behavior problems. A happy, trusting, satisfied cat is the best training partner.

Never "overcue." One or two clicks is enough. If you repeat the cue noise too often, it'll lose its close association with the treat, and thereby lose its effectiveness.

Never coerce your cat—it'll likely sour him on the whole enterprise. *Never* frustrate, frighten, force, or manhandle him.

Never push your cat to perform in front of strangers if he's not ready or would just rather not.

BEHAVIOR MODIFICATION: SENDING THE RIGHT MESSAGES

Your cat craves attention, affection, and approval—but on his own terms. He looks to you for cues on how to behave. Behaviors you respond to with praise or attention—even negative attention—will be reinforced. Ignoring a particular behavior, or diverting your cat to a more attractive activity, may get him to lose interest in the activity you want to stop. Here are some behavior-modification strategies you can try:

1. Leave the room without saying anything. Often, by removing the audience, you're also removing the motivation for the behavior.
2. If a cat on your lap does something you don't want him to, say, kneading your leg painfully with his claws, get up passively, letting him drop gently to the floor. Leave the room for a few minutes. This way, you're not telling your cat that you don't appreciate this affectionate gesture but are simply interrupting a pattern you don't want to reinforce.
3. Immediately divert your cat to a more attractive option. If he's scratching the back of the sofa, for example, toss a small toy across his field of vision. He'll likely give chase and forget about the sofa. But don't make the diversion consist of attention from you, as this may reinforce the bad behavior. The diversion should be something neutral (not associated with you) but attractive to your cat. A small, hand-held laser pointer can be a great diversionary tool—most cats adore chasing that little red dot (never point it directly at his eyes). Keep one handy in your pocket.
4. Cats are sensitive to tone of voice and variations in inflection, so verbal cueing can work if you use it consistently. Yelling in anger or frustration will only confuse your cat or make him fear and avoid you. Devise a particular word or sound and use it only when he misbehaves. Select a special cue phrase and method of delivery, such as a sharply vocalized "Eh,

eh, eh!" When you see your cat misbehaving, speak the cue phrase immediately, or use a diversion not clearly associated with you to interrupt the behavior pattern. Whatever you choose to do, though, be consistent!

The easiest way to correct misbehavior is to prevent it in the first place. Proper socialization of kittens; thoughtful, thorough cat-proofing; and the presence of plenty of safe, cat-attracting climbing-and-scratching surfaces, cozy hideaways, and play opportunities will prevent most feline misbehavior.

Punishment—Useless and Counterproductive

Punishment just doesn't work with cats. Physical punishment is especially ineffective and may be dangerous. Even in the unlikely event that you catch your cat within seconds of performing some undesirable (from your point of view) activity, punishment may do more harm than good. Especially if the activity is normal and natural—like scratching—your cat will have no idea why you're so upset. He may regard you as untrustworthy—someone to avoid.

Even if your cat understands that you don't approve of a particular behavior, punishment won't make him stop it. If he finds the activity pleasurable or necessary, he'll continue to do it—while you're not around. Your cat needs to scratch, and if you haven't provided an acceptable, handy, cat-friendly object, he's going to choose his own. It's unfair to punish him for your failure to plan for his needs.

By punishing your cat, you may be inadvertently rewarding him for misbehavior by paying attention to it. He'll continue, just to get the attention. The misbehavior may be an attempt to communicate. Rather than reacting with anger, annoyance, or punishment, listen to what he's trying to say.

Three Weeks to a Perfect Cat?

The key to breaking your cat's bad habit is to build in his mind a firm relationship between the behavior you want him to stop and something unpleasant—while redirecting his attention to, and rewarding, a behavior pattern you'd rather he follow. A general rule for behavior modification is that it takes about three weeks to break an old habit or form a new one. The first few days will be the hardest.

Safe Aversive Conditioning

Associate a harmless, but unpleasant, result with the bad habit or the location to be avoided. If you're training your cat to stay off kitchen counters while you're cooking, or the dinner table when guests are present, make it clear he's to stay off the counters or the table *all* the time. Make the banned surface itself unattractive. If you merely yell when you see your cat on the counter, he'll associate the unpleasantness with *you,* not the *behavior* or the *location.* As soon as you're not around, he'll be right back up there.

Lay sheets of aluminum foil, double-sided sticky tape, or some other paw-unfriendly material on a spot where you don't want your cat to be. Or devise harmless noisemakers. Place several coins in each of a dozen-or-so empty soda cans and tape them closed securely. When you leave the house, build an unsteady stack of these cans right near the edge of the counter or table. When your cat jumps up, he'll start a harmless but noisy and temporarily scary deluge of cans. After several such occurrences, he'll likely decide the counter or table isn't worth the annoyance.

Remember—no backsliding. Provide your cat with an approved alternative for his jumping, climbing, and exploring urges, such as a tall cat tree with plenty of hideaways and claw-friendly scratching surfaces. Hide some tasty cat treats at the top of the cat tree. Don't unreasonably tempt him by leaving attractive and aromatic foods unattended on the kitchen counter or dining-room table.

Reward and praise your cat when he behaves in ways you approve. While he's not a dog and therefore does not live to please, your cat cherishes his bond with you and naturally wants to keep you happy. Take advantage of his trust in you, and never abuse it. When you get through your kitchen chores without a single pounce on the counter, reward him with lavish praise, a tasty treat, and a rousing interactive-play session. Play can be a great reward strategy—many cats crave play sessions and anticipate them eagerly.

SOLVING COMMON BEHAVIOR PROBLEMS

Is He "Thinking Outside the Box"?

Inappropriate elimination—litter-box avoidance, spraying, urine marking, defecating outside the litter box—probably dooms more cats to euthanasia in overburdened shelters than any other single factor. Elimination-related problems can be enormously frustrating for cat owners and are a source of great stress in many households. But they are solvable. Take your cat to the veterinarian to clear up any medical problem; keep the litter box cleaner; move it to a more cat-appropriate location; change the brand, texture, or odor of the litter; or add another litter box. It's vital to diagnose and solve the problem rapidly before it becomes a deeply ingrained, hard-to-break habit.

Inappropriate Urination

There are three kinds of urine-related cat-behavior problems: *spraying, urine marking,* and *inappropriate urination.* Spraying and urine marking are both territorial gestures, nearly universal in unsterilized male cats. Spraying is directed from the cat rearwards, at about cat height, onto a vertical surface like a wall or corner. (A few female cats spray, too.) Urine marking has a similar territorial function, although it involves a few drops of strong-smelling, concentrated urine on the floor or some other horizontal surface. In spraying and urine marking, very little actual urine is deposited. But the urine of an unsterilized male cat is so pungent that a few scant drops are more than enough.

Neutering and spaying cure most cases of spraying and urine marking, especially in males. Some sterilized cats might spray occasionally, when under stress or at the sight of a strange cat. If your cat always sprays in particular locations (such as near a door or window), block his access to those areas, or cover windows so that he can't see out to whatever is upsetting him. If it's a neighbor cat that frequents your yard, either physically exclude the cat with fencing, or speak to your neighbor about keeping his cat indoors, or at least out of your yard.

To discourage inappropriate elimination, try redefining any areas your cat habitually soils. After thoroughly cleaning and deodorizing the spot (see instructions in chapter 7), place your cat's food and water dishes near it. Or place at the spot something with a strong odor cats generally dislike—fresh citrus rinds, a bar of perfumed soap, or a cat-safe air-freshener canister.

Inappropriate Urination and Litter-Box Avoidance

Inappropriate urination is hard to diagnose and to clean up after. (See chapter 7 for cleanup tips.) It can occur in a cat of any age or gender. It's frequently caused by illness. But a dirty litter box, dislike of litter type, stress in the household, or having had a bad experience while in the litter box can also cause inappropriate urination and outside-the-box defecation. It's vital to track down and eliminate the cause of these problems before they get out of hand and before your ill cat gets sicker or dies. A male cat who's urinating in inappropriate locations may have a painful bladder infection that can easily turn into a complete blockage—a condition that can rapidly kill him.

Rule out illness first. Then closely observe your cat's habits and behavior. Have you switched brands of litter recently? Always make litter transitions slowly and gradually! Perhaps the box has been consistently too dirty or smelly for his taste. If your cat uses the bathtub or sink in preference to his litter box, he might prefer a smooth surface. Try placing less litter in the box, leaving it partially empty. Look for a behavioral cause: Is your cat under stress? Are there new pets or family members? Has there been a change in his routine or environment?

If you have several cats, a bully cat may be keeping other cats from using the box or may be ambushing them while they're using it. (Or perhaps the bully is mistreating only one particular cat in this way.) Provide as many litter boxes as cats, plus one extra—in two different locations, if possible. A loud noise, dog, child, or other stressor may have scared your cat while he was using his box, causing him to avoid it. Try simple solutions first. Chances are, you'll be well on your way to solving the problem.

Fighting and Aggression

There are several distinct types of feline aggression—each with different causes and each calling for different strategies. Sterilizing your cat removes or reduces many of his motivations for aggression and fighting.

Pain-based aggression

Any aggressive behavior that appears suddenly calls for a visit to the veterinarian, who will look for possible medical causes. An injured cat, or one who's in pain due to illness, can lash out at another cat or a person. When handling or moving an injured or ill cat, always be alert to the possibility of unexpected aggressive behavior.

Status-oriented aggression

Groups of cats are often dominated by a "top cat." Although the top cat is usually a benevolent despot, a few become bullies and harass subordinate cats, even keeping them from eating or using the litter box. You can counter some of this behavior by providing multiple litter boxes in different parts of the house and feeding the cats separately. In serious cases of bullying, consult your veterinarian or animal-behavior specialist.

Territorial aggression

When your cat feels that his resource base is threatened by a new cat or kitten in the household, a strange cat he observed outdoors, a new human member of the family, or some other change, he may lash out at the perceived competitor or even at an innocent bystander (human or cat). Introduce new pets gradually and thoughtfully, and never ignore your old-timer in favor of a newcomer. Reassure him that there's plenty of everything—food, toys, litter boxes, attention, laps, sunshine—to go around.

Fear-based aggression

Shield your cat as much as possible from noises, odors, and stresses associated with changes in his life, such as a house move, guests, major renovations, or a new spouse or baby. If he's being bullied, your cat may react aggressively as a defense against the bully, especially if he feels he has nowhere to hide or escape.

Play aggression

Cats, especially young ones, who aren't treated to regular, interactive mock-hunting play often express their predatory urges in playful, stealthy—but possibly frightening—attacks on their owners. This is *not* misbehavior. Predatory play is a natural, normal instinct. Redirect your cat's predatory energy to appropriate targets, such as interactive "fishing-pole" toys and small, preylike solo toys.

Redirected aggression

This can be the most puzzling and difficult-to-diagnose type of aggression. For example, your indoor cat may become angered by seeing, out of a window, a strange cat walking across the yard. Unable to attack or chase off his real "enemy," he attacks whoever is handy—his owner or even a cat friend. If it turns into a serious fight, the two cats may become badly estranged. You could come home to find your previously best-buddy cats at each other's throats—and have no idea why! You may have to completely separate them for a period and then gradually reintroduce them—just as if one were a newcomer in the house. Highly aroused cats can remain so for as long as twenty-four hours. Be careful not to become a target of redirected aggression yourself.

Cat Fight!

Some fights that look serious at first glance are only play. Littermates, especially young ones, often engage in vigorous wrestling matches. Learn to distinguish play fighting from real cat fights. Are the combatants' claws fully extended? Does their body language indicate serious aggression and/or fear? Are tufts of fur flying? Are the combatants screaming and yowling, or emitting guttural growls? If so, it's likely a real fight, and the cats may be in imminent danger of seriously injuring each other.

Never try to break up a cat fight by picking up either of the combatants. You could be badly injured. Make a loud, sharp yell or hand clap, or blow a whistle. This may distract them long enough for one to run away. If you can, toss a blanket or jacket over one of the cats. If they're too tightly entwined for that, toss a soft pillow or a cup of water at them. Then separate the combatants for a period of at least several hours. Afterwards, don't let them interact without supervision until you're certain the battle won't be immediately rejoined.

Give the cats plenty of time to calm down.

Groups of cats are often dominated by a "top cat." Territorial conflicts may be solved by the group (in this case, one drinks while others watch) or may require human intervention.
(FRANTZ DANTZLER)

Never punish a cat for aggressive behavior. Punishment will only confuse and annoy him, cause him to lose his trust in you, and make him fearful.

Once two cats engage in serious combat, they're likely to remain estranged unless you take steps to diagnose and defuse the situation and remove the source of the contention. Don't let the fights continue. Cats are unlikely to just work it out and must usually be separated for their own safety, at least for a while. In extreme cases, the cats can no longer live in the same household unless they can be permanently and completely separated—a difficult practical challenge.

If you have two perennially contentious cats, ask your veterinarian for advice on medications for one or both cats—to be used in conjunction with a professionally designed behavior-modification program. A number of nontranquilizing drugs can safely and effectively quell aggressive behavior and smooth out prickly intercat relationships. Once peace is restored, the cats can be weaned off the drugs. However, some animals never learn to like each other—they tolerate each other at best.

Wool and Fabric Chewing

Predatory play accounts for much wool and fabric chewing—many wool and natural-fiber items smell and feel like prey animals. Or the wool chewer may be bored. Offer plenty of opportunities for vigorous, mock-hunting interactive and solo play with safe, appropriate cat toys. We really don't know whether wool chewing in any individual cat is due to early weaning or genetic disposition. Unless your cat is actually consuming large quantities of textile materials (which can cause dangerous blockages and digestive upsets), your best strategy when your cat is eating, chewing on, or sucking on something you'd rather he didn't is to deny him access to it.

Inappropriate and/or Destructive Scratching—to Declaw or Not?

In chapter 7, we looked at ways to provide your cat with safe, attractive alternatives to inappropriate and destructive scratching, and some cat-friendly strategies for selecting and protecting furniture. In chapter 15, you'll learn how to keep your cat's claws neatly trimmed. With patience, perseverance, and a good scratching post, the problem of destructive scratching nearly always ceases to be a problem. But can declawing be a shortcut or quick fix? No!

Declawing: Is It Really Necessary?

Declawing, or *onychectomy,* is almost never medically or behaviorally necessary, and should never be considered routine or done preemptively. It's the worst sort of cosmetic surgery—done entirely for the convenience and benefit of the cat's owners, and almost always to the detriment of the cat. Although it's still widely believed that declawing is a simple removal of the claws—which most people equate with fingernails—the surgery actually involves full amputation of an entire section of each of the cat's toes. It's the equivalent of having your fingers cut off at the top joint.

To avoid additional time under anesthesia, declawing is often combined with sterilization surgery. Many cats recover from declawing with no or few complications; others experience severe pain, bleeding, claw regrowth, loss of feeling in the toes, and infections that may require further surgery. While scientific studies don't support an increase in defensive and fear-based biting, litter-box avoidance, or other behavior problems in declawed cats, animal shelters report that a large number of declawed cats are surrendered by their owners because of biting and litter-box problems. It's not clear in these cases whether the cat was declawed because he bit and scratched, or that the change in litter-box filler after surgery led to litter-box avoidance. (Shredded newspaper is often recommended as box filler right after declawing to protect tender toes and reduce the chance of irritation from clay or clumping litter.)

Regardless of these controversies, declawing is not a medical procedure that benefits the cat as sterilization does. In fact, The Humane Society of the United States opposes declawing of cats when done solely for the convenience of the owner and without benefit to the animal. While it may be argued that declawing allows a cat to remain in a loving home, it should be considered only as a last resort—when all other behavior-modification and training alternatives have been exhausted.

When It's Time to Get More Help

If your cat develops behavior problems, remember: you're not alone! There's a lot of help and advice available. While your neighbor, work colleague, or chat-room buddy may offer plenty of advice, it's in your cat's best interest that you seek professional help.

Start with your veterinarian. He can either rule out, or treat, illness and medical causes of misbehavior and offer expert professional advice on your cat's needs. He can also discuss with you options for medications that can help you and your cat through the rough patches in your relationship. A number of new nontranquilizing drugs can assist greatly in solving difficult feline-behavior problems.

Before trying medication, always ask your veterinarian to advise you about a behavior-modification program or refer you to a professional cat-behavior specialist. These trained professionals deal with the thorniest feline-behavior problems—and help solve them—every day. These caring experts help keep cats and their owners together. Many make house calls to see the cat and his family in their everyday environment. Though they charge a fee for their services, it's worth it to help get your relationship back on track. Expert observation and advice can mean the difference between a deeply frustrated owner giving up on his cat because of a supposedly intractable behavior problem and a well-adjusted, satisfied cat living in harmony with his family.

Calling for Help

Many colleges of veterinary medicine and animal shelters offer behavior hot lines. When you call, you'll speak to a trained animal-behavior specialist who will help you think through your options and present ideas and tips you may not have considered for solving behavior and other cat-related problems. These are usually free services. They can't solve your problems for you, but they'll offer a caring ear, moral support, helpful advice, and practical information. They can also give you recommendations and referrals to sources of additional help and expertise. Many reliable, recognized authorities, such as colleges of veterinary medicine, veterinary medical associations, professional veterinarians, and animal-protection and cat-fancy organizations, offer informative Web sites as well. The Humane Society of the United States offers a wide variety of cat-specific information sheets on its Web site, at www.hsus.org.

CHAPTER 11

Cats and Children

STRIPEY'S TALE

Oh, Mom, can I keep him? Can I? Please? Bobby's mom gave him to me."

Nora sighed heavily as she considered her earnest six-year-old, who was clutching the tiny bundle of gray-and-black fur. They really couldn't afford a pet right now, not with Jason's little sister ill and another baby on the way. And she was annoyed at Mrs. White, who was always palming off her endless litters of kittens on unsuspecting neighborhood kids. But the tiny tear trickling down her son's face when he saw her wavering did the trick. "OK, Jason, you can keep him," she said. "But you have to take care of him all by yourself. Promise? I'll get some cat food when I'm at the supermarket this afternoon."

Jason beamed. "I'll take the best care of him ever! I promise, Mom! Thanks, Mom!" Clutching his new pet to his chest, he cooed, "I think I'll call him Stripey." The next few weeks went by swiftly. Even Jason's dad was charmed by the sight of the little tyke cuddling up to the kitten as they fell asleep at night. Jason was as good as his word—setting out a little bowl of food each morning and pouring some of the milk from his breakfast cereal into a little saucer for the kitten to lap up. But one evening, Nora noted with horror three vivid red scratches across her little daughter's arm. Naturally assuming the kitten was the culprit, she angrily confronted Jason and Stripey, grabbing the kitten and throwing him out the door with perhaps more force than she'd intended. Jason took off after the now-limping kitten, but Stripey was summarily banished from the house. His little bowl of food now stayed out on the porch, where it accumulated dead wasps and hosted the occasional ant picnic. All summer long, the kitten scratched at fleas and dug furiously at his mite-ridden ears, to no avail. Jason did quite a bit of scratching, too.

As Stripey grew, he wandered farther and farther afield in the neighborhood, often staying away for days at a time. "Oh, he's OK," Dad reassured Jason. "It's normal for cats to wander off like that. They're really more like wild animals. He's having fun." When he was around, though, the swiftly growing cat was increasingly resistant to being grabbed and carried around like a stuffed toy. He occasionally made his displeasure known with his claws, and once, when Jason poked him suddenly to wake him up, he whirled around and bit the startled child—just hard enough to scare him.

The young cat had also clearly tired of being clutched and pounded by Jason's young sister, and hissed and spit whenever she approached him. He developed an alarming tendency to ambush anyone who walked by—wrapping fully extended claws around their ankles, with predictably painful results. As his sweet, cuddly kitten turned into a poorly socialized, undisciplined, increasingly strong, and ever more independent cat, Jason's interest waned, too. One evening, Jason's exasperated dad, trying to get the boy to clean up his room, found him engrossed in a video game. "If you don't clean up your room right now," Dad warned, "Stripey's going to the animal shelter tomorrow." "Fine," muttered Jason, without looking up. "He's just a stupid cat. And anyway, I want a German shepherd."

Benefits of Cat Ownership for Children

For many cat lovers, memories of the dear cats of their childhood are among their fondest. Naturally, they want to share these experiences with their children and help them develop a love for animals, too. Passing on the family tradition of humane sensibilities and responsible pet ownership is, for many cat-loving families, a sacred trust. In sharing their lives and homes with cats, children can learn priceless lessons about love, respect, friendship, loyalty, empathy, and responsibility. In helping to care for a cherished cat, a child can gain a sense of accomplishment and personal competence, and—because it's an important task, with real-life consequences—a real boost to his self-esteem. Responsible, aware pet ownership teaches children to value the lives, natures, and needs of the other creatures with whom we share the world.

But if parents teach the wrong lessons—deliberately or inadvertently—cat ownership benefits neither child nor cat. Jason wasn't prepared to care for a kitten, either physically or emotionally. His parents didn't offer accurate information or emotional support, nor did they act as role models for responsible pet ownership. Jason came to see his growing cat as little more than an annoyance—a toy he'd outgrown. By using the cat as a bribe to try to compel his son to behave in a particular way, Jason's dad reinforced the attitude that pets are disposable and replaceable. Stripey was the immediate loser, but Jason lost, too.

Even as a toddler, a youngster can learn that the family cat—if handled gently and given proper respect—is a companionable playmate. As he grows, guided by responsible adults, a child can gradually learn to respect the cat's fragility and power, appreciate his uniqueness, and come to regard the cat as a friend, a comforting presence, a warm, snuggly sleeping buddy. Older kids, as their sensitivities increase and their bonds with their cats deepen, confide in their cats. Their cats are their best friends, always there through algebra tests, bad-hair days, and teenage broken hearts.

As these precious interspecies relationships grow, mature, and deepen, each child will naturally want to participate more fully and to assume more responsibility in the cat's daily care. A responsible adult should always continue to oversee the pet's well-being, but the adult should also seek to delegate those aspects of cat care they know their child can handle.

Part of this ongoing humane home schooling is continuing education for both parent and child. Age-appropriate books about cat care, history, and lore make splendid gifts for all occasions. Parents can read cat stories to their toddlers. Older children can help maintain the cat's health journal, do simple brushing and grooming, weigh the cat regularly, accompany the cat on regular veterinary visits, and be encouraged to write down questions to ask the veterinarian. Responsible adults can set a good example by keeping up with advances in nutrition, cat care, and veterinary medicine. Learning about cats is a lifelong project that can begin even in the cradle. Make it a project for the whole family.

Cats and Babies

Expecting a baby? A thoughtful, gradual process of accustoming your cat to the sounds, scents, and sights of a baby in the home, together with plenty of extra attention and reassurance, can help make the new arrival an occasion of joy and pleasure for everyone. In chapter 18, you'll learn how to prepare your cat for the household changes—physical and emotional—he'll experience when your baby arrives. Especially if you're expecting your first child, if your cat is already an adult, or if he's particularly closely bonded to you, he'll understandably have concerns. The growing excitement in the household, the arrival of new furniture and supplies, the strange new smells, his favorite people unusually distracted—all can cause him stress. If not sensitively and immediately addressed, the stress can get out of hand, resulting in misbehavior and even medical problems. It's never too early to start getting your cat ready.

Once baby arrives, it's vital that you don't—even inadvertently—make your cat feel he's been supplanted or replaced in your affections by this strange new intruder. As you learned in chapter 10, cats are devotees of routine and ritual, and any change in their familiar activities can upset them. But they're also marvelously adaptable, and will adapt to gradual change if their needs are met and their concerns addressed.

Since the new mother might not be able to maintain her previous level of attention to the cat, it's a good idea for another family member to help care for him during this happy, but possibly stressful, time. Take advantage of your cat's curiosity about the new arrival to help him feel like a vital, loved part of your newly expanded family circle. In addition to their innate curiosity about the infant, many cats relish taking on a baby-sitter role. Encourage your cat to spend time with mother and baby. Let him see family members alternately interacting with, talking to, and cuddling the baby—and playing with him and offering him tasty treats.

Cats' nurturing instincts are sometimes powerfully aroused by the presence of a human infant. Your cat may even attempt to groom the baby. It's best to prevent this by distracting the cat with a game, treat, or toy. A cat's barbed tongue is ideal for grooming kittens but is far too rough for tender baby skin. Don't punish or yell at your cat for his offer to help, though.

It's also not wise to let your cat sleep with the baby. Your cat may be attracted by the baby's warmth or even by the odor of milk on the child's breath. Though the cat and baby sleeping together may make a charming photograph, there's always a danger that a large cat, or even a smaller cat lying on or near the baby's face, could actually suffocate an infant. And if an unexpected sound, light, or other stimulus suddenly startles the cat, he may extend his claws and injure the baby. This is a completely instinctual and normal reaction to an unexpected stimulus, and is not deliberate. Use common sense to prevent such mishaps.

Cats and Toddlers

Toddlers—children about two-to-six years old—are usually fascinated by cats. They're close in size to a child; they run when chased; they jump, roll, and move appealingly; they make cute, high-pitched noises; and they're soft and fluffy, just like stuffed toys. And therein lies the problem: toddlers are often too young to realize that a cat is actually a living animal, not just a particularly appealing, self-propelled toy. Some cats are extraordinarily patient and understanding with the grabbing, poking, pounding, chasing, and hauling toddlers are prone to do when left to their own devices with a cat. But most cats will eventually draw the line.

A cat's natural preference is to remove himself from situations he doesn't like. But even declawed cats are well equipped to defend themselves and to force the issue of escape when held against their will. That's when scratches, bites, and other injuries to their unwitting tormenters can occur. Use common sense to prevent problems. If you're considering adopting a cat and your home includes a toddler, it might be wise to wait until the child is a bit older. Or start well before a new cat arrives to teach your toddler how to behave around the cat, and—especially—what not to do. Start by observing how your child behaves around and interacts with a friend's or neighbor's cat. Successful interspecies relationships require skills that can be taught. The responsible parent teaches his toddler these vital skills.

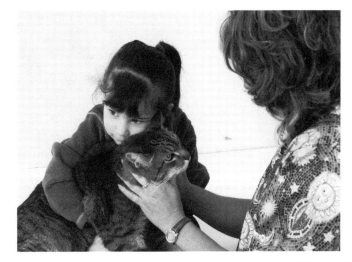

Let your child touch, then stroke, the cat. Monitor her behavior—and the cat's reaction—closely.
(FRANTZ DANTZLER)

Prepare your toddler ahead of time for his first encounter with a cat. Even when he's very young, you can read age-appropriate, but realistic and informative, animal stories to him. Be a good role model in your interactions with all animals, not just family pets. Your child will notice your behavior and emulate you. When you're ready to introduce your toddler to a cat, pick a quiet time, when both child and cat are calm and relaxed. Teach, and demonstrate, how to gently stroke the cat.

Let your child touch, then stroke, the cat. Monitor his behavior—and the cat's reaction—closely. If the child seems frustrated or insistent on pounding the cat with

his hands or fists (common toddler behavior), or if the cat shows any signs of annoyance, stop immediately and divert the child to another activity.

No matter how thorough your preparation, always closely supervise *all* interactions between young children and cats. Be ready to step in and distract the child or the cat, or both, if either seems to be stressed or behaving inappropriately. Watch for signals from the cat such as hissing, a low growl, a lashing tail, dilated pupils, whiskers swept back, and ears swept back. All are signs of growing impatience, fear, or anger. Teach your child to recognize these warning signs, too, and to back off immediately—to stop all petting, touching, and interaction. Teach him to retreat gently and quietly and leave the cat alone. If you notice any of these body-language signals, immediately terminate the interaction. And if you have a choice between bodily removing the cat or the child, pick up the child. Never try to pick up an angry or annoyed cat.

Besides the obvious danger of the cat scratching or biting a child, an overly enthusiastic or poorly trained toddler can seriously injure or even kill a cat. Kittens are especially at risk. If you have toddlers or young children at home, it's particularly important that your cat always have private spaces to which he can retreat at will, safe from unwanted attention. The earliest lessons to teach youngsters about interacting with cats must include the following:

- how to read cat body language that indicates annoyance, anger, and fear
- how to recognize when the cat has had enough and wants to be left alone
- to never hold a cat against his will
- to never corner a cat
- to never prevent a cat from escaping a situation he doesn't like
- to never bother a cat when he's in his safe room
- to never bother a cat when he's eating, sleeping, or using his litter box

If you have young children and are adopting a cat or kitten, choose a cat who's been fostered or socialized in a house with young children. A cat who's been exposed during his critical period of socialization (about three-to-fourteen weeks) to the sights, sounds, and activity levels of young children will be a happier, calmer, and safer companion for your toddlers. (See chapter 12 for more on kitten socialization.) That's why the best "foster moms" for kittens have busy, active homes with children, other cats, dogs, and plenty of attention to go around.

Some cats will never feel comfortable or safe around children, or in noisy, active environments. Others thrive on them. It depends on their temperament, health, and early socialization. Whether you obtain your kitten or cat from a breeder, shelter, or other source, try to find out as much as possible about the environment in which he was raised and socialized.

Every child needs to learn, from an early age, how to interact with animals other than his own family's pets—pets belonging to others and wild animals. Teach very young children to leave *all* animals alone—to never approach or touch them. Teach older children, who can distinguish between pets and wild animals, to recognize body-language cues—especially fear, threat, and aggression cues—of common pets such as cats and dogs. Teach children to *always* ask permission from an animal's owner before approaching or touching a pet of any species. At the same time, teach all children to leave wild creatures strictly alone, particularly if the animal seems overly friendly or accommodating. Such animals are often very ill and therefore extremely dangerous. People-friendly, nonfearful behavior in a wild animal is never normal.

As children grow up, encourage them to learn more about their own cats, their cats' wild relatives, and other animals through reading and study. Teenagers can volunteer to work in a local shelter. Shelters are always looking for extra hands for cleanup, feeding, grooming, and other everyday tasks, as well as extra arms for snuggling and hearts for loving the cats, kittens, and other animals in their care.

The Surprise Gift Cat—Bad Idea!

A live animal is a particularly poor choice of gift or surprise at any time, but especially at a busy, activity-filled holiday or birthday celebration. Too many adults are seduced by an idealized image of the look of thrilled wonder on their child's face when he sees the beribboned cat or kitten for the first time—a charming, if brief, photo opportunity. Unfortunately, this vision often includes unveiling the surprise at a noisy birthday party or amid the chaos of Christmas morning. Nothing could be worse for the animal himself, or for the chances of child and cat developing a healthy relationship and lasting bond. The new cat will likely merge, in the child's mind, with all the other gifts, thrills, and entertainments of the day—no more significant than, and just as disposable as, the latest action figure or talking doll.

If your child has been consistently asking for a cat, and you feel he's both mature and serious enough to understand the big picture, start small. Start with a trip to the library or bookstore to look at some age-appropriate books about cats and their care. Talk to him about the pet he wants. Gradually introduce him to the various aspects of pet ownership, to the notion that a pet is a companion and a commitment for life, and to the daily responsibilities of feeding, grooming, playing, and cleaning. Observe his reactions. Does his interest remain high? As your child's parent, you are in the best position to know whether or not he's ready for assuming even a child-size role in family cat ownership.

A Cat Is Not a Child-Training Aid

Is there a worse reason to get your child a cat than to witness his momentary thrill at a surprise gift kitten? Yes: it's getting your child a cat to try to turn him around if he is recalcitrant or irresponsible or is misbehaving, or to bribe him into behaving better. No animal should ever be used as a bribe, threat, or reward to try to control or modify a child's behavior. If your child has behavior or discipline problems, solve those problems *before* introducing any animal into your home. As wonderful as cats are, the mere presence of one will not somehow magically turn a difficult child into a responsible, caring one.

No young child, however mature and caring, should ever assume complete responsibility for the care of a cat or any other pet. A responsible adult must always vigilantly oversee all feeding, cleaning, grooming, daily-care, and medical needs. The adult must realize that he, not the child, is the cat's owner and primary caretaker—whether it's "the child's cat" or "the family cat." Of course, as a child gets older he'll be able to perform more of the daily-care chores such as feeding, grooming, and routine cleanup. But there must always be an adult responsible for insuring that these tasks are actually performed regularly and correctly. It's the adult who has ultimate responsibility for the health and well-being of the animal. It's unfair to both child and cat to place full responsibility for the cat's health and welfare on a child's shoulders. Many children, unfortunately, lose interest in "their" cat at some point, so an adult must be ready and willing to assume all pet-care responsibilities.

Before adopting a cat or kitten, hold a family conference to decide who will be responsible for various cat-care tasks. As much as possible, let each child choose a particular age-appropriate aspect of cat care as his personal commitment to the new family member. Ask each member of the family to make a promise—to the rest of the family, and to the cat—to perform his chosen tasks as well and as faithfully as he can. Make a chart, and have children check it off when they wash out the food bowls, put the grooming supplies away neatly, or perform whatever other small tasks they have chosen. Part of each child's education in responsible cat ownership is learning to keep their commitments and the promises they made to their family and to the cat.

"Using" a Cat Is Always Wrong

Using a cat (or any other animal) as a gift, bribe, threat, pawn, or reward is always wrong. Don't involve your cat in family discipline—ever. Forcing your cat into the role of pawn, bribe, or weapon is not only unfair to the cat himself but can engender unhealthy responses in your children, from jealousy and resentment to actual cruelty and abuse. Your cat should be a wellspring of comfort, harmony, and peace in your household, not an unwilling source of jealousy, resentment, or pain.

Likewise, never use your cat—or any other animal—as Exhibit A in your family sex-education program. Multitudes of unthinking cat owners fail to get their cats sterilized because they want their children to witness the miracle of birth. Every year, thousands upon thousands of healthy kittens must be euthanized (humanely destroyed) because there are no homes for them. The miracle of birth too often leads to the tragedy of needless death. (See chapter 16 for more reasons to sterilize your cat.) And cats being cats, the chances that your children will actually witness the birth when it does happen are extremely small. Feline mothers-to-be are famous for choosing hidden, out-of-the-way spots for giving birth; they insist upon peace and privacy. Your children will probably be at school or at the mall anyway (much to Mom Cat's relief).

And what about those tiny miracles? Oh, you might keep the cutest one. Even if you have good homes for all the kittens, those are good homes that won't be available for other kittens, who are sentenced, by irresponsibility, to death. Producing litter after litter of surplus kittens—dumped on shelters or palmed off on friends and relatives—teaches only that feline life is cheap, disposable, and endlessly replaceable.

Irresponsible or ill-considered use of animals can too easily lead to abuse. The topic of animal abuse is a touchy one. For too many people, animal abuse is still an acceptable rite of passage, especially in boys, and is dismissed with the old boys-will-be-boys wink.

But researchers have established a clear link between childhood abuse of animals and adult spousal abuse, child abuse, and other serious crimes. Many notorious serial murderers and other violent criminals have histories of childhood animal abuse. In many cases, the animal abuse was open and repeated, yet ignored or rationalized.

Remain vigilant for any signs of a child annoying, provoking, or demonstrating cruelty to, or committing abuse of, any animal, whether the family pet, a neighbor's pet, or a wild creature. Animal abuse is *never* just normal childish behavior. Parents have a particularly solemn responsibility to remain alert to any signs of cruelty or abuse towards animals in their own children and to take immediate and strong measures to stop the abuse and to get help for the child. No animal should ever be introduced into a household in which any resident is known, or even thought, to abuse animals. Thinking that a child who kills neighborhood cats would never harm the family's pet is both wrongheaded and dangerous.

WHAT ABOUT STRIPEY?

What happened to Stripey? As is the case with so many kittens who come into the world unwanted, Stripey's life was short and tragic. Once they realized that threatening to take him to the shelter was ineffective as a disciplinary measure, Jason's parents simply forgot about the cat. Never having made a commitment to cat ownership in the first place, they easily "forgot" to buy cat food. They occasionally saw Stripey wandering the nearby woods, but they thought of him as no longer their cat and therefore not their concern. Eventually, Stripey disappeared—but not before fathering several litters of unwanted kittens and injuring himself and several other male cats in fights over females. Perhaps he became prey to a coyote or a fisher. Perhaps he died miserably, alone in the woods, of a common illness that a simple vaccination could have spared him or of a raging infection from an untreated fight wound.

Too many children get their first experience of pet ownership like Jason did—without planning, without thought, without commitment, without any knowledge or understanding of the nature and needs of the living creature whose life and happiness are at stake. It's not the fault of the six-year-old "owner" when his or her first relationship with a companion animal goes so tragically, disastrously wrong.

And yes, Jason got his German shepherd.

CHAPTER 12

Handling and Socialization

WHAT IS SOCIALIZATION?—
TWELVE YEARS AND TWO LITTERS

Sunshine and Shadow were feral kittens, born in August in a woodpile on a New England hillside. As temperatures dipped and the end of October loomed, a local homeowner, who'd been feeding the little family of five kittens and their fierce mother, managed to trap the whole group and take them to a nearby shelter. There they received ear medication, flea combing, and a general cleanup. The next day, the two tiny females went to a new home. They might have been nine or ten weeks old, at the most.

Once home, they huddled together apprehensively, except when voraciously devouring every scrap of food placed before them, as if no more would ever appear. They showed little interest in self-grooming or even play. After several days of gentle handling, soft conversation, bathing, ear-mite and flea treatment, and lots of attention, they finally made their first tentative steps at connection with their owners. They learned to play with each other, but seldom with that delightfully carefree abandon usually associated with kittenhood.

Shadow eventually warmed up, if quietly, to both of her owners, while Sunshine refuses the attentions of all but her special person. Neither can be persuaded to interact with the family's other cats, and the slightest sound of footsteps at the front door, or an unfamiliar voice, sends them scurrying to their safe haven under a bed. They're safe, protected, pampered, and happy—but their personalities and full potential were circumscribed by their unfortunate early experiences—and especially by the lack of essential early socialization.

Fast-forward twelve years. The same owners adopt a litter of three. This time, though, there's a big difference. Like Sunshine and Shadow, Flash, Rudy, and Abigail were born feral to a fierce mother cat. But in the meantime the shelter had instituted a program of fostering. So when Momcat and her tiny babies are brought in as part of a rescue, the whole family isn't placed in a confining cage but in the home of a trained foster family.

Under loving supervision, Momcat raises and cares for her little family—but instead of an exhausting life of hunting for food, constantly seeking shelter, and defending her helpless kittens from predators and other dangers, Momcat enjoys plenty of nutritious food, warmth, shelter, safety, and precious peace. Her babies prosper, growing up strong and healthy, learning to be cats from the best teacher in the world—their own mother.

At eight weeks, the little ones are treated to their first veterinary checkup. With initial vaccinations and a clean bill of health, the kittens meet the rest of the family, including several resident adult cats and two well-behaved dogs. From then on, they enjoy the run of the house and constant attention, as they grow accustomed to the sights, sounds, smells, and routines of ordinary household life. At fifteen weeks, their foster mom returns them to the shelter, ready for life in a new, permanent adoptive home. Only one step remains: pediatric sterilization surgery. They breeze through this rite of passage, and, oblivious, are running, playing, and exuberantly pouncing on one another the very next day.

And that's when our original owners arrive at the shelter. Having decided it was time to add some kittens to their household, they quickly fall in love with all three. The question of separating the closely bonded group never even arises! In their new home, the kittens enjoy a week or so in private quarters, as they become accustomed to the sensory input in this new environment. Soon, though, it's time to meet the rest of the family.

Already familiar with feline hierarchies and accustomed to respecting the perquisites of rank, the kittens approach the resident cats with friendly interest, but also with respect and deference. The few initial swats and hisses tell them to back off—

and they do, though they are not particularly intimidated. They play vigorously, wrestle like little tigers, bound up and down their new cat tree with stunning grace and athleticism. The owners are careful to offer extra pampering and attention to the resident cats while the newcomers find their way around, and to feed the kittens separately so that the old-timers can continue to dine in their accustomed peace.

Thanks to the enlightened socialization they enjoyed in their foster home, these three feral-born kittens can look forward to a lively, happy life. Their early experiences have insured that their lives will be enriched by deep, satisfying emotional bonds, not only with their owners and other people, but also with their fellow felines—including any newcomers that may join them in the future. And while their owners don't have dogs, it's likely that these three would handle a canine housemate with casual aplomb.

The Sensitive Period for Kitten Socialization

Why did Flash, Rudy, and Abigail's experience after adoption differ so markedly from Shadow and Sunshine's? The answer lies in the critical period of *socialization*—the brief, precious few weeks between the ages of approximately three and fourteen weeks when kittens are most open to adapting to a wide variety of other creatures, of all species, in their environment and making these creatures a part of their extended social circle. During this time, the developing kitten establishes a mental and psychological map of creatures whom he's going to be comfortable interacting with for the rest of his life. This mental mapping function is so powerful that kittens can sometimes be socialized to consider such creatures as birds or rodents as companions rather than prey (though vigilant supervision will always be needed during their interactions, and it may not be fair to the smaller creatures to allow contact at all).

Cats pass through the developmental stages of kittenhood in a remarkably predictable path—and with lightning speed. If a kitten is not handled—daily, lovingly, gently—during this critical period, if he's not

If properly socialized at the right time and in the right environment, a kitten will develop into a tame gentle creature.

(FRANTZ DANTZLER)

HANDLING AND SOCIALIZATION

exposed to a variety of people, sounds, sights, other animals, and other stimuli, it's unlikely that he'll ever be able to form deep, lasting bonds with humans or other creatures.

The developmental pace of kittenhood is breathtaking. By the age of two weeks littermates are already competing for rank and dominance within their group. In the next several weeks, as their senses sharpen, their teeth erupt, and they get steadier on their feet, the developmental pace picks up. By six weeks, they're running, stalking, pouncing, and grooming one another—an important social ritual. It's during this period of extremely rapid development that the "window of socialization" opens.

Cat-behavior specialists have discovered that this stage in the blossoming kitten's psychological development begins around the age of three weeks. To grow up psychologically healthy, a kitten needs as much mental and physical stimulation as possible during this crucial period.

Kittens handled for fifteen-to-forty minutes per day during their first several weeks of life actually develop larger brains and become more adventurous, playful, and socially comfortable adults. They learn faster, too. Skills not developed during this precious early time of life may never be realized fully, or at all. Although each kitten may develop slightly more slowly or rapidly than his peers, by approximately thirteen weeks the window starts to close.

Within this window lies the key to the splendid socialization of Flash, Rudy, and Abigail. Blessed with a rich, supportive environment during their window-of-socialization period, these three lucky kittens bloomed into happy, healthy, psychologically stable animals and unusually companionable pets.

Take Advantage of the Window

If you're responsible for raising a kitten during this crucial period, reinforce (with keen supervision, and camera in hand) your kitten's natural urge to explore, to satisfy his curiosity, to meet and greet his new family, to sample and taste the splendid variety of his new life.

To grow into a happy, adaptable pet, relaxed and friendly, comfortably at home among a variety of humans, animals, and sounds, respectful of other household pets but not fearful or intimidated by them, your kitten needs frequent, loving handling and plenty of stimulation. Take advantage of this priceless opportunity to lay a solid foundation of stability and resiliency. If your kitten is to live in a multispecies household, it's essential to introduce him to dogs and other animals early in life—as early as two-to-seven weeks—before he decides they're either enemies or food.

During this crucial, sensitive period the rapidly growing kittens indulge, while awake, in virtually nonstop play. While this play provides so much delight and wonder for charmed cat owners, it has a number of serious purposes. Through play, the kittens learn how to be cats, and—more importantly—learn how to express their "catness" within the context of the social situation and environment in which they find themselves. As they play, the kittens do the following:

- develop and refine physical coordination
- learn and practice object-manipulation skills: scooping, batting, tossing, pawing, mouthing, holding
- practice social interaction with littermates and the mother cat
- learn how far they can go—the difference between play and real fighting
- establish dominance and social rankings
- practice hunting skills—observation, patience, stealth, the "killing bite"
- reinforce group bonds through allogrooming and mingling of the group scent

Domestication Is Still a Work in Progress

But with each new generation of kittens, the domestication clock turns back a ways—not all the way back to full wildness, but back to a middle ground. A kitten can go either way. If properly socialized at the right time, in the right environment, a kitten will develop into a tame, gentle creature comfortable in human company and possessed of a relatively placid temperament and predictable behavior patterns. He will have the necessary resiliency to adapt to new situations and to take changes in stride, and he will have the stability and confidence he needs to grow and thrive in our world.

On the other hand, a kitten denied appropriate socialization, who does not experience frequent handling and the company of people and a variety of other creatures at the critical formative period of early kittenhood, will likely be forever psychologically handicapped. Depending upon the environment in which he finds himself, he might be fearful, nervous, or clingy; or he might be savage, aggressive, and domineering. It's the lack of appropriate early socialization that makes the prospects for adult feral cats rescued from feral colonies so bleak.

Shelter workers and others who rescue feral cats are painfully aware of how difficult it is—and it's usually impossible—to find adoptive homes for adult cats who have grown up feral. These cats, for the most part, are thoroughly untameable and often completely unhandleable. Even providing necessary medical care for these individuals is a major challenge. If feral kittens are rescued early enough in life, though, there's a good chance they can be socialized and tamed, becoming as sweet tempered and adoptable as any home-raised kitten.

Socialization to People

It's not hard to see why Sunshine and Shadow remain wary cats, despite a dozen years of pampering in a loving, safe home. For example, while at eight weeks Rudy, Flash, and Abigail were enjoying the run of a loving home, plenty of food, and lots of attention, at the same age Sunshine and Shadow huddled in their woodpile, thin, afraid, and tortured by ear mites, as early frost nipped their noses. Being trapped and carried to the shelter doubtless saved their lives, but it was likely a profoundly frightening and unsettling experience. Their window opened, and closed, in vain.

Despite our best efforts and the best efforts of rescuers and shelter workers, the vicissitudes of the real world sentence too many cats to an early kittenhood more like Sunshine and Shadow's than that of our three lucky fostered kittens. Fortunately, cats are extraordinarily adaptable and intelligent creatures. And in many ways most cats are still kittens in both mind and body until they are about two years old. With sensitivity, patience, and persistence, even kittens from severely deprived backgrounds can become happy, well-adjusted, socially comfortable pets, as long as their special needs are respected.

There are lots of helpful strategies you can use to try to make up for developmental and socialization deficiencies in the kitten or cat you adopt. These cats can be challenging and sometimes frustrating—but, oh how rewarding it is when a formerly fearful feline emerges from deep beneath the bed, smooths out his spiky temper and calms his ruffled fur, leans his shaggy head on your arm, gazes into your eyes, and purrs his heart out in love and gratitude!

Poorly socialized adult cats, and even former feral cats, can sometimes be transformed into calm, loving pets—so it pays to try. Don't pass up that adult cat you've fallen for, assuming he'll never be able to bond with you. Go ahead, fall in love. Then follow his lead.

CAT PSYCH 101

Like people, cats come in all sorts of temperaments and personality types, and with all sorts of psychological oddities and vagaries. As with people, these are probably caused by some combination of nature and nurture. And like most people who have difficult temperaments or oddball personalities, most of these unusual cats can live perfectly normal, happy, and satisfied lives—with patience, understanding, acceptance, and love from the significant people in their lives.

It's part of the Feline Covenant to accept our cats for the unique creatures they are. But it's just as important to do as much as we can to try to prevent and lessen the possible adverse consequences of certain behavioral, personality, and temperamental traits through gentle, sensitive, loving desensitization and behavior-modification strategies.

The Clingy Cat

Some cats, because of a combination of natural tendencies and early experiences, become more closely attuned to the people in their lives than to other cats. Perhaps they've always lived as "only cats," or perhaps they're unusually closely bonded to a particular person. A clingy cat can be the ideal companion for a homebound person or one with disabilities, and the perfect laptop muse for a stay-at-home worker. Clingy cats can be enormously gratifying companions, lavish with their love and affection and uninhibited in their demonstrativeness.

The darker side of clinginess is overdependence. A cat attached to one particular person can be devastated if that person suddenly disappears from his life, even for a short time, or if the close relationship they shared is altered or interrupted. A hospitalization, work-schedule change, marriage or divorce, new baby, or other life change can produce a crisis that threatens the clingy cat's mental stability, health, or even life.

It is a mistake to try to change a clingy, overdependent, or highly attached cat (or any cat) into someone he's not. But it's wise to try to gradually and gently lessen his extreme attachment and overdependence. No matter how stable your life or home situation, things happen. An overly dependent cat who's suddenly deprived of his major source of attachment can display signs of extreme separation anxiety: refusal to eat; frantic, destructive self-grooming; hiding and withdrawal; refusal to use his litter box; and depression. In extreme cases, nervous overgrooming can lead to self-mutilation and other serious complications. Separation anxiety caused by overdependence can adversely affect the cat's health and well-being, weaken his immune system, and leave him vulnerable to infection and disease.

The Fearful Cat

Cats who are abused, seriously injured, abandoned, or neglected or who've had other unfortunate experiences can become chronically fearful, skittish, overly wary, and constantly stressed animals. Unlike some other psychological quirks, chronic fearfulness (not to be confused with a lack of socialization) is almost always the result of nurture-gone-wrong, rather than nature. Part of the Feline Covenant is to prevent such horrors from affecting cats in the first place. Another part is doing all we can to help rebuild the fearful cat's precious feeling of trust and comfort in the world and his companions. This can be a long, arduous process.

Although it's never acceptable to coerce any cat, it's particularly vital to avoid any hint of coercion or force with a fearful cat, especially one who's been abused. These cats require, and deserve, the utmost in patience and forbearance. It's vital to give a fearful cat as much time, space, peace, and quiet as he needs to rebuild his shattered trust. Pushing him faster than he wants to go, or forcing him to interact with people before he's ready, can make his fearfulness even worse. Give him plenty of space, time, and love. Let him set the pace.

A chronically fearful cat will benefit from living in a quiet, stress-free environment. He may never be able to tolerate certain stressors, such as dogs, children, loud noises, or frequent changes and upsets in his life. Concentrate on helping him build a loving bond with one person at first, then gradually enlarge his social circle as he becomes more comfortable. Take it slow, and don't expect miracles.

The Domineering Cat

There are two types of domineering cats: those who push other cats around, and those who push people around. Neither type is a particularly pleasant companion. Such behavior may not be healthy for the cat, either. Maintaining a constant high pitch of control and alertness can be very stressful. It can be comical to observe a domineering cat ruling one or two obsequious humans with an iron paw, but that's probably not an ideal model for the human-cat relationship.

An overly domineering cat can make the lives of other cats in his environment completely miserable. Although cats form hierarchies, they are different from the typical pack structure common in dogs. In a group of cats, one will generally emerge as the "top cat." (Often, this is a female.) On the next level down will be one or two second-tier cats who enjoy special privileges and status. Below them is the general rank and file of cats who have roughly equal status.

In most groups, the top cat is a largely benevolent despot—in charge but not aggressively domineering. Occasionally, though, a dominant cat may threaten or even attack a particular subordinate cat. And some domineering cats constantly pick fights with other cats. This causes an unacceptably high level of stress in the other cats and danger to them, and therefore calls for rapid intervention. The aggressive cat may be ill. He should have a thorough physical examination to rule out neurological or other diseases. Your veterinarian can recommend a number of medications that can help smooth out aggressiveness and domineering behavior. Medication is not a panacea, though, and it is not the answer for every cat or every situation. But it's not fair to subject your other cats to the constant stress and threat of attack from an aggressively dominant cat.

Sometimes the conflict is between two particular cats, perhaps the top cat and one that refuses to accept the top cat's authority. These personality-and-status conflicts can become deadly serious and can escalate quickly into all-out wars. In this situation, it's essential to act fast to defuse the situation by separating the contenders completely and, often by isolating the more aggressive cat (who may or may not be the dominant cat) from the rest of the group.

In extreme cases, you might need to consider finding a different home for the domineering or aggressive cat, perhaps a home where he'll be the only cat. That can be a wrenching decision, though. You might find that consulting with an animal-behavior specialist can help you see the problem more clearly. Together you can devise a strategy to try to modify the domineering cat's behavior. This may be a long-term project.

What about the cat who pushed his people around? If the people involved are truly dedicated to changing a cat's domineering behavior (and they sometimes aren't!), a carefully designed program of behavior modification can turn a pushy cat into a more accommodating pet. It may seem hard-hearted to lock your cat out of your bedroom (so he won't demand food at 3 A.M.), play the radio to drown out his insistent meows, and stop play sessions immediately when he claws your ankle. Consistency is essential in behavior modification—any backsliding sets the clock back to zero. See chapter 10 for more tips on training, and retraining, your cat.

The Shy Cat

Some cats, like some people, are shy and retiring by nature. This isn't usually a problem, though our society seems to prefer, appreciate, and reward gregarious and outgoing personalities in both cats and humans. Respect the special nature of your shy cat.

Don't force him to be the life of the party. In fact, don't make him attend the party at all. That's where his safe retreat comes in handy. (See chapter 6.) Your shy cat will appreciate your sensitivity.

If a moderate level of shyness turns into an extreme level of antipathy to *any* company, your cat may be ill or extremely unhappy. Take him to the veterinarian for a complete checkup. Has your normally shy cat become an invisible cat? Does he hide and withdraw from all social interaction with people and other pets? He may feel highly stressed or threatened by something in the environment. Take a mental inventory of changes. Perhaps he needs a few more safe places to retreat from a barking dog, a domineering cat, a grasping toddler, or too many visitors. Have you installed new carpeting or bought new furniture? The odors, sights, and activities accompanying such major changes, while pleasant for us, can send a sensitive cat over the edge.

ACCLIMATIZING YOUR CAT TO YOUR HOUSEHOLD

The happy experience of Flash, Rudy, and Abigail in their foster home is a great model for raising happy, well-adjusted, well-socialized kittens. Whether you are fostering kittens yourself, or have adopted kittens or cats, it's important that they become calm and comfortable with the everyday sights, sounds, odors, activities, and routines of your household.

During your cat's first several days in your home, he'll be staying in a small room that contains everything he needs. During this period, let each member of your family spend time with the new cat or kitten. Help mask unfamiliar noises at first by playing a radio softly, tuned to classical music or a talk station. Supervise youngsters and keep their visits short, especially at first. See chapter 6 and 11 for tips on getting cats used to children, and vice versa.

Otherwise, continue with your normal household activities such as cooking, vacuuming, playing the TV or radio, and the like. The cat's "isolation room" will partially muffle sounds and odors so that he can become accustomed to them without feeling threatened or confused. When interacting with him, maintain a positive, upbeat, and welcoming attitude. Speak softly, especially at first. The cat may hide for a few days. Let him approach you at his own pace. As long as he's eating, drinking, and using his litter box, he'll be fine!

Meeting and Greeting

Once your new feline has a clean bill of health—including all necessary vaccinations and treatments for any parasites he may have arrived with—his veterinarian will clear him for his initial meetings with other animals in your household. Take it slow, at first just exchanging scent-carrying bedding. A screen door on the isolation room can help facilitate early, controlled interactions. Review the strategies outlined in chapter 6 for introducing your new cat or kitten to others in your household and for getting relationships off on the right paw.

Once your new cat or kitten has the run of your house and is comfortable with other family members and pets, take some time each day to integrate him into your daily routines and rituals. If you're an early morning sleepyhead—and your kitten has access to your bedroom—your first "close encounter of the kitten kind" each morning might be a pink nose massaging your chin or a tiny, rough tongue sandpapering your eyelid. It's impossible to ignore this endearing, but insistent, greeting!

Taming the Monsters

Some ordinary household sounds will likely seem frightening to your new cat or kitten at first. These can include the sounds of the vacuum cleaner or the dishwasher, or of a furnace or refrigerator compressor that cranks on noisily and unexpectedly. Most of these will quickly become ordinary background sounds. Remember—your cat or kitten will look to you for reassurance in times of fear, confusion, or new stimuli. If you show fear or alarm, he'll be fearful, too. But if you maintain a cheerful, unconcerned attitude, he'll pick up on your unconcern and quickly become more comfortable. Your cat or kitten will "key" off the emotions and moods of the people in the household to whom he feels the closest.

One household monster many cats never lose their fear or suspicion of is the vacuum cleaner—perhaps because of its uncommonly noisy, mobile, and sporadic appearances around the house. Your cat will likely dash off and hide when the vacuum cleaner appears. This isn't all bad, though; you don't want him chasing around beneath the machine while you're trying to use it! At first, he may hide for several hours. Over time, though, as he sees that there's no real threat, he'll reappear more readily after you're done housecleaning or even observe this curious human pastime with interest—from a high, safe perch.

If your household is a hive of activity with family members constantly coming and going, with complicated schedules and many activities, try to shield your new cat or kitten, especially at first, from as much of the mayhem as possible. Cats are quite adaptable, and he'll eventually become accustomed to your pace of life. Be sure he has plenty of hideaways and a safe room to which he can retreat when things get too noisy or active for his taste.

CHAPTER 13

The Right Veterinarian

YOUR VETERINARIAN—
YOUR CAT'S SECOND-BEST FRIEND

Besides you, your veterinarian is your cat's best friend. You and your veterinarian are partners in maintaining your cat's lifelong health, happiness, and well-being. You make up a team. The victory you both seek is a long, healthy, happy life for your cat.

Your veterinarian is a versatile, highly trained professional. In addition to four years of college or university training, with a heavy emphasis on the sciences, she's had four or more additional years of intense, specialized veterinary education at one of the twenty-seven colleges of veterinary medicine in the United States. It's tough and competitive: in 1999, only 32.8 percent of the applicants to these veterinary schools were accepted. After graduating from veterinary school, your veterinarian passed rigorous comprehensive examinations for licensing in the state where she practices.

Not only does your veterinarian have the training and expertise to treat several species of animals, she's knowledgeable about all sorts of medical specialties: obstetrics, pediatrics, behavior, psychology (human and animal!), urology, nutrition, cardi-

Today's cat owner can choose from a growing number of "cats only" veterinary practices. (FRANTZ DANTZLER)

ology, geriatrics, surgery, dentistry, orthopedics, oncology, pathology, and much more. Every state in the United States requires veterinarians to be licensed to practice, and more than half the states require continuing education credits for license renewals.

As of 1997, there were just over forty-five thousand veterinarians in private practice in the United States. Although 66 percent of these were men, in the future your cat's veterinarian is more likely to be a woman—in 1999, nearly 70 percent of the students entering veterinary school were female. Another increasingly popular trend among veterinarians—and their clients—is specialization by species.

Cats Only

Today's cat owner can choose from a growing number of cats-only clinics. Although the veterinarians at these clinics have received the same broad training that all veterinarians receive, they've chosen to limit their practice to felines. This has many advantages, for both clients and cats. The clinics are generally quieter and are free from the sights, sounds, and odors of dogs and other animals, which can be particularly distressing to ill, stressed cats. Because they work only with cats, the clinic veterinarians and technicians are extraknowledgeable about cat health and behavior, and are particularly sensitive to feline needs and preferences. Equipment, supplies, and other clinic features are optimized for cats—and their owners.

It Takes Teamwork

Despite the splendid advances of modern veterinary medicine, medical intervention can only do so much. Your veterinarian is highly trained in the diagnosis and treatment of animal illness. But one of her most important roles is also one that you, as a cat owner, share—prevention. *Prevention* is always less expensive—and easier on you, your veterinarian, and your cat—than treating illnesses and injuries that could have been prevented. Do your part to help your cat's veterinarian by providing your cat with the following:

- a safe, enriched indoors-only lifestyle (chapters 6, 7, 8, and 9)
- freedom from reproductive stresses through spaying or neutering (chapter 16)
- a high-quality diet appropriate to age, lifestyle, and activity level (chapter 14)
- access to fresh water at all times
- regular home dental care (yes—toothbrushing!—chapter 15)
- weekly at-home, nose-to-toes checkups (chapter 15)
- all appropriate vaccinations (chapter 16)
- a visit to the veterinarian at least once a year
- daily mindful observation and alertness to any changes
- freedom from unnecessary stress
- regular, vigorous exercise and stimulating play (chapter 7)
- plenty of love and attention

Selecting a Veterinarian

Don't wait until you're in the throes of an emergency to find a veterinarian. Using an emergency veterinary clinic as your primary provider of veterinary services is a needlessly expensive strategy. You, and your cat, need to build a relationship of trust and confidence with the veterinarian you choose. Take your time, plan ahead, shop around, and choose wisely.

While it might be nice to have your veterinarian close by, the closest clinic might not be the right one for you and your cat. Here's how to start your search for a veterinarian:

1. Ask cat-owning friends and relatives for recommendations.
2. Check with the American Animal Hospital Association (AAHA). AAHA member hospitals meet certain standards in facilities, equipment, and quality of care. There are seventeen thousand AAHA-certified veterinary-care providers, working at twenty-eight hundred facilities, in the United States (http://www.healthypet.com or 1-800-883-6301).
3. Check with the American Association of Feline Practitioners (AAFP). These are veterinarians with a special interest and expertise in the care of cats (http://www.aafponline.org or 1-800-204-3514).
4. Look in the telephone directory under "Animal Hospitals" and "Veterinarians."

If there are several choices nearby, visit each. Tour the facilities, look around, speak to staff members and veterinarians. Ask lots of questions. Bring a clipboard and take notes. Think about what's most important—to you and your cat.

Evaluating a Veterinary Practice

PROFESSIONAL EXPERTISE AND SERVICES

- How many veterinarians work at the practice? What is each one's education, experience, background, specialties, and interests?
- Are any of the veterinarians board-certified in specialties such as surgery, oncology, dentistry, geriatrics, cardiology, behavior, etc.? If not, do they refer clients to such specialists?
- What kind of support staff is on duty? Are there trained veterinary technicians? What are their training and background?
- What tests and procedures is the veterinarian prepared to do on-site? Will she do X rays? Blood testing? Ultrasound? Complex surgery? EKG? Endoscopy?
- Is there a veterinarian on duty twenty-four hours a day? If not, when a cat is hospitalized overnight, is there a competent, trained veterinary technician on duty—not just an attendant or guard?
- Is there full weekend veterinary coverage, or are weekend calls referred to an emergency clinic?
- Do the facilities look clean, modern, well organized, and well maintained? Is there any obvious odor from animals or other sources?
- Do the veterinarian's employees—receptionists, technicians, and others—seem cheerful, friendly, calm, and competent?
- Do any of the veterinarians make house calls?
- Which emergencies are the veterinarians prepared to deal with on-site? What kinds of cases are referred to a larger clinic or hospital?

FELINE FRIENDLINESS

- Is the practice for cats or small animals only, or does the veterinarian also treat large animals, farm animals, or wild animals?
- Are cats kept in separate wards or rooms when hospitalized and being examined or treated?
- Is there a separate waiting area for cats only?
- Does the veterinarian offer cats-only appointment days?

VETERINARY ETHICS AND HUMANE ISSUES

- Does the veterinarian counsel owners about behavior modification before performing declawing surgery on cats if owners request it, or does she have a policy against declawing?

(cont'd)

You're embarking on a long-term relationship. It's worth it to pay a little extra, and to drive a bit farther, to see the right veterinarian for you and your cat.

Attitude

Although it seems obvious, be sure the veterinarian you choose to care for your cat actually likes and understands cats. Some don't. Fortunately, this prejudice usually becomes quickly apparent. Watch how she approaches and handles your cat (or any cat at the clinic). Is she gentle? Does she speak softly and soothingly to the cat? Ask some of her cat-owning clients for their opinions.

A good veterinarian must be part detective—after all, her patients can't tell her where it hurts! She needs medical skills, people skills, and a special rapport with animals. The best veterinarians are sensitive, patient listeners and effective communicators and possess an ability to explain medical procedures and terms in clear, everyday language.

Being a Good Client

When you visit the veterinarian, your cat is the *patient*, but you're the *client*. Whether your cat is visiting the veterinarian for his annual checkup or because he's not feeling well, you owe it to both your cat and the veterinarian to make the best use of your visit. Be prepared with all the information your veterinarian needs to assess your cat's condition, and be ready to answer all her questions.

It would certainly be convenient if your cat could explain and describe all his aches, pains, and concerns to the veterinarian! But apart from his usual meows (along with those growls and hisses he seems to save for medical situations!), your cat relies on you to communicate his needs and concerns. Your veterinarian, with her experienced hands and wealth of clinical and scientific knowledge, can determine quite a lot from a physical examination of your cat and from analyzing the results of X rays, blood tests, and other tests.

Your veterinarian—and your cat—are relying on you to accurately describe the history and symptoms of any illness your cat is experiencing and to provide information that might shed light on the state of your cat's body, mind, mood, health, and life.

Be sure the veterinarian you choose actually likes and understands cats. (FRANTZ DANTZLER)

Waiting-Room Etiquette

Always bring your cat to the veterinarian in a sturdy, waterproof carrier large enough for him to lie down and turn around in. Cardboard carriers are designed for temporary use and are fine for small kittens, but a determined, injured, or unhappy adult cat can shred one in seconds. Place a washable item that carries your scent, like an old sweatshirt, in the carrier to provide a soft bed and to help calm your cat during the car ride and visit. Check all

latches before you leave home and again before you carry your cat into the clinic.

Once at the clinic, keep your cat in his carrier. No matter how calm a lap cat he is at home, the unfamiliar sounds, smells, and sights of a veterinary hospital can turn him instantly into a yowling, clawing escape artist. This isn't fair to the veterinarian and support staff or to the other clients in the waiting room. Your cat—terrified and disoriented—might escape, either from your car, your arms, or the office, or he might injure you or another client.

First Things First

If you think your cat is in pain, tell your veterinarian immediately. Describe the signs and symptoms you've observed. Cats are notorious for hiding pain and illness, and many cats are especially reluctant to exhibit signs of pain while they're in unfamiliar territory. Your cat may express his pain as hostility or aggressiveness. You know your cat better than your veterinarian ever can. Even with all her training and experience, a veterinarian can miss subtle signs that only someone very familiar with a cat might notice.

Your cat will likely behave differently—perhaps very differently—at the clinic than he does at home. He may feel stressed by the car ride and the unfamiliar smells, sounds, and sights of the clinic, as well as by the discomfort that's brought him there. It's vital to explain to the veterinarian exactly what behaviors and symptoms you've seen in your cat in his everyday life at home.

Has your cat been experiencing seizures, having coughing fits, or exhibiting strange behavior or other symptoms that will probably not show up during his clinic visit? These intermittent symptoms are often valuable clues in diagnosing illness. A video camera may be your best ally—keep one handy at home, if possible. When your cat exhibits the symptoms that concern you, videotape him then and there. Bring the videotape along to show the veterinarian. A brief film can be worth a million words, and can help your veterinarian make a quicker, more accurate diagnosis.

Be ready to tell your veterinarian what your cat's been eating and excreting. The quality, quantity, and contents of your cat's diet have an enormous effect on his overall condition and health. Knowing exactly what he's been excreting, and when, is one more reason to keep your cat indoors and to keep your eye on the litter box—it's full of clues.

Every Clue Is Important

Bring along a list of any medications, supplements, flea-control products, dewormers, ear-mite-control products, or other substances that you've been using on your cat, or that you've used on your cat since his last veterinary checkup—whether prescribed by your veterinarian or another veterinarian or specialist, or obtained over the counter. Better still, pop them all into a paper bag and tote them along. The packaging and labels may contain clues your veterinarian can use to analyze possible interactions. Drugs and other substances can interact in complex ways. Some herbs, supplements, and food ingredients can interfere with or heighten the effects of some medications.

If you've been giving your cat "natural," herbal, homeopathic, or flower-essence remedies, or if your cat's been seeing a chiropractor, acupuncturist, or other alternative health provider, mention this to the veterinarian.

Describe as completely as you can the history of your cat's symptoms. How long ago did they start? What first got your attention? Has the problem gotten worse? Did it come on swiftly or gradually? Was anything unusual going on in your home or life when the symptoms first appeared? Diagnosis of animal illnesses is a lot like detective work. The more complete your cat journal is, the less likely you'll be to miss an important clue your veterinarian needs to make an accurate, timely diagnosis.

Have there been any changes in your life or household that may have stressed your cat? Your veterinarian needs to know. Prolonged stress can weaken your cat's immune system enough to bring on an illness. This is not the time to be shy or to insist on privacy. Your veterinarian is an ethical professional who won't betray your confidences. Any personal questions she asks are aimed at helping your cat—and his health and even life could be at stake.

Don't omit, hide, or fudge facts or time lines out of a misplaced sense of shame or embarrassment. If your cat's been sick for a week, don't say the problem just showed up last night. If he's behind on his vaccinations, say so. The veterinarian needs to know as much as possible to make an accurate diagnosis.

A Second Opinion?

If your veterinarian is unsure about your cat's diagnosis, or you're unsure about the treatment plan she's proposing, or if you still have any qualms about your options, consider getting a second opinion. Your veterinarian likely consults regularly with professional colleagues, either within her own clinic or elsewhere, in analyzing the results of tests, in interpreting X rays, and the like. Sometimes, though, it's worthwhile to take your cat to a different clinic or to a large teaching hospital, where he'll be evaluated by several veterinarians or specialists, or where additional specialized tests or treatments can be performed. Your veterinarian, ideally, will help you find such a facility and give you a referral to necessary specialists.

Practice Makes Perfect

If your veterinarian wants you to give your cat injections or fluids, ask her to demonstrate on your cat or to instruct and assist you in giving your cat the first treatment right there in the office. Performing any unfamiliar procedure first with the veterinarian at your side will give you added confidence when you're ready to medicate your cat at home.

Even administering a pill can be tricky if you're not well practiced at it. If you're going to be giving your cat pills, be sure to ask your veterinarian to show you her pilling secrets before you leave. If you know ahead of time—from past experience—that you'll be unable to give your cat pills, ask if the medication comes in a liquid form. Ask your veterinarian to demonstrate correct administration.

If your cat has rejected all your past attempts to give him either pills or liquids, ask your veterinarian about the possibility of using a compounding pharmacy. These custom pharmacies can incorporate almost any drug or medication in almost any form or flavor, so that you can, for example, mix it in your cat's food. If this isn't appropriate for the medication your cat needs, or if no such service is available locally, or if your cat is a truly difficult patient, your options are more limited. If the medication your cat needs is sufficiently important to his well-being, your veterinarian may want you to bring him back to the clinic to be medicated or even hospitalize him.

Get All the Details

Make sure you know what, if any, follow-up care or additional testing your cat needs. Should you keep him isolated from other pets? Keep him extra quiet for a few days? Keep him warm? Start him on a special diet? Does he have bandages or stitches that require special care or a follow-up visit? Is there a wound you need to keep clean, or an abscess drain you need to tend? Get all the details, preferably in writing, before you leave. If special care or cleaning is necessary, ask the veterinarian, or one of the technicians, to demonstrate the procedure.

Leaving Your Cat

Sometimes you might have to leave your cat at the clinic for a few hours, all day, or even overnight. Be very cautious about doing this, and never do it for mere convenience. When scheduling your cat for minor surgery or another procedure for which he'll have to stay at the clinic for several hours, make your appointment for early morning. That way, you'll likely be able to pick him up at the end of the day, saving both the expense and disruption of an overnight stay.

If you must leave your cat, be sure your veterinarian has complete contact information so she can get in touch with you at any time. Include a backup number or two just in case. Ask a trusted friend to be your backup in case you can't return to pick up your cat when he's ready to go home.

If you plan to leave your cat at the clinic overnight, ask what overnight coverage the clinic offers. Is a trained veterinary technician on duty all night? Does the veterinarian check in periodically? Depending on the care he'll receive, your cat may be better off going home with you overnight and returning to the clinic in the morning for further evaluation or treatment. Depending on the nature of his illness or injury, though, he may be better off spending the night in an emergency animal clinic and returning to his regular veterinarian the next morning.

If you get home and find you're still confused about a medication or a care procedure, or remember a question you forgot to ask, never hesitate to call the veterinarian's office and ask for help. Never just stop giving prescribed medications, even if your cat seems better. Call and ask for advice first.

Money Matters

No caring cat owner wants to put a price tag on his cat. But it's an inescapable fact of life that cat owners must often make difficult trade-offs between doing everything possible for their cats, and caring for their families and meeting other financial obligations. Veterinary care can be unexpectedly expensive, especially in cases of serious injury, emergency, and chronic illness. It's not fair to your cat or your veterinarian to ignore the matter of finances until you receive a whopping bill you can't (or don't want to) pay.

As much as possible, discuss finances, billing, and any financial limitations you have with your veterinarian up front. Will he accept monthly payments? Can you negotiate a discount? This is especially important when you face a veterinary emergency. If your cat is hit by a car, it may cost several hundred dollars in just the first few minutes at the clinic to stabilize him—control pain, place an intravenous catheter, deal with immediate, life-threatening problems such as hemorrhage, respiratory difficulties, and shock, take X rays—and to address his injuries. Further treatment can cost many hundreds of dollars more.

A veterinarian cannot guarantee a particular outcome for such expensive emergency treatment any more than your own doctor can. Unfortunately, many clients feel they needn't pay the resulting bills if their pet doesn't survive. This is unfair and unrealistic. It can be hard to think clearly under the influence of the powerful emotions that arise during an emergency. That's why it's essential to think of money matters ahead of time.

Similar situations, perhaps not as time-critical but every bit as emotional, can arise when your cat is diagnosed with a serious illness that requires expensive, long-term, or specialized treatment. Modern veterinary medicine can offer your cat many of the same advanced diagnostic procedures and treatments humans enjoy: ultrasound, chemotherapy, MRI and cat scans, laser surgery, kidney and other organ transplants, hip replacements, pacemakers, radiation therapy, and more. These procedures can be quite expensive, and some are provided only by specialists or at large teaching hospitals. And, as in emergencies, no particular outcome can be guaranteed.

Planning Ahead

No matter how well you take care of your cat, it's wise and prudent to be ready for anything. Work with your cat's veterinarian. Make sure your veterinarian knows your financial limitations and is aware of how much you're able and willing to pay to maintain your cat's life and health. When your cat is ill or injured, your veterinarian's first priority is to offer him the best veterinary medicine she can. Often, though, there are alternative strategies or less expensive treatments she can propose. It's almost never a stark choice between the best medicine and "economic euthanasia."

One helpful financial strategy is self-insurance. Set aside a sum of money each week or month in a special, untouchable cat-care fund, to be tapped only for veterinary emergencies and serious illness. This requires discipline and planning. Know your own weaknesses. For some cat owners, it's too tempting to dip into this fund to take care of other pressing expenses. Another increasingly popular alternative is feline health insurance.

FELINE HEALTH INSURANCE

In comparison with the health insurance you buy for yourself and your family, feline health insurance is a bargain. But since it's a relatively new concept, many cat owners balk at the idea of paying insurance premiums for their cat. It's not for everyone, but you owe it to your cat to consider it. Health insurance might mean the difference between making a life-or-death decision for your cat from your heart and doing it from your pocketbook.

There are a handful of companies that will insure your cat. Look for one that specializes in pet-health-care insurance. Policies work much like human-health-insurance policies. You pay a monthly or annual premium, and submit claims as you incur veterinary expenses. After fulfilling the deductible, your expenses are reimbursed at the percentages indicated in the policy—perhaps 80 percent for the first few hundred dollars of expenses and 100 percent thereafter. Some policies include "major medical" provisions, with extra coverage for hospitalization and advanced treatments like organ replacements.

Read the Fine Print

Premiums vary, based on such factors as the number of cats you insure and their ages and health histories; the level of coverage you want; and the deductible amount. Read each policy carefully to see what's covered and what's excluded. Some policies have a lifetime maximum limit on coverage; others have annual or "per-incident" limits. Some cover expenses like prescriptions, laboratory fees, dental care, behavior-related problems, conditions related to breeding, and preexisting conditions; some don't. Some pay a fixed amount for particular covered expenses; others reimburse you according to what your veterinarian charges.

Some policies include well-cat coverage, which means they reimburse some or all of your costs for routine health care such as annual veterinary checkups, tests, and vaccinations. Such coverage might cost extra. Buy the coverage that's right for you, your cat, and your situation. Shop around. Costs and coverage levels vary widely. You should be able to obtain a policy that covers from $7,000 to $10,000 in annual expenses for an annual premium of about $100.00 per cat. Be crystal clear on what you're actually buying before you sign on the dotted line.

Before you buy any policy, make sure you'll be able to continue taking your cat to your regular veterinarian. If the plan requires you to switch veterinarians, think hard—is the coverage you'd gain worth giving up the relationship and trust you and your cat share with your veterinarian?

Pet insurance isn't just a fad. Although it's relatively new, one insurer has already issued more than a million policies. Like insurers of human health, pet insurers are subject to both federal and state insurance regulations.

WHAT ABOUT ALTERNATIVE HEALTH CARE?

Alternative health care is a relatively new, rapidly growing, and sometimes controversial area of veterinary medicine. It can be confusing: Does pursuing alternative health care mean giving up your regular veterinarian and the benefits of modern veterinary medicine in favor of herbs, acupuncture, aromatherapy, or homeopathy? Is alternative care safe? Does it work?

Alternative veterinarians take a holistic approach, treating the whole patient, not the disease, and concentrate on prevention and early detection of disease—strategies also used by all veterinarians and responsible cat owners. They also stress proper nutrition—also a concern of every caring cat owner. The list of modalities used in alternative veterinary care is long and varied. A veterinarian who wishes to offer alternative treatment modalities must pursue additional training and study. In 2001, the AVMA (American Veterinary Medical Association) issued its revised "Guidelines for Complementary and Alternative Veterinary Medicine." As the following excerpts show, these guidelines outline an open-minded, sensible, and rational approach to alternative veterinary medicine.

> The AVMA recognizes the interest in and use of these modalities [collectively called "CAVM"] and is open to their consideration.

> The AVMA believes that all veterinary medicine, including CAVM, should be held to the same standards. Claims for safety and effectiveness ultimately should be proven by the scientific method. Circumstances commonly require that veterinarians extrapolate information when formulating a course of therapy. Veterinarians should exercise caution in such circumstances. Practices and philosophies that are ineffective or unsafe should be discarded. . . .

The AVMA does not officially recognize diplomat-status or certificates other than those awarded by veterinary specialty organizations that are members of the AVMA American Board of Veterinary Specialties (ABVS), nor has it evaluated the training or education programs of other entities that provide such certificates. Recognition of a veterinary specialty organization by the AVMA requires demonstration of a substantial body of scientific knowledge. The AVMA encourages CAVM organizations to demonstrate such a body of knowledge. . . .

Diagnosis should be based on sound, accepted practices of veterinary medicine. . . .

Recommendations for effective and safe care should be based on available scientific knowledge and the medical judgment of the veterinarian. . . .

The quality of studies and reports pertaining to CAVM varies; therefore, it is incumbent on a veterinarian to critically evaluate the literature and other sources of information. Veterinarians and organizations providing or promoting CAVM are encouraged to join with the AVMA in advocating sound research necessary to establish proof of safety and efficacy. . . .

Veterinarians should be aware that animal nutritional supplements and botanicals typically are not subject to premarketing evaluation by the FDA for purity, safety or efficacy and may contain active pharmacologic agents or unknown substances. . . .

You might also encounter other alternative treatment modalities such as aromatherapy, magnetic therapy, Reiki, orthomolecular medicine, and traditional Chinese medicine (TCM). Use caution in pursuing these and other nonstandard modalities.

Seek alternative care for your cat only from a licensed veterinarian or from a licensed, certified practitioner your veterinarian recommends. Your regular veterinarian, and any alternative practitioners she recommends, should work together to evaluate and treat your cat.

You can explore alternative or holistic cat care on a small scale, as an adjunct to your cat's traditional veterinary health care. Some cat owners just "dip their toes" into herbs, natural supplements, flower essences, or homeopathic remedies. Cat owners who have seen or read about the benefits of alternative or holistic care and are attracted by them often choose complementary care. They might provide their cat a home-cooked diet, herbal or other natural supplements, and homeopathic remedies to maintain his condition when he's healthy or to treat minor health problems. They turn to more traditional veterinary medicine only in cases of serious injury or life-threatening illness. Some cat owners turn to alternative care when they feel that traditional veterinary medicine has failed their cat.

Is It Safe?

Is alternative care safe? Do your homework. Like some traditional treatments and medications, some "natural" or holistic substances, therapies, and treatments can be dangerous under some circumstances. Chiropractic manipulations, done incorrectly or in the wrong circumstances, can cause injury. Herbal remedies can be toxic if used incorrectly, in the wrong dosages or concentrations, or in the wrong species, or if they're somehow misidentified. There's virtually no federal inspection or regulation of herbal products and nutritional supplements, so buyers must take on faith that the herbs and supplements they buy actually contain what the labels promise.

By placing your faith solely in alternative therapies—some of them unproven—you might deny your cat treatment or surgery he needs. By insisting on so-called natural remedies only, you may deny him pain relief, comfort, or even a cure. Once you've established a relationship of trust with your veterinarian, you can feel confident asking her for recommendations about alternative therapies for your cat or for referrals to qualified practitioners. Never take chances with your cat's health.

CHAPTER 14

Food and Feeding

A QUALITY DIET—"YOU ARE WHAT YOU EAT"

Besides keeping him indoors, the best way to assure your cat's health and longevity is to give him a good diet. It's false economy to skimp on the quality of your cat's food. Offer him the best cat food you can obtain. A few extra pennies for high-quality food will pay huge dividends in the quality of his health and life. Those pennies will save you hundreds of dollars in veterinarian bills.

Meat!

Your cat is an *obligate carnivore*. The primary component of his diet *must* be animal tissue—meat. Virtually everything about your cat, from the structure and function of his body to his biochemical makeup to the behavior blueprint laid down by his evolutionary development, calls for a meat-based diet:

Your cat has a short jaw, designed for gripping and holding prey. He has a relatively small number of teeth, optimized for up-and-down chopping, cutting, and tearing—and incapable of the side-to-side grinding motions typical of herbivores and omnivores.

In the wild, small cats eat about ten small meals in a twenty-four-hour period. This habit of eating frequent but small meals is reflected in the structure of his digestive system.

Your cat's body cannot synthesize certain essential chemicals because he relies on being able to get them from prey. He must obtain these essentials, including the amino acids taurine and arginine, vitamin A, arachidonic acid, and niacin, from his food.

The importance of supplementing cat food with taurine was discovered only recently. A deficiency of this amino acid can lead to retinal degeneration, blindness, and serious heart problems. Adding taurine to cat food has saved the vision and lives of thousands of cats.

Your cat has a high-protein requirement—much higher than that of other mammals. A healthy adult cat's diet should be at least 26 percent protein on a dry-matter basis—that is, excluding the water content of his food. Kittens need even more protein.

Your cat needs a high-fat diet—at least 10 percent on a dry-matter basis—for energy and to transport fat-soluble vitamins throughout his body. (More fat may be even better—cats, unlike humans, can handle large amounts of fat without harm.) Your cat also needs to obtain arachidonic acid, found only in animal fats, from his diet.

The Dangers of Vegetarian Diets for Cats

Many people choose, for ethical or health reasons, to follow a vegetarian or vegan diet. This works for humans, because we're *omnivores*—we can obtain the protein and other nutrients we need through various combinations of nonmeat sources. *But a vegetarian diet cannot work for your cat.*

It's unfair and unrealistic to impose human ethical standards on cats. And forcing a cat to eat a diet that isn't based on meat imperils his health and his life.

Choosing Cat Food

Choosing cat food can be a daunting challenge. Television and magazine advertisements tout dozens of brands, flavors, and varieties. Supermarket pet aisles tempt the shopper with packaging featuring handsome cats and loads of promises. Veterinarians sell special foods for a variety of medical conditions. There are special foods for kittens and seniors, foods that promise to keep your cat's teeth clean, eliminate hair balls, and prevent urinary problems. There are bargain foods, mass-market brand foods, premium brands, and superpremium brands. Health-food stores, mail-order outlets, and the Internet offer still more choices, including "natural," "organic," "raw," and "whole-food" diets. What's best for your cat?

Unless your circumstances or your cat's needs are unusual, you can't go wrong with a readily obtainable, complete, balanced, high-quality food made by a reputable manufacturer, approved in feeding trials by the American Association of Feed Control Officers (AAFCO). Your cat's diet should be appropriate for his health, condition, activity level, and life stage. And—he has to like it!

Life-Stage Feeding

Pound for pound, young kittens (two-to-six months) have twice the energy and nutrient needs as adult cats. Young kittens need to eat at least three meals per day. Until he's a year old, feed your kitten a diet specially formulated for the needs of rapid growth and development. Then, gradually switch him over to an adult maintenance formula. Adolescent cats (six months to one year old) are still growing rapidly and need extra calories and nutrients.

Be alert for any tendency towards overeating. Weigh your cat regularly, using a baby scale to note small changes. If he's putting on too much weight, feed him controlled portions at set mealtimes, rather than leaving food out for him all the time. Obesity can start young and lead to a shortened lifetime of poor health.

Senior cats—ten years old and older—often need easier-to-chew and easier-to-digest foods, and may also have chronic health problems such as diabetes, kidney disease, and weakened immune systems that can be managed through a well-planned diet. Some adult and older cats who've slowed down are prone to gaining excess weight and may benefit from a reduced-calorie or high-fiber diet.

Reading the Labels

If you'd like to know even more about the food you're buying for your cat, learn to interpret the information on the label. Package labels and advertisements for animal foods are regulated by several government agencies, including the FDA (Food and

Drug Administration), the USDA (U.S. Department of Agriculture), and the FTC (Federal Trade Commission). These regulations call for specific information to be listed, in specific forms, on all animal-food packages.

There are several clues to look for on the label of the box, bag, or can of food you're considering buying for your cat. Here are a few important ones:

- *a reputable manufacturer* (Avoid generic and store brands, as well as low-priced discount brands. The few extra cents for a known, quality, or premium-brand food are more than worth it. The label should list a toll-free number, Web site, or other contact information where you can learn more about the company, its quality control, feeding trials, and ingredients.)
- the words *"complete and balanced"*
- food labeled as *appropriate for your cat's life stage*—kitten, adult, senior, or "all life stages"
- food that's been *tested in an AAFCO feeding trial* (The AAFCO evaluates animal foods and runs rigorous feeding tests. If the food has passed an AAFCO feeding test, it can be labeled with the word "feeding" in the life-stage part of the label. This means it's been fed to actual cats in a controlled test.)
- food whose *main dry-weight ingredient is animal protein*—such as chicken, fish, liver, or beef (The ingredients list shows ingredients in order of their relative percentages in the food, according to weight. If the first item on the list isn't real meat, pass that food up.)
- a *dry-weight protein percentage* adequate for your cat's needs (A healthy adult cat needs at least 26 percent protein. Kittens need more.)

Cat-food labels carry all sorts of claims and promises, implied and otherwise. Watch for qualifiers such as "dinner," "entree," and "platter." Using these qualifiers reduces the amount of the main ingredient that must be present in the food. For example "tuna for cats" must be at least 95 percent (dry weight, excluding water) tuna, while "tuna entree" requires only 25 percent (dry weight) tuna.

It's wise to be skeptical about claims on cat-food packages. Foods that purport to be "light" or "natural," or that imply they can treat or cure a particular medical condition, should be taken with a very large grain of salt. Concentrate on determining the composition of nutrients listed in the "Guaranteed Analysis." "Preservative" and "artificial" aren't necessarily dirty words. Preservatives keep foods fresh, and artificial preservatives do this job much better than natural preservatives. Spoiled food may be natural—but it's not good for your cat.

If you have any questions about the ingredients of a particular food, the sources of those ingredients, or the manufacturer's quality or testing standards, contact the manufacturer. Ask your veterinarian to explain anything on the label you don't understand.

"Guaranteed Analysis" and Dry Weight

Commercial cat-food labels include, by law, a "Guaranteed Analysis" that lists the percentage of such nutrients as crude protein, crude fiber, and crude fat. But the percentages you'll see there are shown "as is"—including the water in the product (listed in the Guaranteed Analysis as "moisture"). Canned food contains 60 to 78 percent water; dry food is 6-to-10 percent water.

To figure out the percentage of protein (or other nutrient) in the food, you must determine its dry weight. Here's a simple formula:

1. Let's say that in a can of cat food there's 78 percent moisture, the maximum allowable amount for cat food. Subtract this moisture value from 100 to derive the dry weight of everything else: 22.
2. Look at protein. Let's say protein is listed in the Guaranteed Analysis as 8.5 percent.
3. Multiply 8.5 percent times 100, and divide the result by 22.
4. The result is 38.6 percent—nicely within the range of protein your cat needs.

Do the same calculation for crude fat, crude fiber, and other nutrients.

"Complete and Balanced"

"Complete" means that all nutrients cats require are present in the food. "Balanced" means that these nutrients are present in the food in sufficient quantity relative to the energy content of the food, so that when your cat eats, he gets the required amount of all the nutrients he needs. A "complete and balanced" diet for your cat is high in animal protein and fat, low in carbohydrates, and contains a carefully balanced mix of specific vitamins and minerals. "High protein" doesn't mean all meat, though. In the wild, your cat would eat small rodents and the occasional bird—bones, internal organs, stomach contents, and all. He'd get calcium from the bones and a variety of vital nutrients from the viscera, stomach contents, skin, and even the hair.

Things to Avoid

- In canned food, avoid added preservatives. The canning process preserves the food, so additional preservatives aren't needed. Dry food (kibble) usually requires preservatives. There's no advantage to "natural" over synthetic preservatives such as BHA and BHT.
- In "semi-moist" cat foods, the unusually large amounts of preservatives added to maintain the soft texture can cause allergic and other negative reactions in sensitive cats. Instead, serve a high-quality dry food moistened with warm water or the liquid from tuna-flavored cat food.
- Avoid an all-tuna diet. Your cat probably adores tuna. But an all-tuna diet is very high in polyunsaturated fatty acids, which tend to deplete your cat's supply of vitamin E. Serve tuna cat foods in moderation.

Veterinarian-Prescribed Diets

If your cat has a chronic health condition such as kidney disease or diabetes, or is seriously overweight, your veterinarian may prescribe a special medical diet. Think of these foods as medications. Purchase the exact food your veterinarian prescribes and follow her directions for portion sizes and other details as precisely as you can. These foods are available only from veterinarians, and are generally more expensive than commercial cat foods. But they can greatly increase your cat's quality of life and even lengthen his life considerably.

"Natural," "Organic," and "Raw" Cat Foods

Perhaps no cat-food topic is as confusing and contentious as that of "natural" foods. Many advertisements and anecdotes that promote these products follow the general theory that virtually all mass-market and even premium cat foods are unsafe, unhealthy, or unsuitable for cats. Some foster fear and guilt in cat owners. Many natural and organic products are significantly more expensive than even premium mass-market cat foods, and many are not easily available.

Avoid "raw" diets. Raw meat, especially ground meat, carries a high risk of possibly fatal bacterial contamination. Before deciding on any natural or organic diet for your cat, do your own research—and not just in natural-foods publications. Ask your veterinarian what she thinks. Study the labels. Ask lots of questions. You may decide that you'd prefer organically raised meats, all-natural preservatives, or even "human-grade" food ingredients for your cat. Make sure whatever food you choose is complete, balanced, and nutritionally adequate for your cat's life stage, activity level, health, and lifestyle.

Homemade Diets—Are They Better?

Offering your cat a completely homemade diet has the advantage that you know exactly what he's eating and where it came from. Many cat owners who serve a homemade diet use fresh, organically raised meats and other ingredients. Your veterinarian can advise you about where to find recipes for balanced homemade diets. Nevertheless, many veterinarians discourage their clients from serving their cats homemade diets—and with good reason.

Cats have complicated, specialized nutritional needs, some of which are incompletely understood. It's very difficult, time-consuming, inconvenient, and possibly expensive to design, create, and sustain a nutritionally adequate homemade diet for your cat. Unless you're extremely diligent and thorough in your research, and careful and consistent in the purchase, storage, and preparation of ingredients, you run the risk of harming your cat's health by providing too much or too little of essential nutrients.

If you decide on a homemade diet, have your veterinarian and a qualified animal nutritionist review your diet plan before you start and periodically throughout your cat's life.

Preferences

When it comes to food preferences, your cat pays attention to smell, taste, and texture, all influenced by the temperature of his food. Your cat prefers food that's close to his body temperature (around 101.4 degrees F), or near the temperature of freshly killed prey (around 95 degrees F). That's why he turns up his nose at cold food right from the refrigerator—it just doesn't smell tasty.

Your cat's taste buds are geared to respond to his natural diet—meat. Because of the sensors on his tongue, he's most aware of salty, sour, and bitter-tasting foods. But because he can't detect simple sugars, he's unlikely to develop a sweet tooth like many dogs do. Texture is an individual preference. Some cats prefer crunchy foods, some mushy. For variety, and to prevent finickiness, offer your cat some of each.

Good-quality commercial cat diets are available in both dry kibble and moist canned forms. They are nutritionally equal. Which you serve your cat depends on his personal preference and your lifestyle and schedule. A cat who prefers dry food requires more supplemental water, so make sure he always has plenty available. Dry food offers convenience; it can be left out all day so that your cat can nibble at will. Some cats do well with this. But since modern dry cat foods are designed to be highly palatable, some cats eat too much and risk becoming obese.

Despite claims, a dry-food diet will not automatically solve dental-health problems. It may help, especially if you serve your cat one of the dry foods specifically formulated to scrape tartar from his teeth. But you'll still have to wield the toothbrush regularly.

Set Mealtimes Versus ad Libitum Feeding

Some cats enjoy eating most of their food at set mealtimes; others are natural "grazers," returning to snack on small amounts ad libitum, or at will, throughout the day. Either way is fine.

Serve mealtime cats two meals a day, morning and evening. Kittens under six months old should have three-to-five small meals throughout the day. Canned food is more practical for mealtime cats than for the ad libitum crowd. Unless your cat tends to overeat, you can leave out a small bowl of dry kibble for snacking.

Ad libitum eaters generally prefer the always-fresh dry kibble. Wash all food bowls frequently in hot water and rinse thoroughly. Never just dump more kibble into a half-full or empty (but dirty) bowl.

If your ad libitum cat is packing on the pounds too rapidly, gradually switch him to set mealtimes with controlled-portion feeding. If that's impractical, switch him to a light food or one specifically formulated for less active cats, or measure out the amount of kibble you place in his bowl each day—and don't refill it every time it's empty. Ask your veterinarian how much dry food your cat should be consuming per day, and measure out that much and no more! At the same time, increase the amount of exercise he's getting with plenty of vigorous, interactive play.

Supplements

Supplementing your cat's complete, balanced, and nutritionally adequate diet with additional vitamins, minerals, or other additives is not only unnecessary—it may be harmful. Never give your cat supplements without consulting first with your veterinarian.

Treats, Snacks, and People Food

Cats love treats! But be sensible. Dispense treats sparingly, one at a time. For added fun and exercise, train your cat to jump for his treats. Many cats learn very quickly to leap and catch the flying morsels in midair.

Make sure your cat *never* samples the following:

- onions, onion powder, or any food containing these
- alcoholic beverages—a big no-no—not even a sip!
- salt
- macadamia nuts
- leaves and stems of potatoes and tomatoes (nightshade family)
- coffee, tea, coffee beans, and coffee grounds (Caffeine is very bad for your cat.)
- chocolate
- hops (ingredient in beer)

Some cat owners feed their cats exclusively human-grade tuna in the mistaken belief that it's healthier than tuna-flavored cat food. A diet made up exclusively or largely of human-grade tuna is not only highly unbalanced for feline needs, it can also deplete your cat's supply of essential vitamin E and even lead to *steatitis,* or yellow-fat disease. You and your cat have very different nutritional requirements. A diet consisting entirely of human foods is not a complete or balanced diet for him.

Finicky? ME?

Finicky eaters are made, not born. Sticking to just one favorite flavor and texture all the time isn't wise. Your cat might get tired of it or go on a hunger strike—a dangerous strategy for a cat. He may develop an intolerance for, or food allergy to, an ingredient in his favorite food. If he's totally set on that one food, it'll be difficult for him to switch to one that agrees with him. And it'll likely be more difficult for him to switch if he needs to eat a specific diet for medical reasons.

Experiment with different brands, textures, and flavors. Within the bounds of what he likes, serve him a variety of foods. Varying his diet will keep mealtime interesting and insure that he's getting a good overall balance of nutrients. Your cat's nutritional needs will vary over his lifetime, based on his individual makeup, age, activity level, lifestyle, and health. Getting him accustomed to eating a variety of flavors and foods will keep him from becoming too fussy and set in his ways.

In stressful times, or when he's not feeling well, comfort and pamper your cat with his top favorites. If he needs to be hospitalized or stay in a boarding facility, ask if you can provide a supply of his favorite food to use during his stay. It will greatly help to ease the stress of an unfamiliar environment by evoking tasty memories of home.

Switching Foods

Like other changes in your cat's life, switching foods should be a slow, gradual process. Take at least a week. An overnight switch can not only cause an upset tummy, vomiting, or diarrhea, it might also send your cat on a potentially dangerous hunger strike. Always—but especially when switching foods—make mealtime a relaxed, pleasant occasion, free of stress, distractions, and competitive pressure. Maintain a positive, confident attitude.

Start by mixing a tiny amount of the new food into your cat's regular chow. Each day, add a bit more. If he's going from canned food to dry, moisten the kibble with a little warm water at first.

Don't switch foods without a reason or just because you think your cat must be getting bored with his current staple. Rotating among a small variety of foods he likes will keep his interest up, as well as prevent excessive fussiness. And don't play amateur nutritionist on the basis of a few articles or anecdotes. Never switch your cat's diet for health reasons without first consulting your veterinarian.

Water

Cats who eat mostly canned food require less supplemental water because their diet already contains a large percentage of moisture. But whether you and your cat choose canned or dry food, he needs plenty of fresh water available at all times. A ten-pound cat needs about ten ounces of water per day. If he eats canned food, he may get some or even most of the water he needs from his food, depending on his preferences and the brand of food he eats.

Every day, empty your cat's water bowl, rinse it with hot water, and wipe it completely. If you wash the bowl, rinse it especially thoroughly, as some soap or detergent residue may remain, offending your cat's extremely sensitive senses of taste and smell and keeping him from drinking the water he needs. If you have more than one cat, provide multiple water bowls.

Some cats prefer cold water. If your cat doesn't seem to be drinking much, try adding a handful of ice cubes to the bowl. This is especially welcome during hot weather. Some cats prefer running water. Many cat-supply stores and catalogs carry electric "cat fountains" with recirculating pumps so that your cat can enjoy running water whenever he wants. Clean your cat's fountain every few days to keep the water fresh, sparkling, and healthy.

"My Cat Won't Eat!"

Every cat skips an occasional meal or eats less during hot weather. But if your cat starts consistently turning up his nose at food, or just taking a few bites and wandering off for more than two meals in a row, you have cause for concern. If your cat has a cold or a stuffy nose and can't smell his food, he's likely to lose interest in eating, at least temporarily.

There are also several other medical conditions that can cause your cat to stop eating or to cut back his intake. These include mouth and tooth pain, broken teeth, cavities, tongue ulcers, and sinus problems, as well as more serious conditions like cancer and feline leukemia. Loss of appetite can also be caused by stress, changes, or disruptions in his home, grief, separation anxiety, a too rapid switch of food, or a switch to a food he doesn't like.

Always take any loss of appetite in your cat seriously and monitor it vigilantly. It can be dangerous for your cat to stop eating or to rapidly and drastically cut down on the quantity of food he consumes. If your cat stops eating for as little as three meals, or cuts back severely on his consumption, see your veterinarian at once. Cats can become weak and dehydrated quickly. A fast of just a few days can bring on a serious condition called *hepatic lipidosis* (fatty liver disease), a dangerous accumulation of fat in the liver. Older and overweight cats are particularly susceptible to this often-fatal disease.

FOOD AND FEEDING

FELINE OBESITY

Cat nutritionists, researchers, and clinical veterinarians agree: obesity is the most common nutrition-related disease in cats. Between 25 and 50 percent of U.S. cats are overweight (defined as 10 percent over ideal body weight), and another 5-to-15 percent are obese (20 percent over optimal weight). For cats, as for humans, excess weight brings increased risk of disease; lessens the quality and enjoyment of life; affects mood, hygiene, and emotional health; and can even seriously shorten life span.

Overweight cats are more prone to health problems, suffering an increased prevalence of arthritis, bone and joint disorders, respiratory difficulties, asthma, heart disease, hypertension, pancreatitis, diabetes, urinary-tract disease, stroke, liver disease, constipation, chronic matting, and skin disorders. Overweight and obese cats run a much higher risk of dying in middle age than their slim counterparts.

Heavy cats are prone to sprains, pulled muscles, and other injuries caused by falls

Cat nutritionists, researchers, and clinical veterinarians agree: obesity is the most common nutritionally related disease in cats.
(FRANTZ DANTZLER)

or jumps. As fat cats have increasing trouble reaching all areas of their bodies to self-groom, their hygiene and coat condition deteriorate. Naturally fastidious, cats can become depressed and even ill when they're unable to keep themselves clean.

Overweight cats are at increased risk for complications from anesthesia and take longer to recover from illness, injury, and surgery. Immune function can be impaired. Reduced energy levels, breathing difficulties, and extra strain on joints continue the vicious downward spiral.

Like us, cats get fat when they consume more than they burn off. But there's also a strong psychological component. Cat experts attribute excessive weight gain in many indoor cats to stress, nervous eating, and lack of mental and physical stimulation. Lacking sufficient attention, interaction, and interactive play, as well as adequate exercise, they're bored, frustrated, and depressed. Food becomes the only real pleasure in their lives.

A few medical conditions, such as thyroid- and pituitary-gland dysfunction and diabetes, can cause cats to gain extra weight. But constant access to highly palatable food, combined with too little exercise, is the most common reason. Many owners of overweight cats blame spaying or neutering, and estrogen and testosterone do seem to lower food intake. But sterilized cats may eat more than they need because their owners don't make allowances for their reduced caloric requirements.

Don't overfeed your kitten, even when he's growing fastest, as overfeeding can increase the number of permanent fat cells he develops. Weight problems can start to show up in cats as young as one or two years old, as the high energy needs of kittenhood diminish. In this age group, 25-to-30 percent of all cats are already showing signs of being overweight, and this percentage holds steady for cats up to ages eleven or twelve.

In multiple-cat households, competition at the food bowls may result in one dominant cat becoming overweight because he takes more than his share of the food to establish and maintain his place at the top of the pecking order. And if, as your cat's energy requirements decline in middle age, his food consumption remains unchanged—he's going to put on an extra pound or two. For a ten-pound cat, that extra weight is the equivalent of twenty-five extra pounds for a human.

An overweight cat's ribs have a moderate covering of fat and are difficult to feel. You'll see thickening at the tail base and lack of a "waistline" (abdominal tuck). In an obese cat, you'll feel prominent layers of fat over his ribs and tail base. Look down at your standing cat. An overweight cat has a slightly widened back; an obese cat's back is markedly broadened. From the side, the overweight cat has no waistline, while the obese cat has a drooping abdomen with a grossly thickened fat pad.

Veterinarians find that many cat owners are in denial about feline obesity. It's vital to be realistic and honest about your cat's weight. His health, happiness, and even his life could depend on it.

Slimming Down

A successful slimming program for your fat cat requires time, dedication, and commitment from everyone in your household. Before beginning a diet-and-exercise program for your cat, a complete medical checkup is essential to rule out underlying contributory medical conditions. You and your veterinarian will set a weight-loss goal for your cat and craft an effective strategy. Your veterinarian needs an accurate estimate of your cat's current intake: not just meals, but also treats, table scraps, any other food sources, and those little extras. Once your cat has started his weight-loss regime, your veterinarian will track his progress, periodically reevaluating portion size, brand of diet food, and other factors.

Never put your cat on a crash diet, It might kill him. Overweight cats who reduce food intake too swiftly are at imminent risk of developing hepatic lipidosis. Take it slow. The maximum safe weight-loss rate for your cat is 1 percent of his total body weight per week. In a twenty-pound cat, that's just 3.2 ounces per week. Get an infant scale to accurately track progress.

If your cat is only mildly overweight, serving slightly smaller portions of his usual food, cutting out treats, and increasing his daily exercise may do the trick. If your cat is seriously overweight or obese, your veterinarian will likely recommend a prescription diet food. Most diet foods for cats are reduced-calorie, reduced-fat, high-fiber formulations. Think of these prescribed foods as medicines. Follow your veterinarian's recommendations for portion sizes and feeding schedule to the letter. Don't give your dieting cat supplements, vitamins, or other additives without your veterinarian's approval.

Introduce the diet food gradually, mixing it a little at a time with your cat's old food. Your goal is slow, controlled, gradual, safe weight loss. If your cat completely refuses the diet food, try switching to another brand, with your veterinarian's approval. Never let your cat starve. It's best to go cold turkey on treats and table scraps. Substitute extra attention or a play session. If you must give treats, use a few morsels from his daily measured allocation of diet food, and always place them in his food bowl. Weigh your cat weekly, using a baby scale to accurately track small changes.

Make sure your cat supplements his diet program with daily exercise. If he's been a couch potato, start slowly and avoid overexertion. Even a rollover or two is a triumph for a very sedentary cat. Offer praise and encouragement at every step. Over time, work your way up to one or two interactive-play sessions every day. See chapter 7 for tips on making your play sessions fun and rewarding.

Once your cat has reached his optimal weight, he'll be a healthier, happier, more playful, and more active companion.

CHAPTER 15

Eye on Health: Observation and Action

EDUCATE YOURSELF: YOUR AT-HOME CAT-CARE LIBRARY

To help you understand your cat and give him the best care possible, it's wise to keep a few dependable reference books right at home. You've already made a good start by buying this book. Always ask your veterinarian to clarify any confusion about information you glean from reference books.

Here are a few indispensable volumes for cat owners:

- Johnson-Bennett, Pam. *Think like a Cat: How to Raise a Well-Adjusted Cat—Not a Sour Puss.* (Penguin U.S.A., 2000, paperback, 413 pages, ISBN: 0140288546). A loving, practical approach to cat behavior, encouraging owners to see things from the cat's point of view.
- Mammato, Bobbie, D.V.M., M.P.H. (in conjunction with The Humane Society of the United States and the American Red Cross). *Pet First Aid: Dogs and Cats* (Mosby

Books, 1997, paperback, 109 pages, ISBN: 1 57857 000 X). Lots of clear diagrams and sketches supplement first-aid procedures.

- Milani, Myrna, D.V.M. *The Body Language and Emotions of Cats* (Quill/William Morrow, N.Y. 1987, reissued 1993, paperback, ISBN: 0688128408). Dr. Milani helps you to understand your cat's nature and explains how to understand and solve behavior problems by decoding what your cat is trying to communicate.
- Shojai, Amy D. *The Purina Encyclopedia of the Cat* (Ballantine Books, 1998, hardcover, 480 pages, ISBN: 0345412877). A reliable, easy-to-use, A to Z general cat-care and health reference.
- Siegal, Mordecai, and James Richards (editors) and the Faculty and Staff of Cornell Feline Health Center, Cornell University. *The Cornell Book of Cats, 2nd Edition* (Villard Books, New York, N.Y. 1997, hardcover, 508 pages, ISBN: 0679449531). A clear, comprehensive feline medical reference.

THE IMPORTANCE OF EVERYDAY OBSERVATION

As self-reliant hunters, cats are reluctant to show outward signs when they're feeling ill. As your cat's owner and best friend, it's your job to observe your cat's day-to-day behavior and condition—and to catch any early signs that may indicate illness. By observing what's normal for your cat, and by noticing any changes in his normal behavior patterns, you'll head off many health problems while they're still minor and easily treatable. Here's what you need:

- written records—your cat journal
- insight and intuition
- daily, mindful observation and alertness to changes

Your Cat Journal

Amid the daily pressures of busy lives, details of our cats' activities and routines can fall through the cracks and be forgotten. Take a few moments to start a cat journal. Use a three-ring binder or notebook with pockets so you can insert medical records, photos, and other materials. Keep your journal out and handy, so you'll be more likely to keep it up-to-date.

Your cat journal is a valuable source of information for your veterinarian when you take your cat for his annual checkup and for your pet-sitter when you go on vacation. If your cat gets hurt or becomes ill, you'll have everything you need to immediately tell a veterinarian what he needs to know to effectively treat your cat. Your cat journal should include the following:

- your cat's **name and nicknames** (Include pedigree chart, if your cat is pedigreed.)
- your cat's **weight,** recorded weekly (Your cat's **weight history** is valuable for diagnosing health problems, preventing obesity, and catching early indications of illness.)
- medical records (Keep all records of **veterinary visits** and **treatments.**)
- list of **medications** your cat has taken or is taking
- complete **vaccination** history
- any known **allergies** to foods, medications, plastic, or other materials
- **food preferences,** including normal feeding schedule, preferred brand and flavors of food, and any dietary supplements
- **behavior** notes—quirks, such as hiding when visitors arrive, fear of thunder, fear of dogs, dislike of men, etc.
- **vocalization** notes (Is he very quiet? Chatty?)
- play preferences—favorite **toys, games**
- recent **photographs** (Include closeups that show distinctive markings. Photos are essential for making lost-cat posters and for leaving with area shelters and veterinary clinics that may find your lost cat.)

The Role of Intuition—Better Safe than Sorry!

Never hesitate to report abnormalities or changes to your veterinarian, even if they seem minor. Many a feline life has been saved by an alert owner who had a feeling that something was not quite right. Cats are intensely private, honed by evolution to conceal illness and weakness. Since they are creatures of habit, any change in their daily routine, input, or output is cause for heightened observation and discreet concern. Never be embarrassed to take your cat to the veterinarian for fear there may be nothing wrong, or that your veterinarian will think you're being foolish or overprotective. (If your veterinarian *does* think this, shop around for a new veterinarian.)

What's Normal for Your Cat?

Stay aware of the patterns and trends in your cat's life, and be alert to any changes, however minor. Some changes will be transient, but any change that gets worse or persists for more than a few days is cause for concern—and possibly for a trip to the veterinarian.

Changes in appetite and eating patterns are especially significant. Any change that persists for more than two meals requires increased vigilance.

Review the list of feline emergencies in chapter 17. Never ignore these symptoms. Ill or injured cats can decline and die with heartbreaking rapidity.

Be alert for sudden changes in your cat's appearance, even very subtle changes such as swelling and posture or body language that may indicate pain. Watch for changes in his usual vocalizations, daily routines, sleeping location, or level of sociability. Ill or injured cats often withdraw from social contact, hiding out in a closet or basement. Be alert for stiffness, limping, or favoring of a limb (which may indicate an injury or abscess); breathing troubles or persistent coughing; excessive thirst or urination (possible signs of poisoning or kidney problems); and difficulty in swallowing or eating. If you notice any of these, call your veterinarian right away.

Be a Litter-Box Detective

There are many reasons for keeping your cat's litter-box setup simple and the box in an easily accessible, visible location. One of the best is so that you can easily and quickly spot the health messages your cat leaves there. It's often in the litter box that the first signs of illness appear. Once familiar with your cat's normal daily output patterns, you'll be more likely to instantly notice changes:

1. *more, or less, urine output than normal* (If you use clumping litter, notice the size of the clumps. Much-larger-than-usual clumps, or several tiny ones, could indicate illness. In male cats, urinary blockages—often mistaken for constipation—can prove quickly fatal. If your cat strains in the box but produces no urine, or just tiny drops, it's an emergency.)
2. *blood in urine or feces* (This symptom calls for an immediate trip to the veterinarian.)
3. *"worm" (internal parasite) segments in feces* (These can look like tiny grains of rice, or strands of long thin spaghetti. Tapeworm segments may still be wiggling. Place a fresh sample in a sealed plastic bag and take it to

your veterinarian for testing. Don't give your cat a generic or over-the-counter worm medication. Different parasites, and your cat's age and medical history, call for different medications.)

4. *shape, size, color, appearance, and amount of feces* (Thin, pencil-width feces can indicate a partial blockage. An unusually large amount of hair in feces may mean your cat is grooming himself excessively due to stress, pain, or itching.)

5. *empty box—a very bad sign!* (A cat who appears to be eating, but is producing no urine or feces, is ill. He may be constipated or have a urinary or bowel blockage. He needs immediate veterinary attention.

   (If your cat is eating and acting normally, but nothing is appearing in his litter box, take a flashlight tour of your house, looking in corners, closets, and other out-of-the-way spots—especially in places where he's made unauthorized deposits before. If you find any, you need to determine, quickly, whether the cause is medical or behavioral. An ill or unhappy cat may avoid his litter box because he associates it with pain or stress.)

6. *diarrhea* (Unless it's very transient—gone in twenty-four hours—diarrhea requires at least a call to the veterinarian. Has your cat eaten something unusual? Have you changed brands of cat food? Milk gives many cats diarrhea. Whatever you do, don't punish your cat if he doesn't make it to the litter box in time. The last thing you want to do is to make your cat associate the litter box with pain, or distress, or your own unhappiness.)

7. *unusual odors* (Has your cat eaten something unusual? Is he also scooting on the carpet? If so, his anal glands may be partially impacted, accounting for both his distress and the foul odor. Schedule a visit to the veterinarian if the situation doesn't resolve by itself within a day or so. Some cats have conditions that require their anal glands to be manually emptied. Some intrepid cat owners learn to do this at home, but most prefer to leave this task to a professional.)

If more than one cat is sharing the litter box, any of the above signs calls for enhanced vigilance for any other symptoms in any of the cats. Observe the box shortly after mealtime (when most cats make their deposits) to perhaps discover which cat is leaving the health messages. If you've already noticed a particular cat showing other signs of illness, isolate him—with his own litter box, cleaned first—for further observation.

EARLY WARNINGS—
YOUR CAT'S WEEKLY NOSE-TO-TOES CHECKUP

Watching your cat play and move about your home will reveal much about his condition and health. Do an informal physical examination of your cat at least weekly—without him suspecting a thing! Disguised as a pleasurable grooming, petting, and massage session, a casual, comprehensive nose-to-toes once-over will reveal bumps, lumps, tender or painful spots, weight gain or loss, and external parasites.

Head First

Start at his nose. Any discharge, sniffing, or frequent sneezing? (An occasional sneeze is normal—just like in humans.) Is his breathing ragged, congested, wheezy, or noisy? If so, he may have an upper-respiratory infection—reason for a trip to the veterinarian.

Take a good look at his eyes. They should be clear, with no cloudiness, bulging, redness, or inflammation. Can you see more than the tiniest silver of the "third eyelid" (the white fold of skin that stretches from the lower eyelid to the inner corner of your cat's eye)? Clear visibility of this third eyelid (also called the nictitating membrane) in a fully awake cat is cause for concern, as it often signals illness.

As you play with your cat, be alert for signs of visual problems. Test "visual pursuit" by swinging or tossing a toy across his field of vision. His eyes should track the object rapidly and accurately. If your cat starts bumping into things or missing his jump targets consistently, take him to the veterinarian for an eye checkup. With their multiply redundant sensory systems, cats adapt extremely well to reduced vision and even total blindness. In fact, they adapt so well that owners are sometimes unaware of their cat's visual handicap. A cat who's blind, or who has reduced vision, is at a much higher risk from a variety of dangers. It's imperative that the cat's owner be aware of his condition—and of the need to keep him strictly indoors and to avoid unnecessary changes to his environment.

Sniff your cat's ears. If you smell a sour, rank, or yeasty odor, he may have an ear infection—reason for a trip to the veterinarian. Now, peer into those ears. It helps to gently maneuver him under a reading lamp, or to use a flashlight, so you can get a good look. Any sign of crusty, brownish, or blackish discharge? Do the ear canals look irritated or red? Are there claw marks or scratches? Have you noticed him scratching or digging vigorously at his ears, or shaking his head repeatedly in distress? If so, he may be afflicted with ear mites. And if he has ear mites, he's suffering! Get him to the veterinarian without delay.

Check your cat's mouth and teeth. If you've started brushing his teeth (a great idea—see below for tips) and have accustomed him to having his mouth and teeth touched, this part of the checkup will be easier. Look for red or swollen patches on his gums; swellings in the throat, cheeks, face, or mouth or on the tongue; or broken or cracked teeth. Look for loose or missing teeth. It's never normal for a cat to lose adult teeth. Painful *odontoclastic resorptive lesions,* also called *neck or cervical-line lesions,* can cause teeth to break off at the gum line.

Check for large buildups of calculus or tartar on his teeth. Tartar is a hard, brownish-yellow deposit, formed from mineralized plaque that collects around the baselines of the teeth, especially the rear teeth, when they're not cleaned regularly. This can lead to painful infections and other health problems.

Sniff your cat's breath. Minor tuna breath is normal, but persistent or strong mouth odor is cause for concern. Bad breath can indicate gingivitis or periodontal disease, cancer, or a mouth tumor. An ammonia odor can indicate kidney failure.

Whole Body Once-Over

Run your hands gently all over your cat's body, from his head to the tip of his tail. Be alert to his reactions: does he flinch, vocalize, cry, or otherwise react with displeasure to being touched? Are there particular sore spots? Do you feel any lumps, bumps, or swellings? If so, have your veterinarian take a look.

Look at your cat from above. Can you see his "waistline"? No? He may be overweight. Carrying excess weight is a threat to your cat's health and can significantly shorten his life. It can also diminish his happiness and daily satisfaction. Overweight cats are often unable to groom themselves properly, and their girth and poor condition make them reluctant or unable to engage in health-preserving, vigorous play. See chapter 14 for tips on safely slimming down your pudgy cat.

Run your hands along your cat's underside, paying special attention to his belly area. Does he show any signs of pain or reluctance to be touched there? Does his abdomen seem puffy or distended? Are there scaly patches, lumps, or bumps, especially near his nipples? Are patches of fur missing? Cats with abdominal pain often tear out tufts of fur from their bellies, sometimes stripping their undersides bald. If you notice any of these signs, immediate veterinary attention is a must.

Weigh your cat every week. Use a baby scale to detect small changes. A loss or gain

EYE ON HEALTH: OBSERVATION AND ACTION

of a half-pound or more is cause for concern, especially if it's rapid. Older cats, in particular, can sicken extremely quickly. Rapid weight loss is often the first sign of serious underlying illness. Never ignore it, no matter what your cat's age.

His Crowning Glory

The condition of your cat's coat reflects his diet, health, and mental state. If he's ill or depressed, his coat and grooming will suffer. If he's eating poorly, or eating low-quality food, his coat will reflect this—with dryness, scaliness, excessive shedding, and missing fur. Illness often shows up as poor coat condition before any other symptoms appear. Checking your cat's hair coat frequently gives you lots of clues to his health and well-being.

Grooming is a basic feline instinct. Depressed or ill cats often stop grooming themselves, a danger sign that calls for a complete checkup by your veterinarian.

If your cat has been neglecting to groom his nether regions, it may be because he's overweight and can't reach that far anymore. Review chapter 14 and consult your veterinarian for a safe weight-reduction plan. In the meantime, help your cat with his grooming, using a warm washrag and a gentle touch. Trim his "bloomers" until he gets back into shape and can care for them himself.

Look for signs of external parasites, especially fleas. Comb your cat's fur with a fine-toothed comb, especially over the spine and lower back. Shake the comb on a damp white paper towel. If you see tiny bits of "black pepper" that stain the paper towel pink, your cat has fleas. Those bits of pepper are flea droppings, and they're full of your cat's blood. Happily, there is now a range of modern flea-control products and strategies that are much easier and safer than the weapons of the past. Ask your veterinarian for advice on the best parasite-control products for your cat.

If your cat goes outdoors at all—even if only on a harness and leash or into an outdoor enclosure—he may be exposed to fleas, ticks, and other parasites and insect pests. Ruffle his fur to check his skin for insect bites, ticks, and fleas. And don't forget—indoors-only cats can get fleas, too!

Has your cat been pawing, scratching, or digging at his skin, or pulling out tufts of fur with his teeth? Does he have itchy, scabby raised patches? He may have not only fleas but an allergy to flea bites—*flea allergy dermatitis*, also called *miliary dermatitis*. Get him to the veterinarian. Don't let him suffer.

Does your cat have scaly, reddish patches of missing fur, especially around his face and ears? He may have ringworm, a fungal infection communicable to other cats—

and to humans. Look for scaly patches on his paws and a general moth-eaten appearance to his fur. The earlier you notice this condition, the quicker it can be cleared up and the less the chance for your cat to infect you and everyone else in the household.

GENERAL CONDITION

As you play with your cat every day, observe his gait, movements, posture, and energy level, especially as he starts getting on in years. Does he seem stiffer than usual, especially in his spine or neck? Is he favoring a leg? Does he exhibit pain or limited movement ability? Does he hesitate to make those death-defying leaps he used to make so easily? Is his balance off? Does he seem lethargic or uninterested in life? Does he tire extremely easily, wheeze after just a few jumps, lose interest quickly in once-savored games? Any of these symptoms and changes could be signs of illness, especially in a kitten or young cat.

EVERYDAY CARE

Regular Dental Care

Many health problems can start in your cat's mouth. Mouth infections can migrate to vital organs such as the heart and liver, possibly causing life-threatening complications. Regular toothbrushing can prevent many such potentially serious problems. If you've just adopted a kitten, or if your cat is still a youngster, get him accustomed to regular, at-home dental care. But even middle-aged and elderly cats can learn to sit through regular cleaning—with time, practice, patience, and a positive attitude.

If your cat turns out to be one of those "absolutely not!" types, consult your veterinarian on the best approach to take with your cat, perhaps feeding him one of the many dental diets available. But no matter what your cat's opinion of the matter, never ignore this vital, health-preserving care for your cat.

Start by frequently touching your cat's face, mouth, and gums, to get him used to the idea of your hands near those sensitive locations. Once he's comfortable with this, graduate to a cotton-tipped swab, dipped into any oral antiseptic especially prepared for animals, or a liquid tooth-cleaning formula or toothpaste made especially for cats. To start with, you can even use plain water or the juice from a can of tuna. Never use toothpaste or mouthwash made for humans; these products can irritate and burn your cat's mouth and stomach, or make him very sick.

Another option is rubbing your cat's teeth and gums with a gauze pad moistened with dental paste or liquid made especially for cats. Use a specially made medicated pad (available from cat-supply stores and catalogs), or wrap a piece of sterile gauze around your finger and dip it in a cat-safe toothpaste or cleaner. Ask your veterinarian to demonstrate the proper way to brush your cat's teeth.

Your Cat's Claws—Is This Clip Really Necessary?

Yes! Claws that aren't clipped regularly may inadvertently harm you, your cat, and your belongings. Many a cat has panicked when his claw caught on the scratching-post or carpet. Learning to safely and properly trim your cat's claws isn't difficult. At the very least, regularly check your cat's claws, and clip them if they grow too long.

Nail Clipping 101

Learning to safely and properly trim your cat's claws isn't difficult.
(FRANTZ DANTZLER)

As with toothbrushing, start slowly. Handle your cat's paws frequently and lovingly, to get him used to the idea. Gradually work into pressing lightly to pop out the claws. Do this several times a day, until your cat is totally comfortable with the idea.

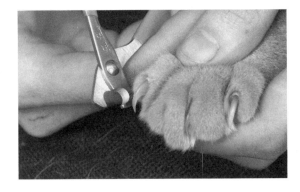

You'll need good-quality, well-sharpened clippers designed especially for cats. If you get dog clippers, get small ones. There are two basic styles: a two-bladed style that operates like a pair of scissors, and the so-called guillotine style. Many professionals prefer the latter, feeling it's safer and more accurate. It has a little opening that you slip over your cat's claw. Once it is in place, you simply squeeze, and the blade slides across the opening, making a straight, neat cut. Have your veterinarian demonstrate safe clipping before you proceed on your own.

Ready to clip? Pick a time when you and your cat are calm, quiet, and relaxed. Maintain a positive, confident attitude. Clumsiness and hesitation will likely alarm your cat. Select a comfortable spot with good lighting; it's essential to see what you're doing. Place your cat on your lap, facing away from you. If you like, wrap him in a fluffy towel, but this shouldn't really be necessary. Especially at first, don't expect to do the whole job in one sitting.

Hold your clippers in one hand. With the other hand, gently press your cat's paw between your thumb and forefinger until a claw pops out. Once you have a good, clear view, slip the clipper into place. Be crystal clear that your cut will be well ahead of the tiny, darker-colored pinkish vein called the *quick,* which is at the base of the claw. If you cut this sensitive area, which contains nerves and blood vessels, it will bleed, and your cat will feel a twinge of pain—not a good idea! If you happen to slip and cut the quick by accident, stop the bleeding with a tiny dab of cornstarch.

Proceed to the next claw. With practice, you'll complete the job so quickly that your cat will hardly notice. Unless he's elderly or is having a problem with them, you don't generally need to trim the claws on his rear feet. He trims these with his teeth and doesn't keep them nearly so sharp as his front claws.

Ear Cleaning

If you have more than one cat, and especially if they're littermates or good friends, you might find little need to ever clean their ears. This is an allogrooming (mutual grooming) task that cats seem to love doing for one another. At your weekly nose-to-toes checkup, sniff your cat's ears and peer inside them. If his ears smell fresh and sweet, and there's no redness, discharge, black or brownish crusty goo, or excessive waxy exudate, he's fine. (A small amount of honey-colored wax is normal.)

Otherwise, take a cotton ball dipped in a medicated ear-cleaning solution (available from cat-supply stores and catalogs) and gently clean out the visible portions of his ears. Never clean further than you can see, and never use a cotton-tipped swap or similar device. Your cat's inner-ear structures are sensitive, delicate, and easily injured.

If you find yourself cleaning lots of wax and discharge from your cat's ears frequently, or if he's scratching, digging at his ears, or shaking his head repeatedly, take him to the veterinarian immediately. He may have ear mites or an ear infection. (See page 226 for more details.)

Basic Grooming

Start early to accustom your cat to the feel of grooming tools and of your hands gliding over and under his body, smoothing his coat and fluffing his fur. Ideally, a grooming session should feel like a combination of massage and petting. Daily grooming is a terrific bonding experience and a great chance to keep tabs on your cat's mood and condition. Health problems often show up first in your cat's coat or on the underlying skin: lumps and bumps, rashes, scaliness, itching, bites, abscesses, dry or ragged fur, mats, or sore spots.

Get into the habit of brushing and grooming your cat for a few moments every day—whether he needs it or not. Daily grooming will reduce the amount of hair your cat swallows as he self-grooms, preventing many hair-ball problems. (Hair balls aren't just annoying—they can cause life-threatening intestinal blockages.) It will also cut down on the amount of cat hair in your house.

Grooming Long, Thick, and Fluffy Coats

If your cat is longhaired, he'll need careful, extensive grooming every single day to prevent mats. If he sports a long, fluffy, thick, or so-called double coat, he also needs attentive daily coat care. Mats are not only unattractive—they can cause pain by restricting movement and keep air from circulating to the skin, encouraging fungal and bacterial infections. A badly matted cat must often be completely shaved.

Start with a confident, positive attitude. Your cat will respond to your good mood and confidence. Alternate between long, petting strokes with your hands, a medium bristle brush, and a wide-tooth comb. A comb with rotating metal teeth works well for breaking up soft mats. Start at your cat's head and work your way around, one section at a time. Be sure to groom his ruff, behind his ears, his underarms, tummy (be gentle!), rump, and "bloomers." Don't forget his tail! Continue brushing and combing until your cat is smooth, fluffy, and free of mats, and you've collected all his easily removable loose hair. Don't test your cat's patience trying to remove all mats at once.

If you brush your cat every day without fail, you should never encounter any but the softest mats, which are fairly easy to comb out. If you do encounter a large or solid mat, don't try to comb it out. Instead, use a tool called a mat breaker to safely split it into smaller pieces, which you can comb out gently. Work slowly and carefully and be certain not to cut or nick your cat's sensitive skin. Avoid using scissors to split or cut mats—it's just too easy to cut your cat's skin inadvertently. Ask your veterinarian or a professional groomer to demonstrate the proper use of the mat breaker and other grooming tools.

Grooming Your Shorthaired Cat

Shorthaired cats need grooming too. Though they're much less likely to form mats, they still swallow quantities of hair while self-grooming. Select a grooming tool like a very soft brush, a fine-toothed comb, or a rubber curry comb that won't poke or irritate your cat's skin. Work gently from head to tail, always brushing with the lie of the fur. For a finishing touch, "polish" him with a chamois, or a piece of silk or velvet. If your shorthaired cat is shedding more than usual, wipe him down with a dampened washcloth to collect loose hair.

Bathing

Cats are remarkably fastidious and spend most of their waking hours grooming and cleaning their fur, using their teeth, barbed tongues, and claws. A cat who enjoys an indoors-only lifestyle, or who ventures outside only occasionally or under supervision, will seldom if ever need a bath. If you have multiple cats, especially if they're littermates or good friends, they'll engage in frequent allogrooming to help one another clean the few spots they can't reach on their own.

   If you plan to bathe your cat regularly for any reason, start when he's young. Have all the tools and supplies you'll need right at hand *before* you pick up your cat. It's unlikely he'll wait patiently in the sink while you run and fetch the shampoo. Here are some tips for successful cat bathing:

- Use a safe shampoo specifically formulated for cats.
- Never allow your cat to become chilled. Bathe him in a warm room, in water close to his body temperature—101.4 degrees F. (Test the temperature first!)
- Place a rubber mat or towel—something your cat can grab onto—in the tub or sink.
- Using a hand-held spray attachment held close to your cat's skin, wet him down thoroughly. Whatever you do, don't spray wildly and startle him! Avoid wetting his face and head.
- Apply shampoo, lathering deep into the fur. (Never put any shampoo on his face.)
- Holding the spray attachment very close to his skin, rinse him thoroughly several times, starting at his neck and working downwards. Rinse, rinse, rinse!
- With a fluffy, warmed towel, remove the cat from the sink. Keeping him warm, wrapped, and close to your body, gently towel him dry.

- If your cat permits it, finish drying him with a hand-held hair dryer, on the lowest heat setting. Some cats adore this; others loathe it. Be extremely careful. Keep moving the dryer back and forth over the cat's body at a safe distance to avoid burning him, and don't overheat him.
- Keep him in a warm room until he's completely dry. Comb and brush out his coat to fluff it.
- Offer a few tasty treats and lavish praise for his patience and cooperation!

If your cat has mats, groom him thoroughly and remove all mats *before* his bath. When wet, mats turn to something resembling concrete and become virtually impossible to remove without shaving the cat.

Parasites

External Parasites

Ear mites

Ear mites are tiny, spiderlike parasites that bite and suck lymph from the skin of your cat's inner ears. They cause enormous suffering, intense itching, and soreness. An affected cat often scratches his ears red and raw trying vainly to soothe the maddening itch. But since the mites live deep within his ear canals, he's helpless against the ravages of these pests. A cat infested with ear mites will shake his head repeatedly and dig at his ears frantically with his hind leg. His ears will exude a crusty black or brown material—mite waste and excess wax.

To get rid of ear mites, you'll probably have to administer drops or medicated ointment in your cat's ears every day, or every other day, for a few weeks. Your veterinarian may also want you to clean your cat's ears daily to remove the dead mites, wax, and mite waste. Do your cat a favor and get started on the treatment right in the veterinarian's office. Ask the veterinarian to demonstrate proper ear-cleaning techniques and administration of the medicated drops in one ear, and practice on the other. If you have more than one cat, your veterinarian may ask you to treat all your cats, as ear mites spread easily from cat to cat.

Fleas? Please!

Fleas have long been the bane of cats—and their owners. Fleas transmit many diseases, including plague, can cause severe allergic reactions, and are responsible for untold miseries of itching. A heavy flea infestation can severely weaken, or even kill, a kitten, by literally draining his blood. And fleas can live almost everywhere, except in extremely dry regions and at extremely high elevations. In warm, humid climates, fleas are ubiquitous all year long. Fleas also bite humans, and transmit diseases, including CSD, or cat scratch disease, to us, too.

When a flea jumps on your cat, she hangs on with six hooklike legs, cuts a hole with her sharp mouth parts, and inserts her feeding tube. After her blood meal, Mama Flea lays a large quantity of eggs, most of which fall off your cat into the environment to begin the cycle all over again. Adult fleas are hard to find in your cat's fur, and tough to crush. The good news is that they live only about thirty days. The bad news? Fully 95 percent of the fleas in a population at any given time are subadults (eggs, larvae, or cocoons) that can lie dormant for several months in your carpeting or cracks in your floor.

Since owners of indoors-only cats usually aren't looking for fleas or expecting an infestation, their flea problem can be quite advanced by the time it's discovered. Once fleas infest your home, you must treat both your home and your cat. If your cat goes out into your yard, even occasionally, you must treat the yard, too. Use environmentally safe products.

In the past, effective flea control meant strong chemical insecticides, many quite toxic for humans and some particularly dangerous for cats. Often, flea products made for cats proved extremely dangerous or fatal if used incorrectly or in certain combinations. Among the insecticide products, those in the *pyrethrin* group, made from a plant in the chrysanthemum family, have proved fairly safe for use on cats. Typical methods of flea control using traditional chemical insecticides include dips, shampoos, powders, sprays, and flea collars. These all have drawbacks.

Later improvements in flea control included *insect growth regulators*, biological substances that interrupt the flea's life cycle. These are much safer for cats and other mammals. They don't kill adult fleas, but keep immature fleas from developing into adults.

A still-newer class of flea-control products is easier to apply and safer and promises other benefits as well. These affect only the insect's nervous system, not the cat's. Some even promise to control other parasites such as ticks and ear mites. Some of these new products are mixed into your cat's food; others are applied topically between his shoulder blades once a month.

Ask your veterinarian for advice and recommendations for using these new-generation flea-control products. Always consult your veterinarian before using *any* flea-control product, especially a chemical insecticide, on your cat or in your home.

You might see advertisements or hear recommendations touting pennyroyal oil (an herbal oil), or pennyroyal flea collars, as "natural" flea-control alternatives. Pennyroyal is a liver toxin and can make your cat extremely ill, and even kill him. Do not use products containing pennyroyal or tea-tree oil on or near your cat.

Ticks

Strictly indoor cats are virtually never plagued by ticks. However, if your cat has access to a fenced yard or an enclosure with natural grass or soil, he may encounter these eight-legged, bloodsucking skin parasites. Ticks can carry several diseases that may or may not make your cat sick—but can cause problems for you.

Because cats are such fastidious self-groomers, they remove most ticks themselves. The ones they miss tend to be on top of their heads, the backs of their necks, or between their toes. If tick-borne diseases are a problem where you live, and your cat has access to the outdoors, check him carefully. If you find a tick, smother it with a cotton ball soaked in rubbing alcohol. This should cause it to loosen its grip. Use tweezers to grasp it firmly, right at skin level. Pull it straight out, then pat a tiny dab of rubbing alcohol on the exit wound. Don't touch ticks with your bare hands.

Internal Parasites

Several internal parasites, often generically called worms, can infest your cat. Although some cause no evident distress or unpleasant symptoms, they are nonetheless harmful to your cat's overall health. One of the many benefits of keeping your cat indoors is the large measure of protection it affords against potentially dangerous internal parasites, including those that can cross the species barrier and make trouble for humans.

Your indoors-only cat has little or no opportunity to hunt and consume prey animals of unknown origin, or to pick up parasites from infected soil, garbage, infected cat feces, or other sources. To further lessen your cat's chances of picking up internal parasites, keep your home free of rodents, fleas, and other bugs.

Signs of internal parasite infestation include diarrhea, frequent vomiting, and the presence of visible worms or worm fragments in feces or vomit. Each type of internal parasite requires a different medication. If you suspect your kitten or cat has an internal parasite, take a fresh sample of his feces and/or vomit to your veterinarian for testing.

Roundworms

The most common cat worm is *toxocara cati,* the roundworm, a three-to-five-inch-long parasite that lives in the small intestine and absorbs nutrients from the intestinal tract. A kitten with roundworms may have diarrhea; a potbelly look with a firm, rounded tummy (often mistaken for kittenish chubbiness); or dull, rough fur or flaky skin; or he may cough and vomit frequently. The worms may show up in feces or vomit. (They look like strings of spaghetti.) Or he may show no symptoms at all. Untreated roundworms can cause intestinal blockage and even death.

Because of potential dangers to humans (including a zoonosis called *visceral larval migrans* that can lead to serious illness or blindness in infected children), researchers at the U.S. Centers for Disease Control and Prevention, and many parasitologists, recommend that all kittens be routinely dewormed—a safe, effective strategy that can prevent much feline and human misery. Periodic microscopic examination of your cat's feces throughout his life will give you a heads-up on any recurrence of infestation.

Tapeworms

These long, segmented worms attach themselves to the intestinal walls and absorb nutrients. There's often no sign of their presence except worm segments shed in feces. You might see them—they look like grains of rice—in the litter box, clinging to your cat's fur, or even on the floor where he sleeps. A tapeworm requires an intermediate host, which is usually a flea, but sometimes a mouse or other prey animal. Over time, the presence of a tapeworm can debilitate your cat. Tapeworms are common in warm, humid climates where fleas are plentiful.

Heartworms

Dirofilaria immitis causes heartworm disease. Cats aren't ideal hosts for this parasite, but under certain conditions, heartworm disease in cats can be fatal. For your cat to become infected with heartworms, there must be a reservoir (usually dogs) of *Dirofilaria immitis,* and there must be mosquitoes. The parasite is transmitted via mosquito bites. If dogs in your area are at risk from heartworm, so are cats.

A cat's immune system is more sensitive to the presence of heartworms and their larvae than is a dog's. The signs are subtler and veterinarians are just now learning how to detect them. A cat with heartworm disease, even if symptom-free, is at risk for sudden death. A cat with heartworm might have no symptoms. More likely, though, he'll suffer intermittent vomiting unrelated to eating; coughing; rapid or difficult breathing; sluggishness; and anorexia or weight loss. The symptoms may first appear four-to-six months after peak mosquito season and can range from minor to severe.

Diagnosis of heartworm in cats is very tricky, and all available treatments are extremely dangerous. You can manage the symptoms with drugs, but the risk of sudden death remains. The best solution is prevention. If you live in an area where heartworm is common in dogs, ask your veterinarian to prescribe a heartworm-preventative medication for your cat.

Coccidia and other parasites

Coccidia are single-celled intestinal parasites. They seldom harm adult cats, but can be deadly to kittens, causing severe diarrhea. *Giardia lamblia* is a one-celled protozoan that lives in the intestine and hampers your cat's ability to process food. This can cause dehydration and weight loss, which can be deadly in already-weak or ill cats.

There are also a number of rarer parasites that can infest your cat. If your cat is suffering from diarrhea, frequent vomiting, or stomach upsets of unknown origin, your veterinarian may want to run more extensive tests on fecal and vomit samples to identify the parasite.

Other Bug Troubles

Even indoors, your cat can encounter problems with creepy crawlies. The venomous bites of black widow spiders, which often live inside buildings, can cause weakness, fever, and paralysis. The bite of the brown recluse spider, also a building dweller, can be very serious, killing flesh around the bite. Effects from such bites can be persistent and severe, including ulcerated wounds that take months to heal. Often, the spider is never seen. If you know, or even suspect, that your cat has been bitten by a venomous spider, take him to the veterinarian immediately. The bites of these spiders should be considered emergencies.

If you walk your cat outdoors, prevent him from frequenting areas, such as woodpiles, stone walls, rodent burrows, and unimproved cellars, sheds, and attics, where he may come in contact with spiders and biting insects. If you live in an area frequented by mosquitoes, restrict your cat's outdoor excursions to a mosquito-proof, screened enclosure.

Cats Have Allergies, Too

Human allergy symptoms tend to center in the respiratory system and mucous membranes, causing sneezing and sniffling. Allergic cats, though, often experience dermatological symptoms, ranging from intense itching to crusty scabs, hair loss, and oozing sores from excessive scratching. Allergies to specific foods can cause diarrhea and vomiting.

Allergies are caused by a poorly understood overreaction of the cat's immune system to particular substances. They can't be cured, though an allergic cat can sometimes be desensitized through lengthy immunotherapy treatment. Determining exactly what a cat is allergic to can be a long, frustrating process, requiring patience, the cooperation of your veterinarian, and lots of detective work. Cats can be allergic to just about anything.

Environmental Irritants

Like people, many cats are sensitive to environmental irritants such as pollen, mold, and dust, and, because they spend so much time close to the ground, they're even more likely than we are to inhale particulate matter. Eliminate these irritants from your environment. Clean and vacuum regularly, wash all bedding in hot water, and invest in an HEPA air filter. Even if your cat is allowed outdoors, keep him indoors during pollen season. Cats are prone to inhalant allergies caused by aerosolized chemicals and other substances wafting through the air.

Many cats are allergic to plastic. Replace plastic food and water bowls with stainless steel, U.S.-made ceramic (glazes on foreign ceramics often contain lead), or heavy glass. If your cat habitually lounges on plastic surfaces, drape his favorite spots with thick, soft towels to prevent skin contact. Plastic allergies are often betrayed by outbreaks of rashes or raised, itchy patches on your cat's throat, neck, and chin—where he touches his food and water bowls.

Newly installed carpeting, and the materials used to glue or fix it in place, can outgas for months, pouring irritating chemicals into the air. Sometimes you can smell these; others are odorless. Home computer systems, televisions, and other electronic appliances can also outgas irritating chemicals, as can furniture made with particle board, many glues, dyes, and building materials; and even such common items as plastic shower curtains. These can cause low-level, but debilitating, allergic reactions in humans as well as in cats. If possible, air out strong-smelling plastic items for several days outdoors before bringing them into your home.

Keep as much fresh air circulating through your home as possible. In modern homes, supersealed for energy efficiency, large concentrations of harmful gasses can build up unless care is taken to monitor airflow and insure that stale air is exchanged and fresh air introduced regularly.

EYE ON HEALTH: OBSERVATION AND ACTION

Cat-Safe Housecleaning

No matter how safe any cleaning or freshening product's container claims it is for animals, keep your cat out of recently treated areas, especially while moisture, powders, or crystals are present. Many common household cleaners and products, especially those that aerosolize or linger on surfaces, can cause allergic reactions. Powdered or crystallized carpet fresheners can cling to your cat's fur, where they can cause skin irritation or mouth irritation (when licked off during grooming), and they can be toxic when ingested.

Keep your cat away from treated areas until all of the product has dried or been vacuumed up. Avoid using chemical cleaners and products. Review chapter 6 for more tips on preventing toxicity and allergy problems.

Food Allergies

Feline food allergies can be maddeningly tough to track down. Food allergies are often signaled by itchiness, especially around the cat's face and ears, and diarrhea. If your cat shows these symptoms, and you've recently changed his diet, go back to his old food and see if the symptoms subside. Keep in mind that it may take weeks for the itching to settle down. If your cat is on a prescription diet for a medical condition, ask your veterinarian to prescribe an alternative formula.

If you're still baffled—and your cat is still itchy and miserable—it's time to get serious. The only really successful method of identifying the culprit may be to put your cat on a strictly monitored "elimination diet" of foods previously unfamiliar to him; then introduce other foods, one at a time, to see which cause symptoms. Consult your veterinarian for advice on selecting the initial diet and carrying out the program. This can be a lengthy, difficult process—no treats, no table scraps, no exceptions. Offer your cat extra cuddling and love, and frequent interactive-play sessions to keep him toned and tuned.

Once you've identified the offending substance or food, minimize or eliminate your cat's exposure to it. Fortunately, many of the lifestyle changes that can minimize your cat's allergy suffering are also the healthiest choices for you, your family, and the environment.

Digestive Woes

Cats have sensitive digestive systems. Diarrhea, constipation, upset tummies, loss of appetite, and finicky eating are well-known to cat owners. Help your cat avoid digestive troubles by keeping him indoors (where he's less likely to encounter prey animals, poisons, and unknown edibles) and by minimizing stress and change—especially rapid change—in his life. Always make dietary changes slowly and gradually. Keep unusual, treat, and holiday foods to a minimum, especially until you know how he'll react. Many cats adore milk but can't tolerate it.

Vomiting

Hair balls, eating grass, eating too much or too fast, eating food that's too cold—all these can cause your cat to vomit. Occasional vomiting—a forceful expelling of material by repeated muscle contractions—is fairly normal. Frequent, copious vomiting, or vomiting unrelated to eating, is cause for concern. If vomiting seems to be transient and uncomplicated, and your cat appears to feel fine both before and soon after the episode, it's likely unimportant.

If your cat crouches as if in pain or clearly feels bad for more than a few brief moments, or makes typical vomiting motions with repeated muscle contractions that produce nothing, if there's blood in the vomit, or if he vomits repeatedly, he may have a serious problem. Call your veterinarian right away.

Diarrhea

Diarrhea—frequent, loose, or liquid feces—isn't a disease in itself, but a symptom with a wide variety of possible causes, including stress; an abrupt change in diet; a virus, colitis, inflammatory bowel disease, or other underlying illness; parasites; poisoning; consumption of poorly tolerated food like milk or too-rich table scraps; consumption of diseased rodents or other prey animals; food allergies; hair balls—and the list goes on!

If there's blood in his feces, or if you have reason to suspect your cat has swallowed poison or a foreign object, take him to the veterinarian immediately—after calling first to make sure the veterinarian is in the office.

In persistent or severe cases, your veterinarian might recommend an antidiarrheal medication. Don't medicate your cat with an over-the-counter product—you might do more harm than good. If the diarrhea episode is severe and your cat has become dehydrated, your veterinarian may recommend supplemental fluid therapy.

Constipation

A cat who's constipated is in pain. He produces small, hard, dark-colored, dry feces, sometimes accompanied by a thin, dark brown liquid. Or he may squat and strain for long periods with no result. He may stop eating and lose weight rapidly, risking dehydration and other complications. Offer nonmedicated petroleum jelly or an over-the-counter hair-ball remedy, but be vigilant for results. Veterinary intervention, including enemas, suppositories, or manual removal of impacted feces, may be required.

Stress, old age, drinking too little water, getting too little exercise, or a diet with too little fiber can all cause constipation. Ask your veterinarian about offering plain bran or a bulk-forming laxative that contains cellulose. Switch to a high-fiber food. Canned food is good for chronically constipated cats, as it has a higher moisture content.

Obstipation

Obstipation is the inability to defecate. It's very serious and painful and requires an immediate trip to the veterinarian. Although the causes of this backup of fecal material are poorly understood, the result is that your cat's intestines become dilated and unable to push feces out of his body. Signs of possible obstipation are straining or crying out while trying to defecate and lack of feces in the litter box. Sometimes, obstipation appears initially as diarrhea. This is because severe irritation causes the intestines to generate large quantities of mucus and watery fluid, resembling loose stools.

Hair Balls

In the course of daily grooming, your cat ingests some hair—sometimes a large quantity of it. Most of the time, this passes uneventfully through his digestive system and ends up in his litter box. Sometimes, though, it forms a cigar-shaped mass that he throws up—probably right where you'll step on it in the middle of the night.

Occasional hair balls are normal. Frequent, large hair balls aren't. If your cat is regularly throwing up large masses of hair or having trouble expelling hair balls, you can help him out by treating him to daily brushing so he won't swallow so much hair, and by giving him an over-the-counter hair-ball preparation or nonmedicated petroleum jelly. If he has a chronic hair-ball problem, increase the fiber content in his diet by feeding him a high-fiber food or offering a teaspoon of canned pumpkin, plain bran, or other fiber supplement along with his meals.

Half of all cases of feline constipation are caused by impacted hair balls. In severe cases, a large hair ball can become impacted, causing constipation or obstruction of the cat's digestive tract. This is an emergency. If your cat is vomiting frequently and has diarrhea, loss of appetite, a retching cough, and a swollen belly, get him to the veterinarian immediately. In some cases, the blockage must be surgically removed.

To protect your carpets from hair balls and the inevitable puddles of cat vomit, use inexpensive, washable throw rugs and runners. Clean up cat vomit immediately, as it contains hydrochloric acid that can rapidly stain carpets. If the vomited matter is fairly solid, pick it up with a paper towel and blot the spot with a cat-safe deodorizing cleaner or plenty of hot water. For the more common, thinner vomit, scrape up as much as you can with a spoon or kitchen knife. Don't spread it—scrape towards the center to minimize the affected area. When you've picked up all you can get, blot (don't rub) the area with a clean cloth or paper towel moistened with hot water and/or deodorizing cleaner. Or try commercial pet-stain-and-odor removers. Follow label instructions. Rinse thoroughly and keep your cat away from the area until it's thoroughly dry and deodorized. (Be sure to pretest any cleaner you plan to use in a nonconspicuous spot.)

Major messes require a wet-dry vacuum cleaner or carpet-cleaning machine and plenty of hot water. For older, dried, set-in stains, you'll likely need the help of a professional cleaning service. If the vomit is on an expensive fabric or carpet, it might be wise to call in a professional immediately, lest your own efforts do more harm than good.

AT-HOME CARE OF AN AILING OR RECUPERATING CAT

Unless he's in need of constant monitoring or frequent veterinary attention, your recuperating cat will be happier, and recover much faster at home, with your comforting presence and all his safe, familiar sights, sounds, and odors. Set up a quiet, comfortable sick room equipped with everything he needs. To avoid unnecessary stress and excitement, keep other cats and pets and young children out of the sick room.

If your cat needs medications, pills, injections, wound cleaning, or other home treatment, administer these as quickly and gently as you can. Don't agonize or feel guilty; your cat will pick up on your distress. Speak softly and reassuringly to him as you perform these care rituals. Nursing him can be an opportunity to enhance your bond. Any brief unpleasantness will be long forgotten when he's back to his old self. Struggles, fights, coercion, and tears, on the other hand, will hamper his recovery and make you feel worse.

Giving Medication

Medicating your cat can be tricky business. Pilling your cat, in particular, often requires speed, self-confidence, a practiced technique, and—if you have a fractious cat—body armor and a brave helper. Surprisingly, giving your cat medication via injection is often easier than giving him a pill. Many cats who hate pills just ignore needles. If you've had problems pilling your cat in the past, ask your veterinarian if the mediation you need to administer at home can be given via subcutaneous (under-the-skin) injection. The technique is straightforward and easy to learn. Ask your veterinarian to demonstrate and to watch while you practice by preparing the medication and giving your cat the first injection right there at the clinic.

Whether you're administering pills, injections, ointments, or drops, always accompany your ministrations with plenty of praise and soft, soothing, reassuring talk.

Administering pills often requires speed, self-confidence, and a practiced technique. Avoid placing your fingers in the cat's mouth, so that the cat can't bite down on your hand.
(FRANTZ DANTZLER)

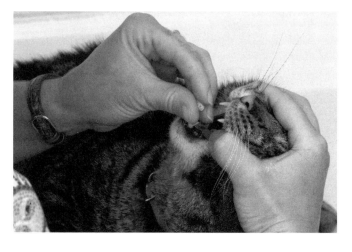

Tips for Successful Pilling

Obtain some extra pills, as you can expect to lose a few along the way as you perfect your pilling technique. Many cats are expert at pretending to swallow a pill, while concealing it in a cheek pouch for spitting out later in some out-of-the-way place where you won't find it for months.

First, make sure the pill is within reach. Restrain the cat (that's often the hardest part). Kneel on the floor with your legs about eight-to-ten inches apart. Tuck the cat between your legs, facing away from you. This limits his escape options. With one hand over the top of his head, point his nose at the ceiling. His mouth should fall open naturally. With your thumb and middle finger, gently apply pressure to the corners of his mouth. Now, with the other hand, drop the pill down his throat. Aim right down the middle. He has little choice but to swallow the pill if you get it past the hump in his tongue. Now, massage his throat to make sure he swallows. Once he swallows the pill, give him lots of petting and praise.

For Tough Cases

Is your cat a tough case? Once you *think* he's swallowed the pill, don't let him go just yet. Stroke his throat, pet him, fuss over him—then, really fast, clap your hands loudly or make some other sudden, loud noise. The surprise will almost certainly cause a swallowing reflex. Or try placing the pill in a dab of tasty food. Although some experts recommend coating the pill with a slippery substance like butter, many cats find this makes it easier to spit it out. Plus, it makes the pill greasy and hard to handle. Here's another approach:

1. Put out a plate of some really irresistible, goopy treat your cat loves (like juicy oil poured from a can of tuna cat food).
2. Let your cat start eating it. Wait until he's really involved in his snack!
3. Grab him (gently!) and pop the pill down his throat. (Use the technique above, or do it right there, treat-side, if you're quick.)
4. While still holding him, let him go back to his treat. With luck, he'll just resume eating his tasty snack, not even minding the brief interruption. After he's swallowed a few bites or licks, you can be fairly sure the pill went down, too.

Pill Guns—Don't Let the Name Scare You!

Pill guns, also called pill poppers, can make medicating your cat easier and safer for you both. By using a pill gun, you can give your cat a pill without actually placing your fingers in his mouth. Pill guns are about the size of a pencil and made of plastic, with a rubber-tipped pill receptacle on one end and a plunger on the opposite end. The rubber tip prevents you from harming your cat when you place the pill gun in his mouth. Place the pill in the receptacle end of the pill gun, and you're ready.

To use the pill popper successfully, place one hand over your cat's head (as described in the section on pilling your cat). As you gently press in on the corners of his lips (causing his mouth to open), place the pill popper far back on his tongue. Press

EYE ON HEALTH: OBSERVATION AND ACTION

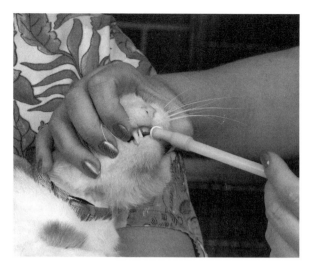

A pilling gun sometimes make administering pills easier.
(FRANTZ DANTZLER)

down at the back of his tongue (towards your cat's jaw, *not* towards his throat) with the pill popper, depress the plunger, remove the pill gun, and stop pressing in at the corners of his mouth, but with that same hand gently hold his mouth closed. Pressing down gently on his tongue as you deposit the pill causes his tongue to pop back up into its normal position when you remove the pill popper—and improves the likelihood of him swallowing the pill. Ask your veterinarian to demonstrate this helpful and inexpensive technique for pilling your cat.

Ear Medications

Most ear medications are ointments or liquid drops. The trick is to get enough of the medicine down into your cat's long, curved ear canals for it to do its job. Your cat's ears are very sensitive, and even more so when he has an infection or ear-mite infestation. Be prepared for resistance. It might be wise to wrap your cat in a large, thick towel before attempting to medicate his ears.

Have the medication ready at hand. Arrange your cat (towel-wrapped if necessary) on your lap so that the opening in his ear is facing more or less upwards. With one hand, gently squeeze the required number of drops, or the required amount of ointment, straight into the opening. Then, quickly grasp and fold over his ear flap to prevent your cat from immediately flinging all the medicine right back out again (and all over you). With your other hand, massage the base of your cat's ear to work the medicine down deep into his ear canal. In the case of ear mites, application of the soothing medication often brings virtually instant relief, so your cat may stop struggling after the first few moments.

Eye Medications

Like ear medications, most eye medications are either drops or ointment. Administration techniques are similar, too. Wrap your cat in a towel on your lap, with the eye to be medicated pointing straight up. With one hand, pull your cat's lower eyelid back. With the other hand, and without touching the tube or bottle to the eye, squeeze out the required number of drops right into the little pouch made by the retracted lid. As soon as you let go, your cat will naturally blink several times, spreading the medication over the eye surface.

Taking Your Cat's Temperature

Fever is an important symptom. When you call your veterinarian, he may want to know your cat's temperature. The normal temperature range for an adult cat is 100-to-102.5 degrees; for a very young kitten (under three-to-four weeks old), it's lower. Unless your cat is uncommonly placid and cooperative, taking his temperature will require a helper.

Lubricate the tip of a thermometer (preferably digital, not glass and mercury) with baby oil or petroleum jelly. Have your helper hold the cat firmly. (You may want to wrap the cat in a towel. Leave his tail free.) With one hand, raise your cat's tail. With the other, insert the thermometer about one inch into his anus. Hold it in place for at least three minutes. Then remove it, quickly wipe it clean, and read his temperature. Be sure to clean the thermometer thoroughly with alcohol after each use.

A digital thermometer is worth the investment. It reads in much less time than does a glass thermometer, and there's no danger of contact with glass and mercury should the conventional thermometer break. Ear thermometers are also available, but they're not as accurate as the rectal variety.

Caring for Healing Wounds

If your cat has had surgery that involved an incision, including dental surgery, or is recovering from an injury, it's important to keep him confined, quiet, and calm. Set up your sick room in an area with no tall furniture or other items that may tempt your cat to climb or jump. Watch him carefully. If he shows any tendency to pick at the sutures or the wound itself with his teeth or claws, your veterinarian may need to fit him with a restricting collar. One style, the *Elizabethan collar,* is funnel shaped, is usually made of flexible plastic, and fits loosely around the neck. It prevents your cat from reaching most of his body with his teeth. If he's clawing at his wound or sutures, trim his claws.

Your veterinarian may have instructed you to clean a wound periodically. Ideally, she demonstrated the procedure. If you have any doubts about how to perform required care, call the veterinarian and ask for clarification. If you try to muddle through, your cat will sense your uneasiness and be disinclined to cooperate, putting you both under unneeded stress.

If your cat is recovering from an abscess wound, your veterinarian may have placed a drain through the skin over the abscess to continue to purge any remaining pus and fluid from the site. The drain must usually be cleaned several times a day. Call your veterinarian for clarification if you have any doubts about how to perform this procedure.

All such wound-care procedures are, like medicating your cat, easier and quicker with the help of a second person. One person can wrap and hold the cat securely, while the other performs the wound care or administers the medication. Both nurses should be people the cat knows well and trusts.

A FEW MEDICAL MYTHS DEBUNKED

Myth: Herbal remedies are best, because they're harmless.

Fact: This is a very dangerous myth. Just because herbs are "natural" doesn't mean they're automatically safe, let alone effective. Some herbal "knowledge" is simply unreliable, unscientific folklore, dating from times before modern veterinary medicine could provide the safe, effective treatments we now have for a host of feline maladies.

Many herbs can have powerful—and sometimes toxic—effects on cats. For example, oil of pennyroyal, often mentioned as a flea preventative, is a liver toxin. Before using any "natural" or herbal remedy on your cat, discuss your plans with your veterinarian.

Myth: Fleas can be controlled by adding Brewer's yeast or garlic to your cat's food.

Fact: These folk remedies, while relatively harmless, have never been shown, in controlled scientific or clinical tests, to have any effect whatsoever on fleas.

Myth: If your cat's nose is cold and wet, he's healthy.

Fact: The temperature and moisture of your cat's nose have more to do with the room temperature and humidity than with the state of his health. If other symptoms are present, don't assume a cold, wet nose means all is well.

Myth: "Carpet scooting" means your cat has worms.

Fact: Most scooting in cats is caused by impacted anal glands or dermatitis caused by dried fecal matter that's collected around his anus. A scooting cat is itchy and uncomfortable. If your cat is having trouble keeping his rear end clean and groomed, perhaps because of long fur, obesity, or inflexibility due to age, help him out by clipping away excess fur. Check frequently and wipe the area with a warm, damp washcloth. Persistent redness, itchiness, and scooting call for a trip to the veterinarian to check for impacted anal sacs.

Myth: Cats get "worms" from bad food.

Fact: Your cat may acquire intestinal parasites, commonly called worms, when he eats prey, undercooked or raw meat, or dirt from outdoors. Keeping your cat strictly indoors eliminates or greatly minimizes these risks. Spoiled food *can* make your cat sick with bacterial infection. Fortunately, your cat's extremely acute sense of smell will usually cause him to reject spoiled food.

CHAPTER 16

A Few Ounces of Prevention

NEUTER OR SPAY, IT'S THE KINDEST WAY!

In just seven years, one unspayed female cat and her offspring can found a family tree of about 420,000 cats. Many of these must be euthanized (humanely destroyed) in animal shelters because there are no homes for them. Many others will meet sad ends through accident, abuse, neglect, and illness. That's a lot of feline misery—all completely avoidable. If there's one thing that distinguishes responsible cat owners from irresponsible ones, it's their dedication to sterilizing their cats. Unless you're an experienced breeder involved in a responsibly planned, organized breeding program designed for the continuing benefits of pedigreed cats, there is no reason not to sterilize your companion cats. None. Not one.

Health Benefits of Sterilization

Sterilized cats enjoy longer, healthier lives. Spaying your female cat eliminates her risk of uterine and ovarian cancer, birth complications (including Cesarean sections), pyometra (pyometritis, uterine infection), and ovarian cysts. She won't be burdened by repeated heat cycles, which are wearing and frustrating for both cat and owner. She'll avoid vaginal tears and prolapses, and eclampsia. If she's spayed before her first heat, she'll enjoy a greatly reduced risk of breast cancer.

Neutering your male cat before he reaches sexual maturity reduces his risk of prostate enlargement, prostate cancer, and testicular cancer. Neutering will also make him more affectionate and less likely to roam, get in fights, or get lost.

Behavior Benefits of Sterilization

An unsterilized cat of either gender can be a very problematic, frustrating, frustrated, expensive, and unhappy pet. Unaltered male cats habitually and instinctually spray—marking their territories with an overwhelmingly pungent and offensive-smelling, hormone-laced urine brew that can quickly make your home uninhabitable. Cat breeders who keep intact or stud males for their breeding programs generally house them in specially constructed, escape-proof quarters where the pungent spray does not impinge too intrusively upon daily life.

Unsterilized male cats have a phenomenally heightened sensitivity to the odors exuded by female cats in heat, and can detect these scent calls from considerable distances, indoors or out. Your unsterilized male's urge to follow his instinct means a constant battle of wits to keep him from escaping. And when he does escape (and he will), he'll likely meet up with numerous potential competitors, whom he'll feel compelled to fight. The resulting bite wounds, abscesses, torn ears, scratched eyes, infections, and other battle damage can rapidly rack up hefty veterinary bills.

Your unsterilized female cat will cycle through heat periods several times a year, several days at a time. She'll roll, moan, wail, call, and try desperately to escape. And if she does—even for a few moments—you can bet that there's at least one male eagerly awaiting her. The repeated stress of these heat cycles—not to mention the probability of the resulting pregnancy and kittening—can take an enormous toll on her health. A spayed female cat, free of the complications of mating and reproduction, is a calmer and happier companion.

Social Benefits of Sterilization

Overpopulation is the greatest killer of dogs and cats in the United States, and a major cause of animal pain and suffering. Four-to-five-million cats and dogs are euthanized (humanely destroyed) each year in shelters. Animal shelters want to be in the business of sheltering, not killing, adoptable animals. Imagine being an animal lover working at a large animal shelter. Now imagine that a huge percentage of your daily tasks involve killing healthy, adoptable cats. Is it fair to ask shelter workers to carry this heavy burden, behind closed doors for society?

The killing of so many surplus healthy adoptable animals sends a message to society, and especially to young people, that these lives are cheap, worthless, and disposable. Is this a message we want to send our children? Too often, witnessing the miracle of birth is followed shortly by witnessing the convenience and tragedy of easy disposal. Many of those little miracles end up dumped at the nearest shelter or off in the woods, or offered to anyone who responds to a "free to a good home" ad—to die needlessly, perhaps after a life that's, at best, "nasty, brutish, and short"—or to start the cycle all over again.

What Are Spaying and Neutering?

Spaying, or *ovariohysterectomy,* is the surgical removal of a female cat's uterus and ovaries. It's performed under general anesthesia. Spaying is considered relatively simple, routine surgery. It requires a small incision in the cat's abdomen.

Neutering, or *castration,* is the removal of a male cat's testicles from his scrotum. Like spaying, it's performed under general anesthesia and is considered a simple, routine procedure. Routine neutering (where both testicles are descended into the cat's scrotum) doesn't require an abdominal incision, so it's usually less expensive and quicker than spaying.

Spay and neuter surgeries are very safe procedures, with complications appearing only extremely rarely. Healthy cats tolerate general anesthesia extremely well. Gas anesthesia is usually used, although male cats are often neutered under injectable anesthesia. Cats are closely monitored during and after surgery. Most cats can go home the same day. Occasionally, your veterinarian will want to keep a cat overnight, but this is increasingly rare, especially for pediatric (early age) sterilization. After awakening from the anesthetic, your cat might be groggy for a few hours. This is normal. Your veterinarian will give you instructions on caring for your cat after surgery, and will tell you if there are stitches that need to be removed. Most cats bounce back from this simple, vital procedure very quickly.

Pediatric Spaying and Neutering

Pediatric spaying and neutering (often called early age or juvenile sterilization) are the performance of surgical sterilization procedures on kittens as young as eight weeks (and at least two pounds in weight). (The traditional approach is to perform the procedure just before or after the cat reaches sexual maturity at about six months.) When practiced by animal shelters and rescue groups, juvenile spay and neuter surgery is often linked with a policy of SAA—sterilization at adoption.

Statistics show that there's a very poor compliance rate in sterilization of cats adopted from shelters and rescue groups. Though most adopters sign forms promising to sterilize their pets before sexual maturity, there's no practical way to enforce these agreements. Many cat owners, especially those with little or no previous experience with feline reproduction, wait too long to have their cats sterilized. Or, because of financial or emotional considerations, or belief in old myths, or even procrastination, they never have the surgeries performed at all. The results? In some cases, it's an "Oops!" litter. And even if these owners subsequently have the cat spayed, yet another litter of surplus kittens has been born.

Some owners deliberately postpone sterilization in the mistaken belief that their cat will be somehow happier or healthier if she's allowed just one litter. Or they want their children to witness the miracle of birth. These beliefs are based on myths—myths we demolished in chapter 3. Owners of male cats often skip the surgery, believing that any kittens resulting from their cat's adventures are not their problem.

Pediatric sterilization is a neat, safe, practical, and inexpensive solution to all of these problems. However, some cat owners, and even some veterinarians, still harbor fears that early age sterilization might be disadvantageous to the future health of the animal or that it might even be dangerous. But pediatric spaying and neutering have been endorsed by the American Veterinary Medical Association: "AVMA supports the concept of early (eight to sixteen weeks of age) ovariohysterectomies and gonadectomies in dogs and cats, in an effort to stem the overpopulation problem in these species." It's also been observed that kittens (and puppies) sterilized before twelve weeks of age had fewer complications from surgery.

People Problems

When it comes to spaying and neutering companion animals, it's the people issues—not the simple matter of the surgery—that cause the most problems. For one thing, there's the persistent belief in those myths we demolished in chapter 3.

Another, more vexing problem, is cat owners who feel that neutering their male cat will make the cat feel like less of a male or will somehow take away his opportunity for fun. But animals don't have a sexual identity or an ego based on mating prowess or success. Cats mate because of an innate, instinctual compulsion that has nothing to do with pleasure or personal identity. Being an intact (unsterilized) male cat is a tremendous stressor all by itself. Your male cat won't plot revenge against you because you deprived him of his manhood. He won't suffer an identity crisis or psychological trauma because he's neutered. He'll be a happier, calmer, healthier, safer animal and a better pet and companion.

YOUR CAT'S ANNUAL CHECKUP

Every cat needs to visit his veterinarian at least once a year for a "well-cat" checkup. Senior cats (over ten years old) should receive routine checkups twice a year, or as often as your veterinarian recommends. Bring your cat journal along and ask your veterinarian all those questions you've been wondering about. Before your cat's annual checkup, review his weight records. Has his weight gone up or down? Has he been eating well? Any changes in dietary preference? Water consumption? Litter-box habits? How's the hair coat? Talk to your veterinarian about any concerns you may have about these essential health factors.

Bring any behavior changes, however minor, to your veterinarian's attention. Use your veterinarian's time and attention wisely during the well-cat visit. It's a sterling opportunity to let the veterinarian see how your cat looks and acts when he's healthy and fit. When your cat turns eight years old, your veterinarian might suggest taking a baseline blood panel. This is a complete set of blood tests that gives your veterinarian a look at how all your cat's systems—kidneys, liver, heart, muscles—are functioning. It will establish a set of normal values for your cat—an invaluable resource for comparisons if your cat becomes ill later.

Read chapter 13 to discover how to prepare for your cat's visit to the veterinarian, and how to get the most out of that visit.

VACCINATIONS

Vaccinations appropriate to your cat and his lifestyle, combined with high-quality nutrition and veterinary care, are your best bets for insuring him a long, healthy life. Vaccinations are vital to your cat's health and well-being. *Don't be misled by irresponsible, uninformed, or fear-mongering claims that vaccinations are unnecessary or even harmful.* While it's true that occasional side effects and problems have been associated with routine vaccinations in the past, new data and new vaccination protocols are helping to make vaccinating your cat safer than ever before. The tiny possibility of side effects is greatly outweighed by the benefits of regular, appropriate vaccinations. Prevention is always more cost-effective—and easier on you and your cat—than treatment of avoidable diseases.

Although most of the rumors and fears about feline vaccinations are unfounded, there is some cause for concern. Studies have shown that about one in ten-thousand cats develops a *sarcoma*—a fibrous tumor of connective tissue—within a few months of receiving routine vaccinations. Though these tumors have been known to appear at other locations, they most often develop at or near the injection site. These tumors are troubling because even when removed, they quite often reappear. And in about 25-to-30 percent of cases, the tumor eventually metastasizes, or spreads to other organs and areas of the body. The resulting cancer can kill the cat.

A group of veterinary scientists, researchers, and clinical veterinarians formed the American Veterinary Medical Association Vaccine-Associated Sarcoma Task Force (AVMA-VASTF) to examine the known facts about the sarcomas being reported and to try to track down the causes. It was determined that sarcomas most often appeared after administration of the rabies and feline leukemia (FeLV) vaccines. Work and research on the problem are still ongoing and have already led to a new set of guidelines, issued by the American Association of Feline Practitioners and the Academy of Feline Medicine Advisory Panel on Feline Vaccinations, for routine vaccinations of domestic cats.

One major recommendation was to discontinue the use of polyvalent (combined) vaccines—that is, several vaccines combined in a single injection. While such combination shots are more convenient, and possibly cheaper, the Task Force determined that these shots were forcing additional vaccines on cats who didn't need them and also were producing an unacceptably high number of side effects. Many of the observed side effects are poorly understood and are possibly due to interactions among the various vaccines and the cat's immune system.

Another recommendation was to minimize or eliminate the use of adjuvants, substances added to vaccines to increase their effectiveness in the body. Some research has shown that use of adjuvants seemed to cause more adverse reactions than unenhanced vaccines. Adjuvants have also been implicated in vaccine-associated sarcomas.

Which vaccinations your cat needs, and how often they should be given, depend on a number of factors, including your cat's age, health, medical and behavioral history, and living situation. When you take your cat or kitten for his checkup, rather than just poke your cat with a needle, your veterinarian will first ask lots of questions about your cat's individual circumstances. Then you can decide together which vaccinations your cat really needs. Some are essential for health, some required by law, and others optional—depending on your cat's situation.

In brief, here are the vaccine guidelines:

Rabies

Rabies is a fearsome disease. Once symptoms appear, rabies is invariably fatal. Cats are infected with rabies more often than any other domestic animal. Rabies can be transmitted to cats from other mammals, and to people from cats and other mammals. Therefore, the rabies vaccination is highly recommended for all cats, whatever their living situation. In many states, it's required by law. These laws often specify the required frequency for booster shots, usually one or three years. Ongoing research to determine how long the various available rabies vaccines remain effective may, in the future, cause these laws to be modified.

Feline viral rhinotracheitis (FHV-1) and feline calcivirus (FCV)

These viruses cause upper-respiratory illnesses. These illnesses are easily spread via exposure to infected cats, either from aerosolized droplets of saliva from an infected cat (as in sneezing or hissing) or from contaminated objects such as water and food bowls. Symptoms can include fever, inflamed eyes, discharge from the nose and eyes, and mouth and nose sores. These respiratory infections can be serious and even fatal, especially in kittens. A cat who's infected may never completely shake the infection—and may continue to infect other cats even after his own symptoms subside. Therefore, this vaccination is highly recommended for all cats. After the first vaccination series, a booster is given at one year, followed by boosters every three years thereafter. The boosters are important because the vaccine doesn't confer complete immunity from these viruses, but merely lessens the severity of illness if the cat catches one of them.

Feline panleukopenia (often called feline distemper)

"Distemper" is really a misnomer, as this is a totally different disease than canine distemper. Feline panleukopenia is a serious intestinal virus that causes lethargy, fever, dehydration, vomiting, weakness, appetite loss, tremors, and severe diarrhea. It's especially dangerous to kittens, and often fatal. In fact, 75 percent of kittens who get this disease die of it, often very rapidly—within one week. Therefore, this vaccination is highly recommended for all cats. After the first vaccination series, a booster is given at one year, followed by boosters no more often than every three years thereafter. The feline panleukopenia vaccine is often combined with the FHV-1 and FCV vaccines; the combined shot is called FVRCP or FDCVR.

Feline leukemia (FeLV)

This vaccination is recommended only for cats considered at risk for FeLV infection—those allowed outdoors unsupervised, those living in shelters, or those living in situations where new cats enter the environment frequently. Cats can catch feline leukemia only from direct contact with an infected cat. Mother cats can also pass it to their kittens. Researchers point out that the best way to protect against FeLV is to prevent exposure to possibly infected cats, as the vaccine isn't perfect and doesn't confer protection on all cats who are vaccinated. At-risk cats should be revaccinated every year. Initially, kittens are given two doses of the vaccine three-to-four weeks apart, starting at age eight weeks.

Feline infectious peritonitis (FIP)

FIP is a fatal disease caused by a coronavirus. A cat can catch it by inhaling or ingesting the virus while actually exposed to an infected cat, or by coming in contact with an infected cat's bedding or food bowls or other items an infected cat has touched (such as an owner's clothing). For reasons not yet understood, only a small percentage of cats who become infected with the virus actually develop the disease, but they remain carriers. This vaccine is currently not recommended to be given routinely. While it appears to be safe, it's not yet known whether the available vaccine actually confers any protection against the disease.

Chlamydia

Vaccination for *Chlamydia psittaci*, which causes conjunctivitis in cats, is not recommended to be given routinely. The disease is uncommon, relatively mild, and easily treated with antibiotics. In addition, the available vaccine has produced an unusually high rate of adverse side effects. In multiple-cat environments where *Chlamydia psittaci* is causing disease, its use should be considered.

Ringworm

This vaccine does not confer protection or immunity against the fungal skin infection, also called dermatophytosis, caused by *Microsporum canis*. In multiple-cat environments where *M. canis* infection is present, use of the vaccine may be appropriate. The vaccine is also sometimes used to treat extremely persistent cases of ringworm in individual cats.

Bordetella bronchiseptica

Routine vaccination against this respiratory infection is not recommended. But in multiple-cat environments, such as shelters and boarding facilities, where the disease has been shown to be actively present, vaccination should be considered. Further research is still necessary to determine how long this vaccine is effective.

Giardia

Routine vaccination against the intestinal parasite *Giardia lamblia* is not recommended. But the vaccine has been shown to lessen an infected cat's symptoms, and to render him contagious for a shorter period of time. In multiple-cat environments where *G. lamblia* infection is present, its use may be appropriate as one component of an overall control program. (Giardiosis can be transmitted to humans and other animals.)

Although most cats do little more than flinch when vaccinated, there's a small possibility of anaphylactic shock following vaccination. This severe allergic reaction to some component of the vaccine usually occurs within the first half hour after vaccination. Symptoms include salivation, vomiting, difficulty breathing, lack of coordination, and collapse. Rush back to the veterinarian if your cat shows these signs. Better yet, hang around for a while until you're sure your cat is doing well.

After Vaccination Day—Keeping Watch

After receiving their vaccinations, some cats display temporary symptoms such as diminished appetite, lethargy, crankiness, or a minor fever. Some will also develop a small amount of tenderness or swelling at the injection sites. These symptoms should be minor and subside quickly, usually within a day or so. Keep your cat, and your household, quiet and peaceful for the first few days after vaccinations. Let your cat rest as much as he wants. If he still seems lethargic or depressed a few days later, a call and return visit to the veterinarian may be in order.

In the weeks and months following your cat's annual checkup and vaccinations, be especially alert for any unusual lumps, bumps, or swellings anywhere on your cat's body, but especially near any of the vaccination sites. Report any bumps you find to your veterinarian immediately. One reason for the new recommendation for giving vaccines at separate sites on your cat's body is to more easily identify which vaccines may be causing problems. Many cats get a small amount of swelling at their vaccination sites in the weeks following their vaccinations, but the cat doesn't seem to notice or care, and the swelling usually subsides quickly. Of special concern are lumps that are pea-sized or larger and still getting bigger a month after the vaccination, and lumps that persist for three months or more after the vaccination. Tissue samples of such lumps should be sent to a laboratory for testing.

If your cat develops a vaccine-associated sarcoma, your veterinarian will usually recommend surgery to remove both the sarcoma and a wide margin of surrounding tissue—to make sure all the tumor tissue is removed, and to keep it from spreading. If the tumor is large, your veterinarian may recommend radiation treatments as well and may refer you to a veterinary oncologist (cancer specialist).

Don't Skip Vaccinations!

The risks to your cat from the diseases against which he's routinely vaccinated are far greater than the chances he'll suffer an adverse reaction or develop a vaccine-associated sarcoma. Never let your fears, or rumors you hear, keep you from giving your cat the best protection veterinary medicine can offer him. Keeping him healthy and protected from disease is part of the Feline Covenant.

IDENTIFICATION—YOUR CAT'S TICKET HOME

Does your cat need identification, even if he never ventures out the door? Yes! No matter how careful you are, your cat might still slip out one day. Or some disaster—a house fire, earthquake, or other calamity—may overtake your cat when you're not there to evacuate him safely. If your cat escapes, he may save his own life, but he's likely to be frightened, disoriented, or even injured. Without identification, his chances of returning to you are greatly reduced. Identification is your cat's ticket home. Very few cats without identification are ever reunited with their owners.

Your Cat's First Line of Defense

There are many ways to identify your cat. Perhaps the easiest is a collar designed especially for cats. Some cat owners might have concerns about the safety of cat collars. Using a properly sized breakaway-type collar reduces any risk of injury to the cat if his collar gets caught on something. These collars have a section that's designed to break under pressure or weight—such as your cat's weight hanging from the collar. You should be able to fit two fingers between the collar and your cat's neck. Check the fit frequently to insure it's not too tight.

Although you can indelibly inscribe your phone number or other contact information right on the collar itself and forego tags (which can seem heavy or noisy), you run the risk that the information will be obscured by fur and that whoever rescues your cat may not even realize the information is there. Lightweight, sturdy tags are much more reliable and noticeable. A collar with tags is reliable, safe, inexpensive, and easily visible to anyone who finds your cat. As a backup, you might consider a second method of identifying your cat, such as microchipping.

And remember, while the experts at The Humane Society of the United States are not aware of a single documented instance of a cat strangled by a collar, they're all too aware of the millions of documented deaths of cats euthanized because they didn't carry any identification.

Identification That's Skin-Deep

In microchipping, a tiny (rice-grain-size or smaller) microchip, in which is encoded a unique identifying code, is injected into your cat, usually right below the skin behind his shoulders. The needle used for the injection is only slightly larger than the needle used for routine vaccinations. Cats tolerate the procedure extremely well. With a special reader, like a supermarket checkout wand, shelter workers can read the encoded identifier and send your cat on his way safely home. Efforts are underway to standardize these microchip identification systems, and to solve other technical problems, such as chips that "migrate" away from their original locations, making them harder to detect.

Think of the number encoded in the microchip as being like the VIN (vehicle ID number) for your car: it never goes away, and no one can alter it. Having a microchip implanted can cost anywhere from twenty-to-forty-five dollars plus an annual registration fee. *Registering your cat's microchip ID with the registry is crucial!* Many shelters now routinely microchip adopted cats. Because of this high-tech innovation, many cats who would have been euthanized have instead gone safely home.

CAT LICENSING

Efforts are underway in many localities to enact legislation requiring registration and licensing of cats. Many cities and counties have required cat licensing for decades. Other areas are pursuing educational and voluntary-compliance approaches. Partly because mandatory licensing of cats is a new concept for some cat owners, and partly because many people still believe so many of the cat myths we demolished in chapter 3, there's a great deal of resistance to the idea. The Humane Society of the United States promotes licensing all cats, under a strategy called differential licensing—charging significantly more for a license for unsterilized cats than for spayed and neutered cats.

YEAR-ROUND HOLIDAY SAFETY

Because your cat is so sensitive to change and upset in his familiar routines, his health and safety can be at the most risk at the very times you're distracted by other matters—like holiday celebrations. Many holiday traditions, while fun for people, are inexplicable and stressful for cats. Noise, overstimulation, unusual food and decorations, stress, and invasions of his territory by strangers can, if not sensitively managed, endanger your cat's health and safety and bring on misbehavior. Unsupervised access to unusual or rich foods, candy, poisonous plants, and breakable or swallowable decorations can threaten his health and even his life.

Although many holiday throughout the year present similar threats—possible escape, stress from unfamiliar smells or loud noises, digestive upsets from candy or unusual foods—each holiday also presents its own unique hazards. Summer holidays, with doors opened frequently, increase your cat's risk of escaping. Explain to visitors and guests that your cat is an indoors-only pet so that they don't innocently let him out. Your cat should always wear a safe, properly fitted breakaway collar with your phone numbers clearly inscribed either on the collar itself or on tags attached to the collar. Identification is his ticket home if he becomes lost.

Whatever the holiday, always try to anticipate and shield your cat from loud or unfamiliar noises with white noise such as soft music. This is particularly important during celebrations that include fireworks, trick-or-treaters, or yelling, loud music, and noise. Amid busy holiday celebrations, it's particularly important to maintain your cat's normal schedule—regular mealtimes, playtime, and litter-box cleaning.

For holidays that include decorations and special foods, it's much easier to ban potential dangers from your home than to try to keep your cat away from temptation, constantly chase him away from decorations—and worry whenever you're not nearby to supervise. Explore safe, simple, inexpensive, or homemade alternatives to such dangerous decorations as tinsel (which can cause serious abdominal damage in cats), shatterable glass ornaments (which can cut paws and mouths), candles (easy to tip over, causing burns and house fires), and toxic or irritating plants such as holly and mistletoe.

Chocolate may cause your cat gastrointestinal upsets at least; at worst, it's toxic. Keep candy in safe, closed containers (like cookie tins with tight-fitting lids), never in open bowls.

Hosting a holiday gathering? Install your cat in his safe retreat (see chapter 6) well before party time. Provide food, water, litter box, toys, and a tape player or radio playing soft music to mask unfamiliar sounds. Warn your guests to not open your cat's safe-retreat door, and explain why it's a bad idea to offer him party foods. After your party, carefully clean up all food and drink before letting your cat out of his safe retreat (alcoholic beverages are bad for cats). Then, enjoy your own private party, complete with special cat treats and a play session with a favorite interactive toy.

Holiday decor often requires extra electrical wires for lights, decorations, or sound systems. Be vigilant around these setups. If your cat shows any tendency to paw at or chew the wiring, render all wiring inaccessible by running it through PVC pipe, or (as a last resort) paint wires with pet-safe bitters to prevent chewing. Better still, install your cat in his safe retreat until the decorations and wiring have been dismantled.

TRAVELING WITH YOUR CAT—A GOOD IDEA?

Before you hit the road (or the skies) with your cat, ask yourself: Is this trip really necessary for your cat? Unlike many dogs, cats tend to be poor travelers. They find change, disruption, and alteration of their accustomed schedules stressful and disorienting. Away from his familiar, comfortable home base and routines, your cat is unlikely to feel happy or secure. It can be difficult to find hotels and motels that allow feline guests.

If you travel with your cat by air, your best choice is a carrier that allows your cat to fly in the passenger cabin with you, in a carrier that fits beneath the seat in front of you. (FRANTZ DANTZLER)

Cats are not allowed on most, if not all, public buses and trains. If you need to get your cat from point A to point B, your options are, in most cases, limited to a car trip or a flight aboard a "common carrier" airline. As a prudent, responsible, and caring cat owner, be sure you know your cat, your options, and the pros and cons of your chosen method of transportation well before you embark on your trip. Fortunately, there are alternatives to taking your cat on the road with you. The first is to hire a professional pet-sitter.

Professional Pet-Sitters

You could hire the neighborhood teenager or a friend to come in twice a day to check on your cat, feed him, and scoop the litter box. If you know and trust the person in whose care you place your cat, this may work well, especially for very short absences. But for your cat's sake, and for your own peace of mind, consider hiring a professional pet-sitter. Contact the National Association of Professional Pet Sitters (6 State Road, #113, Mechanicsburg, PA 17055; 1-717-691-5565; Fax 1-717-3381; http://www.petsitters.org) or Pet Sitters International (418 East King Street, King, NC 27021-9163; 1-336-983-9222; Fax 1-336-983-3755; http://www.petsit.com) to find a qualified, accredited pet-sitter in your area.

Members of these organizations abide by a code of ethics, have demonstrated professional experience and cat-care expertise, and have completed a home-study course in pet care. Many keep their skills sharp through further study and attendance at professional conferences. Have the pet-sitter visit your home before your trip. (If she's a professional, she'll insist on it!) She'll meet your cat and take written notes on his needs, personality, preferences, behavior, habits, and routines. Ask the pet-sitter plenty of questions, too:

- Is she bonded? (to protect you from theft)
- Does she have proof that she carries commercial liability insurance?
- Does she have a reliable backup in case she's unable to care for your cat?
- How much experience does she have caring for cats?
- Does she offer a written service contract, spelling out fees and services?
- Can she refer you to other clients of hers?
- Does she provide other services such as live-in service, plant care, etc.?
- Will she verify that you've actually returned home before stopping her visits?
- Will she continue to care for your cat if your return is delayed?

While you're away, the pet-sitter will not only attend to your cat's needs, she'll also spend quality time with him. She'll recognize if he needs veterinary attention and make sure he gets it. Many pet-sitters also offer such additional services as plant care, bringing in mail and newspapers, turning lights on and off, and giving your home a lived-in look while you're away.

Give your pet-sitter the tools and information she needs to effectively care for your cat and your home in your absence. Do you have a security system? Emergency shutoffs? Different keys? When is the regular trash pickup? Are all cat supplies (cat carrier, food, litter, medications, etc.) in stock and easily accessible? Are there extras, in case your return is delayed? Is your cat current on all his vaccinations? Does he have complete ID (collar and/or tags)? Does your pet-sitter have complete contact information both for you and for a trusted relative or friend as backup?

Boarding Your Cat? Be Picky!

When choosing a boarding facility, be very, very picky. Get recommendations from trusted friends who own cats. Find out if pet-boarding facilities are licensed or inspected by your state or municipality. If so, insure that the facility has its certification and inspections up-to-date.

Visit the facility ahead of time. Sniff around. If the place smells—leave. It's not for your cat! Here are some questions to ask:

- What are the qualifications of the staff?
- Are all animal residents required to be current on their vaccinations?
- Is there a veterinarian on call? Do you know the veterinarian?
- Does each cat have a roomy, comfortable, individual cage or enclosure, with plenty of room for a litter box, and with a separate food area and exercise area?
- Is the facility properly heated or air-conditioned for the animals' comfort?
- Can the staff handle medications and special diets?
- Can your cat eat his usual brand and type of food?
- Will the staff adhere to your cat's usual feeding schedule?
- Can your cat use his regular brand and style of litter?
- How much individual attention will your cat get?
- Is regular grooming provided?
- Is it "cats only," or will the barks and odors of dogs stress your cat during his stay?
- How much does the facility cost per day? Does that include all services, or are there extras or add-on charges you may not expect?

Even at the best boarding facilities, many cats do poorly, refuse to eat (a potentially perilous health risk), or are in danger of picking up airborne illnesses from the other cats in residence. Like some catteries, boarding facilities often harbor perennially recurring illnesses such as respiratory and skin infections. And the stress and change to familiar routines can bring on hard-to-solve behavior problems. If you can arrange it, your cat will probably be much happier staying in his own home, attended by a qualified pet-sitter.

Hitting the Road with Your Cat

Cats being individuals, some truly enjoy car trips with their owners. But most cats strongly dislike the feeling of motion and the stop-go nature of car travel. Unlike dogs, who seem to revel in hanging their heads out the car window, cats are rapidly disoriented by the sight of the world whizzing by. Some even get carsick. Sometimes, though, a car trip with your cat is unavoidable. If you're traveling by car with your cat, keep these precautions in mind:

- Your cat must carry clear, visible identification at all times. Road accidents happen, and your cat could easily escape or be thrown from your car. Even if he's in a carrier, the carrier might shatter or open during a collision. Consider using a more permanent form of ID, such as a microchip, as a backup.

- While riding in your car, your cat should always stay in a sturdy carrier that's large enough for him to stand up and turn around in. Place a soft, washable pad (like an old sweatshirt that carries your familiar scent) in the carrier. If your cat seems distressed or upset, cover his carrier with a towel or blanket, but allow for air circulation and don't let him become overheated. The darkness will help calm him and muffle the sounds of the engine and the wind. If he's been accustomed to wearing a harness, keep his harness on him so that you can easily attach a lead for occasional rest and exercise breaks.

  A cat loose in a car can become a danger to the driver (crawling under the brake pedal, for example) and thus to others in the car and others on the road. He could panic because of an unexpected sound or event. He could become a missile during a collision or rapid stop—possibly injuring himself and others. No matter how calm and well traveled your cat is, he should always ride in his carrier.

- At rest breaks, never open car doors or windows until you're sure your cat is confined and securely in his harness and lead. He could easily escape and become quickly lost and disoriented, which would be especially dangerous near a busy highway.

- If possible, keep a litter box in the car for emergencies. You can purchase disposable plastic or coated cardboard litter boxes made just for the traveling cat.

- Resist the temptation to medicate or tranquilize your cat. Many cats respond poorly or unexpectedly to such medication while stressed by unfamiliar sights, sounds, or odors, or by the movements of the car. Instead of calming them down, these medications make some cats aggressive, frightened, or hyperactive. Maintain a calm, positive attitude, cover his cage, and speak softly and soothingly. Keep the car windows closed, and play soft music to mask road noises.

- If possible, bring water from home to avoid any possibility of adverse reactions to unfamiliar chemicals or chlorination in water you find on the road. Bring along a supply of your cat's usual food—and make it his favorite flavor. It will help ease the stress of travel.

- Never leave your cat unattended in your car—even for a few moments. Dangers include your cat being stolen, your car (along with your cat) being stolen, and your cat becoming dangerously overheated. A car's interior temperature can soar quickly to levels deadly to your cat. He can suffer serious heat exhaustion or heatstroke within minutes.

The Feline-Friendly Skies

Traveling by air can be a scary proposition—for cats and their owners. But a short plane trip can be easier on your cat than a long, multiday car ride. Think through your options ahead of time. If you must travel by air with your cat, do your homework and planning well in advance. Contact the airline you plan to use and make sure you know its complete, current policies on flying pets. If you must travel by air, by far your best choice is to fly with an airline that allows your cat to fly in the passenger cabin, in his carrier beneath the seat in front of you. You'll have to make arrangements and reservations at least a week in advance and transport your cat in an airline-approved carrier that can fit under a seat. You'll also have to buy him a special cat ticket.

On travel day, don't rush. Arrive in plenty of time to get yourself and your cat to the airport and settled. Don't let your cat go through the scanner with the luggage; carry him, in his carrier, through with you. If security personnel ask that you take your cat out of his carrier, insist on seeing a supervisor. If you can't avoid taking him out of his bag, use a harness and leash for security. Don't rely on being able to hold him in a busy, noisy, crowded airport terminal. Pay close attention to your cat during the flight, but never take him out of his carrier.

Cargo Cat

What if you have absolutely no choice but to ship your cat as baggage? Is this safe? Lots of cats fly safely and uneventfully around the United States in the cargo holds of major airlines every year, but five thousand animals are killed or lost on commercial flights annually as well. Do your homework. Make your plans and reservations in advance. In hot weather and warm climates, schedule a cooler early morning or evening flight. Avoid flying your cat in very cold or uncertain weather, when delays and cancellations are more likely.

If you're flying too, try to fly on the same plane as your cat. Consider scheduling a nonstop flight—even if it's more expensive. Especially if your cat is traveling solo, avoid using multiple airlines that might involve lengthy transfers or delays on the ground. If you can't avoid transfers or stopovers, investigate options for having your cat hand-carried from plane to plane. This service is well worth the extra cost. When shipping your cat, you'll have to drop him off and pick him up at a special cargo terminal—not the regular passenger terminal. Find out ahead of time where this is, at both the local airport and at your cat's destination.

Your cat may need a health certificate from his veterinarian within ten days prior to his trip. This is usually required by both government and airline regulations.

As with car travel—and for the same reasons—avoid using tranquilizers or similar medications. Don't leave food or water in your cat's carrier, even if you're tempted. It will just spill and make a mess your cat will have to lie in. Feed your cat a light meal four hours before the flight.

The airline will require your cat to be transported in a solid, leak-proof carrier that meets its standards. If your cat's carrier has wheels, you'll probably have to remove them. Label your cat's carrier clearly, on all sides, according to airline regulations. Add an additional, large label with your cat's destination airport conspicuously and clearly written on it. Include your name, address, and contact information. Add a clear warning to airline personnel instructing them that they are not to open the carrier for any reason. Don't give your cat the chance to escape in a dangerous and unfamiliar location!

Legal requirements and restrictions on shipping pets and other animals by air are continually changing. In addition to government regulations, individual airlines have regulations, policies, and restrictions. Some airlines will not carry live animals at all. Be sure to check well in advance of your trip (or your cat's trip). Check again a few days before the flight and again on the day of the flight itself, to make sure your flight plans are still valid and that your cat can safely and rapidly reach his destination.

CHAPTER 17

Emergency!

N o matter what the emergency—natural, human-caused, environmental, or
medical—advance planning can mean the difference between life and death for
your cat.

IS THIS REALLY A MEDICAL EMERGENCY?

Samantha is a four-year-old black-and-white cat with a permanently quizzical look.
Early one morning her owner, Mitzi, was startled—and alarmed—to see Samantha
staggering around in circles as if drunk. Every few moments, Samantha would sit
down suddenly, close her eyes, and stay very still for a few moments—then resume her
drunken circling. Emergency?

Lindy was taking some clean laundry out of the dryer when she heard a cross
between a yowl and a shriek emanate from the corner where the litter boxes were.
Rushing over, she found Boris, her big, healthy two-year-old tabby, crouched just out-

side the box, crying out piteously, clearly in distress. Every few seconds he'd hop in the box, circle rapidly, squat, raise his tail, cry out, and then hop back out, lick furiously at his rear end—then start all over again. Emergency?

Champer, an indoor-outdoor cat, returned home one day obviously the worse for wear, with three evil-looking gashes in his flank. Blood still seeped through his fur, crusted as it was with dirt and already-dried blood. He walked with a sort of bunny-hop, one hind leg dragging uselessly behind him. Emergency?

Cleo, a plump fourteen-year-old calico, took one bite from her breakfast, walked away, and sat down across the room. Her owner, Marcia, suddenly realized Cleo hadn't eaten more than a few mouthfuls in three days. Emergency?

Mark came home to find his cat Bob stretched out on the kitchen floor, barely breathing, eyes glassy. Nearby, a cabinet full of cleaning supplies was wide-open. Emergency?

While dishing up dinner, Paula noticed that one of her kittens, Biff, looked funny. His head was tilted to the left, and he was holding one eye tightly shut in a comical-looking squint. When he tried to run to his food bowl, he ran into a wall and fell down. Emergency?

In all these cases—yes! These are all true veterinary emergencies. Samantha may be having seizures, showing signs of neurological damage or disease, or may have ingested poison. Boris is likely experiencing a painful urinary blockage—a condition that can kill him within hours if he doesn't get emergency care. Champer, in addition to his visible injuries, likely has a broken bone or two, and he may have suffered internal injuries as well.

Cleo is in imminent peril of developing hepatic lipidosis, an extremely serious liver condition that strikes cats whose food intake drops suddenly for more than a few days. As an older, overweight cat, she's especially at risk for this condition. Cleo needs immediate veterinary care and supplemental nutrition.

Bob has likely ingested poison, probably by licking at a pesticide or cleaning product. Mark's best bet is to call his veterinarian or emergency clinic at once. If he can't reach them, he should call the National Animal Poison Control Center. (See chapter 6 for details.) He also needs to try to discover exactly what substance his cat consumed. Every second counts.

The squinting kitten, Biff, likely has an eye injury—a scratched cornea or a foreign object embedded in his eye.

Each of these cats needs immediate veterinary attention. These are scary situations, and some of them, at least, could have been prevented by rigorous cat-proofing or by an indoors-only lifestyle. No matter how careful and conscientious you are, emergencies can arise. Kittens will wrestle; a tiny claw will scratch an eye. Urinary blockages can occur at any time, especially in male cats. Older cats will stop eating for a variety of reasons and risk hepatic lipidosis.

MEDICAL EMERGENCIES: PREVENTION, OBSERVATION, INTERVENTION

Handling medical emergencies requires prevention, observation, and intervention. Though your ultimate goal is to prevent all emergencies through wise choice of lifestyle, rigorous cat-proofing, and everyday vigilance, even the most conscientious efforts won't prevent all emergencies. That's where observation comes in: Part of the Feline Covenant is becoming familiar with your cat's normal looks, sounds, habits, rituals, moods, activities, and haunts. Any change in these calls for heightened attention and immediate intervention when needed.

When to Call the Veterinarian

If you're concerned about your cat, call your veterinarian. Perhaps your cat's face suddenly looks funny to you, a bit puffy or asymmetrical. He may have an abscess on his cheek or chin. Tiny claw injuries can heal superficially, but become badly infected underneath—hidden by a thick ruff of fur. A slight drag of a leg could be a sign of a pulled muscle, broken bone, or muscle weakness that signals underlying disease.

There are a number of symptoms that *virtually always* constitute true feline emergencies and call for immediate veterinary intervention:

- **bleeding from any part of the body,** especially bleeding that doesn't stop on its own within a very few minutes
- **broken bones,** either obviously broken or evidenced by signs such as lameness, dragging of a limb, or difficulty bearing weight or walking
- **unconsciousness** for any reason
- **breathing difficulty,** including cessation of breathing, a blue tongue, extreme shortness of breath, noisy breathing, or sustained panting
- **sudden onset of weakness or extreme listlessness,** especially if accompanied by dilated pupils, rapid heartbeat, or shallow breathing

- **any evidence of electric shock,** such as electrical burns in the cat's mouth or on his paws, especially in the presence of chewed electrical cords
- **seizures,** evidenced by staggering, circling, collapsing, uncoordinated movements, loss of balance, mental confusion
- **any major trauma,** even if the cat seems fine—including being hit by a car, a fight with another cat or other animal, a serious fall, or an accident of any kind
- **poisoning,** including any evidence that the cat has ingested a poison, whether a plant, chemical, or other substance
- **straining and crying out in the litter box,** whether depositing nothing or only tiny bits of urine
- **sudden-onset squinting** or holding an eye tightly shut, sudden copious flow of tears, or any kind of drainage from the eye
- **evidence of pain,** including crouching, crying out, reluctance to be touched, or unusual aggressiveness or other reaction when touched
- **diarrhea** that lasts for more than a few hours
- **bloody diarrhea**
- **bloody urine**
- **crying out or howling while urinating or defecating**
- **persistent or copious vomiting,** or vomiting accompanied by diarrhea, unusual behavior, or other changes
- **extreme or sudden behavior or mood change,** such as violent attacks or aggressiveness
- **open wound or gash** that is large or bleeds heavily
- **heatstroke or heat exhaustion,** evidenced by panting, drooling, rapid pulse, temperature up to 106 degrees F, staring, bright red gums, diarrhea, bloody nose, severe weakness, or coma (Wrap your cat in a cool, wet towel or immerse him in cool water immediately to lower his temperature. Then call the veterinarian.)

Some emergencies—the ones with unconsciousness, blood, and broken bones—are obvious. Others are less messy or scary, perhaps, but no less life threatening. For example, Boris's urinary blockage, Samantha's staggering, and Cleo's refusal to eat can all cause rapid death without emergency intervention. Never hesitate to call your veterinarian or an emergency veterinary clinic for fear of appearing foolish or overreacting.

First Response for Medical Emergencies

A life-threatening emergency involving your dear companion cat is tremendously scary and confusing. Don't let your own fear, panic, or confusion keep you from helping your cat as best you can. The best way to help your cat is to be prepared, calm, methodical, competent, reassuring, and brave. Hope for the best, but be prepared for the worst.

Your Feline-First-Aid Book—Read It Before You Need It

Don't let an emergency situation be the first time you open a good feline first-aid guide and reference book. The Humane Society of the United States and the American Red Cross jointly have published *Pet First Aid: Cats and Dogs,* a handy first-aid reference for cat and dog owners. It's available from The Humane Society of the United States, 2100 L Street, NW, Washington, D.C. 20037.

Part of the Feline Covenant is being prepared to do all you can to keep your cat alive in an emergency situation until you can deliver him into the care of a veterinary professional. Review the contents of your first-aid book several times a year, and be sure you stay up-to-date on the latest recommended emergency and first-aid procedures. Some procedures once routinely taught were found to do more harm than good. If you have any questions, ask your veterinarian to clarify or demonstrate a procedure. Keep your first-aid kit stocked and handy. Check the contents periodically, and replace items that have been used or removed. In an emergency, you'll be glad you took the time.

Remember Your ABCs

If and when you experience a feline emergency, your advance preparation, along with calm, clear thinking, will help you to keep your priorities in order. These priorities may seem obvious—but with a badly injured cat whose life is at stake, it's easy to become confused and distracted. Any cat who has suffered an accident or has been subjected to trauma of any kind may be in shock, may be bleeding uncontrollably, may have ceased breathing, or may not have a heartbeat. These matters must be attended to first, and immediately. Always assume, and treat for, shock. Then, just remember your ABCs:

- airway
- breathing
- circulation

Your first priority is treating life-threatening conditions: protecting the airway, breathing and circulation. Your next priority is to treat less-threatening injuries that are causing pain or distress. Reducing shock, getting the cat to a veterinarian, and reducing pain are all more important than treating lesser injuries, cleaning up wounds, or washing blood from fur. In an emergency, it's vital to safely transport the cat to a veterinary clinic as rapidly as possible. *Be sure to call ahead to make sure the veterinarian is there.* No matter how well you know first-aid procedures and techniques, they're just stopgaps. Your cat needs professional assessment and care as soon as possible.

Protecting Yourself from an Injured Cat

No matter how well you know your cat and how close your bond, when he's injured or ill he may become a stranger temporarily. Pain, fear, stress, and shock can all cause your usually mellow cat to strike out, bite, and thrash. If you become injured yourself—and a cat has the weaponry to cause you serious damage extremely quickly—your ability to help your cat and transport him to medical aid may be greatly reduced. Don't take this chance.

If you're the least bit suspicious that your injured cat may have tangled with a rabid animal, it's vital to protect yourself from possible exposure to the rabies virus. The rabid animal's infective saliva may still be present in your cat's wounds. Wear thick, heavy gloves, avoid touching any fluids or blood present on your cat, and wrap him securely in a thick towel for transport.

Shock

In any emergency, especially following injury or trauma, assume your cat is in shock. Shock can range from mild to severe, and can be life threatening in itself. Signs of shock include rapid, shallow breathing, pale gums, and weakness. The cat will seem cold to the touch. Keep him quiet and warm. Speak softly and avoid sudden movements and loud noises that might further stress or frighten him.

Airway

If your cat is unconscious, make sure his airway is unobstructed. Roll him over on his side with his head tilted slightly backwards. Keep his head slightly lower than the rest of his body. Make sure that neither his tongue nor any foreign object or material is obstructing his airway.

Breathing: Artificial Respiration and CPR

If your cat has stopped breathing, begin mouth-to-nose artificial respiration immediately. Consult an up-to-date first-aid reference, or ask your veterinarian to demonstrate this life-saving procedure.

If your cat has no detectable heartbeat, veterinary assistance is not immediately available, and you know how to perform the procedure correctly, initiate feline CPR, also called cardiac compression. If the cat has both stopped breathing and has no discernable heartbeat, ideally a two-person team should alternate with mouth-to-nose artificial respiration and cardiac compression in a synchronized pattern. This can also be performed by one person, alternating techniques. Consult an up-to-date first-aid reference, or ask your veterinarian to demonstrate and train you in this life-saving procedure. The American Red Cross offers classes in CPR for pets. Call your local Red Cross chapter to find out when a class may be offered in your area.

Circulation: Stopping Bleeding

To stanch uncontrolled bleeding, establish a secure hold on your cat—either wrap him in a thick towel or blanket, or grasp him by the scruff of the neck and hold down his rump. Apply firm pressure directly to the bleeding site, either with your finger or with a pad of gauze or other soft cloth. If the bleeding wound is not in a location where you can easily apply pressure, wrap some ice in a towel and place the ice pack directly over the wound. Press, don't rub. Stroking, dabbing, or rubbing tends to increase bleeding. Don't worry about cleaning the wound until you've controlled the bleeding.

Call Your Veterinarian

Part of your preparation for emergencies is knowing your veterinarian's policy on handling emergencies, especially when his office or clinic is closed. Does he have a twenty-four-hour pager number? Do you know it? Is it written down by every phone in your house? Does he have a colleague on call when he's not available? Do you have that phone number? Does he use a referral to an area veterinary emergency hospital? Do you know where it is? Knowing this vital information ahead of time will give you peace of mind and help you stay calm and in control should a feline emergency arise.

If you think you may have a feline emergency on your hands, call your veterinarian, or the veterinarian who's covering for him, first. Be prepared to explain exactly what you've observed, why you're concerned, any symptoms you're seeing, and any other relevant information.

Poisoning—Getting Help Fast

If you suspect poisoning, call your veterinarian or emergency animal clinic first, and follow their instructions. If you cannot reach either, call the NAPCC, the National Animal Poison Control Center. (See chapter 6 for details.) Always keep the phone numbers of the NAPCC and a twenty-four-hour emergency veterinary clinic posted by every telephone in your home.

Broken Bones

Fractures are very painful. Expect pain-related aggression and protect yourself. Never attempt to push a broken bone back into place—you could harm your cat further. If you're more than thirty minutes away from veterinary help, splint, or at least pad, broken limbs to try to reduce movement and the resulting pain. Don't try to straighten the limb—you may get bitten and end up stressing your cat even more. Pad the limb with a roll of soft towelling and use a rigid item such as a rolled-up newspaper or magazine to immobilize it. Wrap it loosely with plastic wrap, panty hose, or elastic bandage to hold everything together. In any case of fracture or suspected fracture, concentrate on getting your cat to the veterinarian safely and as rapidly as possible.

Transporting an Injured Cat

Although it's vital to get your cat to a veterinarian as soon as possible, it's also important not to further stress or frighten him, worsen his injuries, or put yourself in peril. If your cat is in imminent danger of death—for example, if he's stopped breathing or is bleeding uncontrollably—your first priority is to stabilize his vital functions. Remember your ABCs. *Always* treat for shock.

Always call the veterinarian or hospital and tell them you're on your way. Tell them the age, gender, and condition of the cat and what injuries or symptoms you're seeing. If the symptoms are immediately life threatening, the veterinarian may have you initiate first-aid procedures if you haven't already done so.

Once you've stabilized the cat's ABCs, prepare him for transport. Never grab an ill or injured cat, or even pick him up as you would normally do. He could lash out in pain or fear. Speak softly and soothingly, and approach him slowly. Gently cover him with a soft, thick towel, blanket, or coat. Have a carrier ready. A carrier that opens from the top is best; use a large cardboard box in a pinch. Don't try to force or maneuver an injured cat into the small door of a side-opening carrier.

Injured during Hurricane Opal, a cat is comforted by a Florida shelter worker after being rescued.
(LAURA BEVAN)

Gently lift the wrapped cat and place him in the carrier or box. Carefully support his entire body as you lift and move him, especially if you have reason (such as floppy or dragging rear legs) to suspect an injury to his spine. Avoid twisting or turning him. When you're ready to head to the veterinarian or emergency hospital, try to find a companion so that one of you can drive while the other watches and tends the cat.

PREPARING FOR NATURAL AND MAN-MADE DISASTERS

When it comes to disaster planning, any plan is better than none. But a well-thought-out, comprehensive plan that includes every member of your family offers your best chance of surviving mayhem as unscathed as possible. Including your cat in your disaster plan is part of the Feline Covenant.

What kinds of disasters might threaten your home and life? A house fire can happen to anyone. Depending on where you live, other disasters may include earthquakes, floods, brushfires, forest fires, mud slides, chemical spills, and industrial explosions and accidents that release chemical gasses or radioactivity. Then there are the rare, random occurrences, like a plane or meteorite crashing into your home. (They do happen!) Any of these disasters may require you to evacuate your home with little or no notice.

Find out what hidden threats may lurk in your vicinity. Is there a warehouse full of pool chemicals nearby? A dammed reservoir? After the 1971 earthquake in the San Fernando Valley near Los Angeles, California, thousands of families had to evacuate at very short notice because a dam was in imminent danger of breaking, and the water would flood their homes. Most residents had no idea of the existence of the reservoir looming over their heads!

Be Prepared!

The more widespread the disaster, the more you'll have to rely on your own skills and preparations. In a residential fire, you can usually count on swift, comprehensive aid from firefighters and authorities. But in a major earthquake, you may be on your own for up to several days. Be sure your planning reflects this.

Be ready for what you hope will never happen. Start right now to formulate a plan and assemble the supplies and equipment you'll need to evacuate your family and your cat at a moment's notice. Here are the three major questions you need to consider:

1. How will I transport my cat?
2. What should I bring with me?
3. Where will I go?

In addition to the supplies you'll need for your human family members, plan ahead for your cat. Keep everything you'll need for a quick evacuation, including your cat carrier(s), packed near the entrance to your home so that you can grab it quickly. Don't stash your disaster gear off in a corner of the basement. Here's what you'll need:

1. a sturdy carrier for each cat (Don't rely on cardboard carriers.)
2. a supply of cat food that will last at least a week (more is better), for as many cats as you have (Buy extras of your cat's favorite, and rotate your stock regularly so that emergency supplies are always fresh and ready to go. If you use canned food, don't forget a hand-operated can opener and a spoon or two.)
3. several jugs of bottled water (Check frequently for leaks.)
4. a portable litter box and enough litter to last at least a week or two
5. extra copies of your cat's identification (tags and paperwork)
6. your first-aid and emergency kit, including your cat's medications, medical records, and recent, clear photographs (See below for the complete list of contents.)
7. a supply of plastic garbage bags
8. a supply of clean old towels and rags

This sounds like a lot of supplies. But everything except the cat carriers can be neatly packed into a large or medium-sized plastic storage tub (available at home stores and discount stores). Collapsible plastic cat carriers are available from pet-supply stores and catalogs. If you have several cats, this might be a worthwhile option. It's vital to keep everything easily accessible.

Evacuation

Depending upon the situation, you may be given from a few moments to a few hours to evacuate your home. The cardinal rule is: *take your cat with you.*

Never leave your cat behind if you have to evacuate. If it's too dangerous for you to stay, it's too dangerous for your cat to stay!

If your cat enjoys an indoors-only lifestyle, it should be relatively easy to find him on short notice, pack him into his carrier, grab your emergency supplies, and be on your way. Be sure you know—ahead of time—all the locations in your home where your cat likes to hide. If your cat is allowed outdoors, train him, in advance, to respond

Although rescue workers, firefighters, government employees, or other authorities may be able to help some animals in a natural or manmade disaster, never rely on them to save your cat. (HSUS)

to a special call, whistle, or clicker noise. Use a cue noise that summons him unfailingly to your side. Make sure your cat is wearing his collar and ID tags (as he always should be, especially if he ventures outdoors). If you've trained him to walk in a harness with leash, fit him with his harness before you place him in his carrier. Keep the leash handy.

If you can't find your cat, but are required to evacuate, notify rescue workers, authorities, local rescue groups, and local shelters as soon as possible that your cat is missing. Provide a recent, clear photo and complete contact information so that your cat can be returned to you as soon as he's found. Unfortunately, many cats who can't be found when their owners have to evacuate are never reunited with their owners.

Set aside time every few months for your family to go over your disaster plans and practice safe, rapid evacuation—of humans and pets alike.

It's Up to You

The primary responsibility for securing your cat's safety in any emergency or disaster, large or small, lies with you. *Never count on the government, rescue workers, firefighters, or other authorities to save your cat.* In a disaster, they're often hard-pressed to deal with human problems. Be sure to place *nonpermanent* "Please Rescue my Cat(s)" signs, specifying the number of cats you have, prominently on several locations around your home. (Keep the pet count on these signs up-to-date. Remove the signs before you move or if you no longer have pets to prevent emergency personnel from being injured—or worse—trying to rescue pets no longer in the home.) Firefighters may rescue companion animals when they're able to (and brave firefighters have saved many feline lives), but they're there to save human lives first.

Never count on anyone else to rescue your cat. It's up to you.

Working Together

Health and safety laws prohibit companion animals (except service animals) in most American Red Cross and other emergency shelters. Hotels and motels, especially if they accept pets, are likely to be filled quickly. So where can you and your cat go? Local shelters are often overwhelmed during emergencies. Your cat could get lost in the shuffle. And the stress of being placed suddenly in a noisy, scary shelter could cause behavior or even health problems. Selecting a temporary caretaker ahead of time will not only give you more peace of mind—it's also much better for your cat.

Form a cat-rescue pact. Get together with a few trusted friends and relatives who live within a driving radius of about three hours. Agree to open your homes to other members of the pact during any emergency when they have to evacuate with their cat. Each member of the pact can agree to take in cats only, human evacuees, or other pets—it's up to each individual. If there are five different homes, in five different locations a few hours apart, in your cat-rescue group, it's likely that not all will be affected by the same disaster at the same time. Communicate frequently—an E-mail list is a good way—to coordinate your plans. You could even go in together on buying supplies, cat carriers, and first-aid gear, perhaps getting a discount for bulk purchasing.

What If the Worst Happens?

If you and your cat are inadvertently separated during a disaster or evacuation, don't panic. And don't wait. Start searching for him immediately. After a disaster, shelter personnel and pet rescuers are often allowed into the affected area to search for lost or injured animals. Be sure searchers know your cat is missing, and give them a clear, recent photo of your cat, and all contact information for you, including backup phone numbers. Be persistent. After a disaster, displaced cats continue to arrive in shelters for weeks and sometimes months. And don't give up. After the massive fires in Oakland, California, it was nearly a year before some cats and their owners were finally reunited.

Your Feline-First-Aid Kit

Pack your feline first-aid kit in a sturdy, waterproof, portable container. You might need to take it with you in a hurry; for example, while evacuating your home during a disaster. Every few months, check the contents and replace anything that's been used or that has an expired date. Check the flashlight bulb and batteries, too. Keep a supply of several old, clean towels and rags with the kit, perhaps in a large plastic bag or canvas tote bag.

Always store your first-aid kit out of the reach of children and cats!

Keep emergency supplies handy. (Depiction of individual products does not imply endorsement by The Humane Society of the United States)
(FRANTZ DANTZLER)

CONTENTS INFORMATION

- clear, recent photo of each of your cats, showing any distinctive markings
- copies of prescriptions for medications your cat is taking
- extra collar with ID tags
- feline first-aid manual
- feline medical-reference book, with diagrams

- medical records and descriptions of each of your cats
- phone numbers for local emergency animal hospital(s)
- veterinarian's phone number, and after-hours or pager number

SUPPLIES

- absorbent cotton cloths (like handkerchiefs) to help stop bleeding
- activated charcoal tablets
- adhesive tape, one-half-inch and one-inch widths
- antibiotic ointment for eyes and skin (Neosporin®, neomycin, bacitracin)
- antidiarrhea medication, cat-safe
- baking soda
- bandage scissors
- cat muzzle
- cornstarch or bar of cat-safe, unscented soap (for nail-clipping errors)
- cotton-tipped swabs
- elastic bandage and fasteners
- Elizabethan collar
- flashlight, small, plus extra bulb and batteries
- gauze bandage rolls, one- and two-inch widths
- gauze pads, small and large
- grooming tools (brush, comb) for cat
- hair-ball remedy
- harness and leash (if your cat is accustomed to these)
- heavy, thick gloves
- hot-water bottle
- hydrogen peroxide, 3 percent
- magnifying glass
- mineral oil
- nail clippers (for clipping nails)
- needle-nose pliers, small
- nonstick wound pads, variety of sizes
- nonsting iodine solution (dilute with water) for cleaning wounds
- 1 percent hydrocortisone cream
- paper towels
- petroleum jelly
- plastic cups
- plastic eyedropper
- plastic or rubber gloves
- premoistened antibiotic towelettes (for human cleanup)
- rectal thermometer (preferably digital)
- rounded-tip sterile cotton balls
- rubber gloves
- rubbing alcohol
- safety pins
- scissors, with safely rounded tips
- sewing needles
- splints (old magazines, sticks)
- triangle bandages
- tweezers, square tip
- wire snips, small
- wooden tongue depressors

CHAPTER 18

Life Changes

THE FELINE FEAR OF CHANGE

Cats are highly intelligent, adaptable, and flexible creatures who nonetheless often do poorly with change. Your cat regards any change in his familiar, comfortable circumstances as a possible threat to his survival. He's highly territorial and sensitive to potential threats to his resource base. Life changes that are pleasant, welcome, and thrilling to us can be deeply unsettling to our cats.

Understanding how your cat perceives change is half the battle. One of your tasks as a responsible cat owner is to sensitively shepherd your cat through the sometimes scary and unsettling changes in your household, routines, and life. Often, times of change are times when our attention is focused anywhere but on our cat's feelings. Paying mindful attention to your cat's needs, feelings, and sensitivities during times of change—whether difficult and painful, or pleasant and thrilling—is part of the Feline Covenant.

New Baby, Old Myths

In chapter 3, we demolished the old myth that cats suck the breath from babies. But common sense, and consideration for the safety, health, and happiness of both baby and cat, still require sound judgment. If you're considering adopting a cat or kitten and your household includes an infant, it might be best to wait a few years until your youngster is ready to interact safely and comfortably with a cat.

If you already have a cat and are expecting a baby, you'll likely hear advice from everyone from your physician to your friends and relatives that you should give away your cat before the baby arrives. For owners who consider their cats as disposable or as convenience pets, this may seem acceptable. But no responsible cat owner who has formed a loving bond with a cat is willing to simply toss him out because life in the household is about to change!

Unless your circumstances are very unusual, there are no valid health reasons for giving up your cat because a baby is on the way. Physicians usually advise pregnant women to delegate litter-box cleanup to a spouse or other family member, because of the small risk of toxoplasmosis. Even though infection from the parasite *Toxoplasma gondii* is relatively rare, its possible effects on your developing fetus are serious enough to call for caution.

Most cases of toxoplasmosis are caused by eating undercooked meats, particularly lamb and pork. Unpasteurized dairy products and raw, unwashed vegetables are other potential sources of infection. In rare instances, infection can occur through the ingestion of soil contaminated with the parasite's oocysts. Get someone else to handle litter-box maintenance, and always wear gloves while gardening. If you've lived with cats all or most of your life, chances are excellent that you've already developed immunity to toxoplasmosis.

Planning, preparation, and sensitive attention to your cat's needs and feelings can insure that he and your new baby will be happy, healthy housemates. Recent research has shown that the presence of a cat in the household can even help protect your baby from allergies. A study of seven-year-olds raised from birth with a cat (or dog) showed they had less allergic sensitivity than those who had had no early contact with pets!

Preparing for Changes

Start early to prepare your cat for the baby's arrival. Gradually accustom him to the new sounds, smells, sights, and activities he'll experience. As you acquire clothing, equipment, baby furniture, and other supplies, let your cat see, smell, and touch them.

Engage all his senses as he learns about these new stimuli in your home. Ideally, the new items will lose their mystery, novelty, and potential threat (in the cat's mind) before the baby arrives.

Scent

Early in your pregnancy, or several months before the baby is to arrive, start using baby powder, baby oil, and baby lotion yourself. Let your cat come to associate those scents with your presence, with extra cuddling and attention, and with tasty food treats. Let your cat become accustomed to the scent of baby formula and other baby-specific odors.

Vision

Show your cat the room you're preparing for the baby and let him see the clothes, blankets, furniture, and supplies. At first, let him explore the room freely, so that it holds no mystery (and thus, less attraction). As your due date nears, convert the room to a cat-free zone, while providing some irresistible attractions (a new cat tree, a snacking garden of fresh wheat sprouts, a new bird feeder just outside a favorite window) in other parts of the house.

Hearing

Obtain a recording of baby sounds—crying, laughing, giggling—and start by playing it at low volume for a few minutes every day as "background music." (A friend with a baby will likely be happy to make a recording for you.) Over time, play the recording louder and for longer periods, until your cat learns to ignore it. You'll be able to tell because he'll no longer startle or show much of a reaction when the tape starts. Put the tape on a timer so that it plays at random times of the day. Get some cat-safe baby rattles and squeaky toys and let your cat play with them to accustom him to these kinds of sounds.

Activities

As baby time draws closer, engage a friend to visit with a baby. Your cat will likely observe from a discreet distance at first. Let him see you cuddling and interacting with the infant, talking to it and playing with it. While you fuss over the baby, have your spouse or other family member snuggle or play with the cat and give him treats. Then, change places. Ideally, you want your cat to associate the presence of an infant with extra love, attention, praise, and rewards.

Above all, share your joy at the baby's impending arrival with your cat. Cats are very sensitive to the moods and emotions of the people closest to them. Your cat will naturally pick up on your excitement and joy. He'll also be there to help you through those inevitable moments of stress and worry. Share lots of extra time and closeness both to deepen your mutual bond and to reassure your cat that he has a permanent place in your heart.

As soon as your baby is born, send your spouse or another family member home with an article of clothing or a receiving blanket that carries the baby's scent. Let the cat smell this item, or even sleep on it. Once Baby is home, never leave him unsupervised with the cat. Review chapter 11 for tips on providing a safe, happy, harmonious environment that will bring out the best in both your cat and your new baby, and on helping your child and your cat learn to delight in one another's company.

Empty-Nest Cats: When the Children Leave

With the increasing longevity of domestic cats—especially those who enjoy a safe indoors-only lifestyle—a cat adopted during childhood may still be an active, healthy adult when his young human companion is ready to leave home. It's often a wrenching decision for a young adult to leave a cherished feline companion—often even more difficult than the decision to leave home and parents. But most college dormitories and many city apartments don't allow pets, and removing the cat from his comfortable, familiar home environment is usually not in his best interests anyway. Cats are highly attached to their territories, familiar environment, and daily rituals. Removing a cat from a home he knows well is generally a poor idea, unless he's so closely bonded to his owner that neither cat nor person will consider separation and he'll continue to receive optimum care in his new home.

Though the young person will undoubtedly visit as often as he can, the relationship he had long shared with his cat is bound to change. This can be a difficult transition for the young adult, for the cat, and for the cat's new primary companions, usually the parents. If not handled sensitively, it can cause fear, confusion, depression, and even grief for the cat—stressors that, especially in an elderly animal, can cause serious health problems.

If you're a parent whose child has left home, minimize physical changes in your home, especially at first. Leave a few articles of clothing or perhaps a used towel that carries your child's scent around where the cat can sleep on them. If the cat has been accustomed to sleeping with the child, be sure he still has access to the bed, with its comforting, familiar feel, texture, location, and scents.

Keep household routines unchanged. Avoid changes in feeding, grooming, and cleanup schedules. Don't move the litter box. And resist the urge to reclaim the child's room or convert it to another use. Make any changes gradually, and monitor the cat's reaction and moods. Be especially alert for any signs of depression such as apathy, withdrawal from the family circle, and loss of appetite. Keep up the cat's normal exercise and play schedule, and offer as much attention and snuggling as the cat wants.

New Spouse, Partner, or Housemate

As with any change in your cat's life, take it slow. Don't haul your cat out from under the bed to introduce him to your new boyfriend, girlfriend, or roommate. Let the relationship develop naturally, for the sake of both your cat and your human friend. Keep your expectations realistic. Don't pressure either your cat or the newcomer to become friendly so rapidly that either of them become uncomfortable. Let your cat determine the pace. He may surprise you by pouring on the charm and quickly winning the newcomer's heart!

Be Prepared

Prepare your cat ahead of time for the new resident. Many of the techniques for getting your cat ready for the arrival of a new baby will work equally well for a new spouse or housemate. Borrow an item of well-worn clothing and leave it in a spot your cat frequents for napping to help accustom him to your new friend's scent signature. Keep a box of treats by the door so that the new resident can offer your cat a treat whenever he arrives and leaves. Always keep a positive, upbeat attitude—this relationship *will* work out!

Let the new resident feed your cat. Present this opportunity as a special privilege! It will help them form a mutual bond based around a daily, pleasurable, satisfying activity. If your new friend has little or no experience living with a cat, be sure to let him read this book. Offer to answer any questions your friend may have. Many people, especially those who haven't lived with cats, still believe the old myths we demolished in chapter 3.

Take every opportunity to teach your friend about cats and their behavior. Use your cat's activities and behavior as informal teaching moments. For example, when your cat hops up on your lap and starts to knead and purr, explain how this is a loving gesture reminiscent of the kitten–mother cat relationship.

If the newcomer is bringing cats or other pets of his own, introduce the two groups very slowly and gradually, just as you'd introduce any new pet to the family. (See chapter 6 for tips.) Be sure all animals have a complete veterinary checkup and are given a clean bill of health before you begin introductions, and keep all animals current on their vaccinations. Give each pet plenty of time and daily, loving attention. Never let an old-timer feel he's being supplanted by the new pets in the family.

Each pet should have his own water and food bowls, toys, bed, and other supplies. If you're adding one or more cats to your household, be sure to add enough litter boxes. One per cat, plus one extra, is a good rule. Set up two separate litter-box stations to lessen competitive pressure and remove the potential for bullying. Make sure every cat, new and old, feels his resource base is secure. Demonstrate, by your actions every day, that there's plenty of everything, especially love, to go around.

Do Cats Grieve?

Of course they do! Cats are aware of the absence of a beloved companion, whether human or animal, from their lives. But they have no clear way of distinguishing a permanent loss, such as the death of a human or animal companion, from a temporary separation. Some cats treat every separation, however brief, as a total break and begin to grieve immediately. Others seem to wait long periods for the expected reunion, only gradually coming to the realization that their friend isn't going to come back after all.

Grief and Health

Once you and your cat have forged a close, loving bond, any prolonged absence can seriously affect your relationship and even harm his health.

One of the most common manifestations of grieving in cats is appetite loss or complete refusal to eat—a potentially deadly reaction. Closely monitor a grieving cat. Offer plenty of supportive care and attention. Keep his daily routines as normal as possible, under the circumstances. If you need to be away from home, emphasize to your cat's temporary caretaker how important it is that your cat continue to eat and drink normally. Instruct him to notify the veterinarian at the first sign of trouble.

What If You Die First?

Though we too often outlive our cats, sometimes a cat outlives his owner. What then? Who would step in to care for your cat? Where would he go? Plan carefully for this possibility! If a person who has animals dies suddenly, authorities often turn the animals over to a municipal shelter, where they may be euthanized (humanely destroyed) before the deceased's relatives or friends are even aware of the situation. Don't let this happen to your cat! Designate one or more trusted friends or relatives willing to take in your cat at a moment's notice. Carry on your person, and post prominently in your home, their names and phone numbers.

You can't leave assets directly to your cat in your will. And there's no way to leave a certain sum of money specifically earmarked for his care with any kind of guarantee that the money will indeed be used for that purpose.

If you want to have any control over what happens to your cat after your death, especially if you die suddenly, consult with a competent attorney and write out clear, unambiguous instructions. Carefully choose at least one potential caretaker for your cat. Designate a few backups, just to be sure. These persons should love and understand cats, and be reliable, trustworthy, and in a position to care properly for your cat. Talk to each of your designated cat caretakers ahead of time and secure their permission to name them as potential cat caretakers. Leave a sum of money to your designated caretaker(s), along with clear instructions to use those funds to care for your cat for as long as he lives in a way in which you would approve. Don't leave anything to chance.

Moving Day

Your cat is extremely attached to his accustomed surroundings—the sights, sounds, odors, routines, furnishings, and daily activities of your home. If you're treating him to an indoors-only lifestyle, your home is his whole world. Moving turns this world upside down. Make moving decisions with his needs in mind.

Getting Ready for the Move

The sights, sounds, and disruptions of packing up your household can be disturbing for your cat. Leave his essential equipment—litter boxes, scratching post, favorite bed, feeding area—alone until the last possible moment. Stick to his regular routine as much as possible. Maintain the familiar times for play and meals and the same feeding location.

If you're moving to a different state, check ahead of time to see if you need a veterinary health certificate. If you'll be changing veterinarians, get copies of your cat's medical records well before moving day. Make sure your cat is up-to-date on all his vaccinations.

The Big Day

On moving day, confine your cat to a small room with everything he needs. Include an article with your scent, and a familiar chair, cat bed, or other piece of comforting furniture so that he can relax. Make sure he has a safe place to hide. Post a prominent "Do Not Enter" sign on the door and also verbally warn movers and others to keep out. Play a radio or a soothing tape softly to mask strange voices and scary noises.

During the move, make sure your cat is wearing his collar with full identification, your old and new locations, and the backup phone number of a trusted friend, just in case. If your cat is accustomed to a leash and harness, have him wear his harness during the move. Have the leash ready.

If you are driving to your new home, transport your cat in a sturdy carrier.
(HSUS/MEDIA SERVICES)

If you're driving to your new home, transport your cat in a sturdy carrier in your car. Stop often to offer your cat a chance to use the litter box and drink some water. Be sure the cat carrier is securely closed, and never remove your cat from his safe place. He could panic and be hit by a car, or become permanently lost in an unfamiliar location. Never leave your cat in the car alone—even for a few moments. If your trip will require an overnight stay along the way, seek out and book a room in a pet-friendly hotel or motel. Don't expect to find one at the last minute or after you're already on the road.

If travel to your new location requires an air journey, be sure your cat has any necessary veterinary documents in time for the move. Investigate the policies of various airlines to select the most animal-friendly carrier for your trip. Book your flight early to maximize the possibility of getting a nonstop flight and of transporting your cat right in the passenger cabin with you, under the seat in front of you. If you cat must fly as cargo, book your own travel on the same flight, if possible. Always minimize the time your cat is out of your control. See chapter 16 for tips on both car and airline travel.

At Your New Home

Arrange to have your cat's litter box, food bowls, bed, and other needed supplies arrive in your new home as early as possible. Select a room that won't get much traffic, such as a small bathroom. Install your cat's supplies and equipment. To enhance his comfort and sense of continuity, set up his old, familiar litter box (use the same litter so it will smell familiar), bed, and food and water bowls. Place a few items of well-worn clothing, such as old sweatshirts that carry your scent, in the room. Play a radio or tape softly, and post a large, conspicuous "Do Not Enter—Cat Within!" sign on the door. And verbally warn movers and others to keep out.

Carry your cat, still in his carrier, directly into his safe sanctuary. Don't let him out of the carrier until you know he's securely in his safe room. Feed him at the usual time and offer extra treats and praise. Once the movers have gone and you've restored some of your living arrangements, don't just give your cat the run of your new home. The first night, either keep your cat in his safe room or allow him into your bedroom. (Be sure he has everything he needs right at hand.)

In the following days, as you gradually unpack and settle in, give him more and more freedom within the house. He'll need to thoroughly explore each and every room and closet, sniffing out who's been there before—especially cats. If the previous owners owned a cat, pay particular attention to any areas in which your cat shows a great deal of interest. If he sniffs a corner of a room, then displays the "flehmen" reaction (that odd, open-mouthed cat grimace), he may be detecting an old urine mark. Be ready with a supply of enzyme-based stain-and-odor remover to clean up any old urine-marked areas your cat finds to prevent him from trying to "overmark" them.

If you previously allowed your cat unsupervised access to the outdoors, moving to a new home is the perfect opportunity to introduce him to the pleasures of a safe, indoors-only lifestyle. Review chapter 8 for plenty of reasons your cat will be safer, healthier, and happier indoors. Review chapter 19 for tips on making the big transition.

OLD FRIENDS—YOUR SENIOR CAT

The normal maximum feline life span is about twenty years. Some cats beat those odds; one lived to be thirty-four! The age your cat achieves depends on his luck, genetic makeup, lifestyle, and the care he receives throughout his life. The best way to keep an older cat healthy is to keep him healthy when he's younger.

When is your cat considered a senior? It varies. A six-year-old cat is the physiological equivalent of a forty-year-old human; by the time your cat is fifteen, he's in his mid-seventies in human terms. Your twenty-year-old cat is like a ninety-six-year-old human. Veterinarians generally treat cats about ten and older as seniors. Since senior cats can sicken more rapidly than youngsters, many veterinarians like to see senior cats twice a year instead of once.

Baseline Blood Tests

As your cat approaches his senior years, your veterinarian will likely suggest obtaining a baseline blood panel. "Baseline" simply means values that are normal for your healthy cat. Each of the chemicals and values checked can fall anywhere within a normal range, but each healthy cat's values will vary within that range.

At your senior cat's checkups, your veterinarian will check for enlarged thyroid gland, liver swelling, and heart abnormalities such as murmurs, elevated heartbeat rate, and abnormal heart rhythms. He'll pay particular attention to the size and shape of your cat's kidneys, and check for abdominal swellings, constipation, and other gastrointestinal irregularities.

A lifetime of sound preventive care will make your cat's senior years much happier and healthier. In particular, regular dental care can head off many serious health problems, since so many infections start with poor dental hygiene and deteriorating teeth. To provide your cat the best chance for a healthy old age, start brushing his teeth when he's a kitten. Sterilizing your cat can also prevent a number of diseases that can plague unsterilized cats later in life.

Senior Changes

Especially after he turns ten, any change in your cat's daily habits, food intake, elimination patterns, or behavior calls for a visit to the veterinarian. Cats age gracefully, but they're adept at hiding pain and illness until they're quite sick. In your senior cat, any lump, bump, wound, swelling, increased thirst, change in appetite, drooling, bad breath, or other physical change needs to be looked at immediately.

As your cat gets older, he'll naturally slow down and start to show some of the same signs and symptoms of old age seen in humans. As long as these changes are gradual and don't adversely affect the quality of his daily life, they're perfectly normal. Rapid or dramatic changes always call for immediate attention from your veterinarian, though. Here are some changes to expect as your cat eases into seniorhood:

- weight loss (It's normal for senior cats to lose weight over time. But any rapid or dramatic change may signal serious illness. Weigh your senior cat frequently on a baby scale, and bring any weight loss of more than one-half pound to the attention of the veterinarian. Never ignore weight loss in a senior cat—even if you think it might be a good thing because he was a little pudgy before.)
- increased susceptibility to stress (For the sake of your senior cat's peace of mind and health, minimize stress of all kinds in his environment.)
- decrease in tolerance for changes in routine
- tendency towards constipation, diarrhea, and other digestive upsets (Talk to your veterinarian about switching to a more easily digestible senior diet and more frequent, smaller meals. Many elderly cats prefer "grazing" throughout the day, rather than eating two big meals.)
- decrease in ability to metabolize medication (Make sure any veterinarian who prescribes medications for your cat knows how old your cat is.)
- personality changes, mental confusion, restlessness, memory loss, loss of interest in once-favored toys or activities (Be especially patient with your senior cat. Never laugh at him when he misses a jump or stumbles.)
- cognitive dysfunction, including aggression due to pain or loss of vision, hearing, and sense of smell (In addition to myriad physical changes, aging cats can experience cognitive deterioration that leaves them confused and disoriented.)
- blurring vision; cloudy look to eyes; pupils that turn grayish or bluish
- decreased hearing acuity (Many aging animals lose their upper-range hearing first. If your cat seems to be having trouble hearing you, try speaking in a lower-register tone.)
- decrease in muscle mass and skin elasticity
- increased need for sleep
- decreased ability to regulate body warmth (Be sure your cat has plenty of warm places to sleep. He'll appreciate dozing in the sunshine or by a heating duct, espe-

cially in chilly weather. Provide thick blankets or mats to keep him up off chilly floors. Look in pet-supply stores and catalogs for safe heated cat beds.)

- increased thirst (This can be a sign of several illnesses, including kidney problems. Alert your veterinarian. Many senior cats appreciate a "cat fountain" with an electric recirculating pump for access to fresh running water whenever they want it. This can encourage them to drink enough to get the moisture they need to flush their kidneys.)

- dry thinning coat, flaky skin (As your cat ages, he may need help with his regular grooming. Offer gentle assistance.)

- teeth yellow and worn down, possibly causing trouble chewing crunchy food (If your cat is having trouble eating, and your veterinarian has ruled out medical causes, offer a canned food formulated especially for senior cats. Senior foods are usually easier to chew and digest.)

- stiffness in joints, arthritis, slower moving (A safe electric heating pad (one made especially for pets) can help alleviate stiffness and sore muscles. Your senior cat may appreciate a carpeted ramp or a few steps up to his favorite perches.)

As your cat ages, he may need modifications to his environment to help him with his daily routine. If your arthritic cat cannot negotiate the high sides to enter his litter box, cut one side low enough for him to enter but high enough so that litter remains in the box.
(FRANTZ DANTZLER)

- drop in efficiency of immune system; greater susceptibility to infection (Be especially alert for signs of bladder and urinary-tract infections, such as straining and crying in the litter box, blood in the urine, or passing only minute drops of urine. These symptoms require immediate veterinary attention.)

- decrease in efficiency of major organ functions (especially kidneys)

Diseases of Age

Be alert for these symptoms in your senior cat, especially if they appear suddenly or are dramatic. They require immediate veterinary care:

- *Heart disease* lethargy; weakness; irregular or rapid breathing; abdominal swelling (These can be signs of congestive heart failure.)
- *Hyperthyroidism* loss of weight even though eating well; excessive thirst and urination; unkempt, ratty coat and general appearance; nervousness and hyperactivity

- *Arthritis* limping; hot or swollen joints; stiffness upon waking; greatly reduced activity level; hesitation to jump or run (*Never give your cat aspirin or any other pain or arthritis drug designed for humans.* Always consult your veterinarian for a cat-safe arthritis remedy.)
- *Kidney disease/kidney failure* loss of appetite; excessive thirst and urination, or complete lack of urination; weight loss; vomiting and diarrhea; seizures and stumbling; extreme listlessness
- *Cancer* abnormal swellings or growths that get larger; sores that don't heal; appetite loss and weight loss; bleeding of unknown cause; offensive mouth or body odor; difficulty swallowing or eating; persistent lameness; difficulty with any normal body function such as breathing, defecating, urinating, or walking, especially when combined with other symptoms
- *Dental disease* refusal to eat; mouth pain; bad mouth odor; pawing at mouth; drooling
- *Diabetes mellitus* increased eating accompanied by weight loss; excessive drinking and urination; behavior changes; litter-box "errors"
- *Liver disease* refusal to eat for forty-eight hours or more; persistent loss of appetite; jaundice (yellowish tinge on skin inside ears and whites of eyes); listlessness; vomiting and diarrhea

Saying Good-bye

Aging, and the changes it brings, are a normal part of life, not cause for despair. As long as your senior cat is happy and comfortable and enjoys a good quality of life, there's no reason he can't remain at home with you right up until his last moments.

Your most difficult decision, as a responsible cat owner and a humane person, is deciding when your cat's quality of life has deteriorated to the extent that keeping him alive is actually unkind. Many people have a deep fear of death and are willing to spend huge amounts of health-care resources in the last few days and even hours of life—in a vain attempt to cheat death. Although a human has every right (as long as he's consciously able to do so) to insist that every possible medical intervention be performed to prolong his life, it may not be fair to impose that same standard on our cats.

Veterinary medicine can offer many of the same life-saving and life-prolonging treatments available to humans. But while a human can make the decision to trade off pain or intrusive procedures for a few more days or weeks of life, your cat can't. Think very hard before subjecting your elderly, ill cat to painful, confusing, invasive, and "heroic" life-prolonging interventions. Are you doing it for your cat—or for yourself?

Letting Nature Take Its Course

If your cat is fading slowly and gradually, but isn't in pain and still enjoys a reasonable good quality of life for his age and condition, let nature take its course. As long as your cat can get around, groom himself, take care of his own bodily care functions, and is eating and drinking—even at a diminished level—take the opportunity to enjoy the gift of extra time you have together. He may need some assistance from you in his daily activities. He may need medications, fluid therapy, or other treatments you can administer at home. Pay close attention to how well he tolerates these interventions and to how much he seems to be enjoying life and your company. Be alert for rapid or dramatic changes and signs of pain, but let him enjoy life as much as possible.

Euthanasia: How Will You Know When It's Time?

There's no one right way to know when it's time to let your cat go. It's a difficult decision that you, your family, and your veterinarian must make together, paying special attention to the condition and needs of your cat. If your cat is suffering from intractable pain or has taken such a sudden or dramatic turn for the worse that there's no chance for a turnaround, your choice is clear. But in many cases, it's not that clear-cut. Here are some factors to consider.

- Has your cat stopped eating? Is he experiencing persistent vomiting, diarrhea, or other painful and distressing symptoms? Has he lost control of his bowels and bladder? These symptoms, especially together, indicate that your cat is suffering.
- Is your cat suffering from a terminal illness, such as cancer, in which only very expensive or invasive treatment can prolong his life? If you can't afford to follow through with the entire course of treatment, or if the treatment will only buy your cat a small amount of additional time, it may not be fair to your cat to begin the treatment at all.
- Does your cat require more-or-less constant medical intervention to remain alive? If so, it might be kindest to let him go peacefully.
- Is your cat crying or vocalizing constantly, as if in confusion, distress, or pain? Does

he cry out when trying to eat, walk, or use the litter box? When these basic life activities become painful or extremely difficult, it may be time.

- Has your cat retreated from all social contact, perhaps into a closet, the basement, or under a bed? When a cat knows he's near death, he'll often withdraw in this manner. This withdrawal is a clear sign he's ready to go.
- Has your cat lost the ability to walk around independently, to groom himself, or to eat and to use the litter box independently?

No one can make this difficult decision for you. Many cat owners who had dreaded this decision report that when the right time finally came, it was clear their cat was ready for peaceful, gentle release. Once you make the decision, take your time saying good-bye in your own way. Spend those last few days or hours with your cat in whatever way is most meaningful to you personally. Let children and other family members have a chance to say good-bye in their own ways, too.

Your cat has no real understanding or fear of death. He does, however, understand pain and loss of personal dignity. He'll suffer no emotional trauma or spiritual doubt about his impending death, but he will pick up on your mood and feelings. Although it will be very difficult, try to keep a loving, positive attitude throughout. Your loving support will help your cat feel safe and cherished right up to his last moment.

Details to Consider

Euthanasia is a term derived from the Greek for "good death." In the case of cats, an overdose of barbiturate is given by injection and is followed by painless, rapid unconsciousness, cardiac or respiratory arrest, and death. Once you've made the decision to euthanize your cat, there are several other decisions you need to make:

- Do you want the euthanasia procedure done in your home or at the veterinarian's office? Some people opt for home euthanasia so their cat will be in his safe, familiar surroundings until the end. Others would rather not. It's up to you. Find out if your veterinarian will make a house call for this purpose. Home euthanasia is much easier on many cats, as it avoids subjecting your cat to the stress of travel and to the strange smells and sounds of the clinic.
- If you want the procedure done at your veterinarian's office, schedule the appointment for early in the morning or late in the day, when the clinic is least busy. Some veterinarians offer special "comfort rooms." These rooms are quiet, comfortable,

and away from the bustle of the regular clinic environment, allowing a cat owner to share his cat's last moments of life in a quiet, dignified, supportive, safe setting.

- Request that your cat be given an injection to sedate him. He won't be aware of the final intravenous injection.

- Do you want to be present throughout the euthanasia procedure? Some cat owners do; others opt to stay just until their cat is sedated, then leave. Again, it's up to you. This is a very personal decision. If you have any questions or concerns about the actual procedure, the drugs used, how your cat might react, or what to expect, ask your veterinarian beforehand. She may also have informational materials you can review ahead of time.

You can have your cat's remains buried in a pet cemetery.
(FRANTZ DANTZLER)

- What do you plan to do with your cat's remains? There are several options. Your veterinarian can have your cat cremated individually, or in a group with other pets. You can have your cat's ashes returned to you, or buried in a pet cemetery. Or you can bury your pet's body in a pet cemetery, or in your own yard (although local regulations may prohibit this in some areas). Ask your veterinarian about your options and think them through beforehand.

THE HUMANE SOCIETY OF THE UNITED STATES COMPLETE GUIDE TO CAT CARE

WHEN YOUR CAT IS GONE

Grieving for your cat is natural and normal. The human-animal bond is one of the strongest, deepest relationships many people ever form. Unfortunately, grieving for a pet is still not fully accepted in our society. You may find you have to endure some harsh and extremely unkind comments from relatives, friends, and coworkers who simply don't understand the depth of your feelings over your tremendous loss.

Guilt is a common, understandable reaction when a beloved pet dies. It's natural to ask such questions as "Could I have done anything differently? Should I have seen sooner that he was so ill? Could I have prevented the illness? Should I have waited longer for euthanasia?" Responsible cat owners, dedicated to their cats' health, happiness, and well-being, feel particularly helpless in the face of a beloved cat's death. But many cat owners torment themselves needlessly, blaming themselves for their cat's pain, suffering, illness, and eventual death. Like grief, guilt is normal and natural, but it can be overwhelming. In some cases, especially if the cat owner doesn't have a source of supportive, understanding help, this guilt can turn into full-blown, health-threatening, long-term depression. If this happens to you, seek out professional counseling and care without delay.

Understanding and help are available. Many schools of veterinary medicine and other organizations offer pet-loss-support hot lines and other services. Ask your veterinarian for a recommendation. Many local veterinary clinics and animal shelters conduct regular pet-loss support groups and offer counseling that can help you both before and after your cat's death.

Getting Through the Pain

Take your time. Give yourself permission to grieve for your cat. Seek out understanding, supportive, cat-loving friends. Talk about your cat. Remember the good times, the funny stories, the cute anecdotes. Talking about your cat will help reinforce those happy memories and keep them alive in your mind.

There's no better way to memorialize your cat than by making a donation in his name to a local shelter or animal-welfare organization. If you adopted your cat originally from a shelter, make a gift to that shelter.

Now What?

Should you rush out and adopt another cat? Probably not. Give yourself time to work through the stages of grieving. Regain your emotional equilibrium before embarking on a new relationship. Take your time—just as you probably knew when it was time for your beloved cat to leave life peacefully, you'll know when you're ready for a new cat. Sometimes, a cat owner might feel that adopting a new cat would be somehow unfair or disloyal to the memory of their departed cat. But wouldn't your cat want you to be happy and to enjoy again a close, loving relationship with a dear feline companion? Of course! Your cat always did want what was best for you!

When you're ready to adopt, be realistic and fair. You'll never find a cat or kitten just like the one you loved and lost. Every cat is an individual right down to the tip of his tail. No cat can ever replace another, and you can't ever replace the dear friend you lost. But you can make a new friend. And yes, you can fall in love again.

CHAPTER 19

Another Cat
on Your Doorstep

NOBODY'S CAT? ARE YOU SURE?

You've seen them: slinking around the Dumpster behind a fast-food joint, dashing down an alley or vaulting a cinderblock wall, disappearing into dense roadside weeds, peering from a broken window in an abandoned building, flashing across the headlights' glare on a busy thoroughfare, stalking a backyard bird feeder, or contemplating infinity on a park bench.

Is that somebody's cat? Whose? Why is he here? Is he in trouble? Lost? Abandoned? Sick? Hungry? Injured? Feral? Should you intervene?

Intervention is a formidable responsibility, fraught with risk and replete with challenging trade-offs. But it can also be rewarding. It calls for common sense, patience, caution, sound judgment—and soul-searching. It can seem overwhelming. But you *can* help—one cat at a time.

Although each situation is unique, always take a logical, orderly approach:

- Observe the cat.
- Analyze the situation.
- Seek information.
- Locate the owner, if possible.
- Detain and isolate the cat, if appropriate.
- Ensure the cat's health and safety.
- Secure a permanent place for the cat.

Is the cat in imminent danger? A kitten stranded on the median strip of a busy highway definitely is; a sleek, full-grown tabby trotting purposefully through your yard probably isn't. Absent imminent peril, observe the cat as closely as you can. Is he wearing a collar? Does he look sleek and healthy, or scraggly and sick? Are there any obvious wounds, limps, or other signs of distress? Keep a pair of binoculars handy to observe the cat without scaring him away or putting yourself in danger by approaching too closely. Note his coloration, pattern of markings, eye color, fur length, size, and gender. If possible, take a photograph (a zoom lens helps). Write down the date, time, location, and your other observations.

Is that somebody's cat? Whose?
(FRANTZ DANTZLER)

THE HUMANE SOCIETY OF THE UNITED STATES COMPLETE GUIDE TO CAT CARE

Protect Yourself—and Your Cats

Because of rabies and other zoonoses (diseases transmissible from cats or other animals to humans), approaching a strange animal, especially one that looks sick or is acting odd, can be hazardous to your health. If you must remove a cat from imminent peril, wear thick gloves and cover all exposed skin. A frightened or injured cat might lash out at you unexpectedly.

After handling any unknown cat, wash your hands and all other exposed skin thoroughly with antibacterial soap before going near your own cats. It's a good idea to change your clothes, too. Never expose your own cats to blankets, carriers, food bowls, or other supplies that have been touched by a stray or unknown cat.

If you see a cat in danger but feel the situation is beyond your ability to intervene—active abuse, a desperately ill cat, a cat trapped in a collapsed or burning building or on a rock in the middle of a raging river—summon aid from your local animal-control agency or police department.

Is he in trouble? Lost? Abandoned?
(HSUS/RONALD MCNEES)

Are You New in the Neighborhood?

Let's look at a common situation: an unknown cat shows up in your neighborhood. You have two tasks that can call upon your skills as an observer, sleuth, and diplomat:

1. Determine if the cat belongs to someone or is unowned (stray) or never owned (feral).
2. Locate the owner or find a permanent, secure place for the cat.

If the cat is friendly, approachable, and in reasonably good shape, or is wearing a collar, you can tentatively assume that he belongs to someone, or did until recently. If the collar has tags, you're in luck. There may be a phone number or other identification. Some cats have had a microchip carrying a unique identifier code implanted between their shoulder blades. Some shelters and veterinarians have the equipment to retrieve information from the chip.

Seek information from neighborhood children (who spend lots of time outdoors) and neighbors who are home all day. Ask about repeated sightings and behavior patterns: does the cat come around every afternoon, then disappear? Weather and the surrounding environment should figure prominently in your analysis. The case of a healthy-looking cat traipsing through a rural woods in summertime is less urgent than that of a thin young kitten lost on an urban street corner in a snowstorm.

Whose Cat Are You?

It's critically important to realize that not every unknown, wandering cat is a stray in need of rescue. Some cat owners believe strongly in giving their cats the freedom of the streets. By hustling a cat directly to a shelter, you may be endangering the future of someone's beloved pet. And by bundling the cat into your car and taking him home, you may upset his routine and completely disorient him.

Use the phone. Call neighbors, local veterinarians, and other resource persons. If you live in a small town, ask police officers or town office personnel—who usually know everyone and everything, including who owns animals, and who might be looking for a lost pet. Call local shelters to see if anyone has been looking for a lost cat similar to the one you've found. Describe the cat and the exact location where you saw him. Check local bulletin boards for "Lost Cat" posters and the local paper's "Lost Pet" column. But don't assume the cat's owner is frantically looking for him. Some owners wait days or even weeks before initiating a search for a missing cat.

Once you locate the owner, the case should be closed with a happy reunion. But that is not always the case, unfortunately. Confronted with his missing pet, the owner may be anything but grateful. He may be resentful, chagrined, accusatory, or even hostile. Perhaps he transported his unwanted cat out of the area, and, in some mysterious feline manner, the cat found his own way back. Perhaps the owner was relieved when his neglected or misbehaving cat disappeared. Perhaps the cat has been left behind by a child who left home—and whose parents don't want the bother or responsibility of a cat. Maybe the cat is ill, and the owner can't afford veterinarian bills. Your diplomatic skills could be sorely tested. If the owner refuses responsibility, your only humane course is to proceed as if the cat were a true stray.

Decision Time

Once a cat's homelessness has been established beyond a reasonable doubt—a process that can take time—other decisions still loom. If the cat has a "tipped" ear (a tiny but noticeable bit of the ear tip cut off cleanly) or a tagged ear, he may have come from a managed feral-cat colony. Locate the colony managers and let them know you have the cat. Or the cat may be part of an unmanaged or formerly managed feral colony—a colony whose presence may be unwanted by its neighbors.

If the cat is a solo stray, should you bring him to a shelter? Which one? Should you adopt him yourself? Find him a home elsewhere? Is a foster home an option? Or should you sterilize and vaccinate him and release him near the location where you found him? Don't try to solve the problem alone, especially if it involves an unmanaged group of feral cats. Contact a responsible animal-welfare or cat-rescue organization for advice and assistance.

In some areas, you must, by law, take any true stray to an animal shelter, where he will have a chance of being reunited with his owner. Once the cat has remained in lost and found for the time required by law, he can be put up for adoption if he's healthy. Many shelters allow the Good Samaritan who brought the cat to the shelter to place a "finder's hold" on the animal. This means that you may apply to adopt the cat after he's fulfilled the time mandated for his owners to claim him. And if you can't keep him and aren't knowledgeable about screening potential adopters, it's best that he be left to the professionals at the animal shelter. Unfortunately, some shelters must euthanize cats because there are simply not enough homes or financial resources to care for them.

A Cat in the Hand . . . ?

If your next move is to safely detain and isolate the cat, you'll need—in addition to a sturdy carrier—a secure place, completely separate from your own cats and equipped with all the necessities: food, water, cat bed, litter box, and assorted accessories. (None of this equipment should be used again until the stray cat is given a clean bill of health and until everything has been thoroughly cleaned and disinfected.) Getting the cat into the carrier may be as simple as carefully picking up a friendly feline and confining him or as complex as several attempts with a humane trap.

If you decide on trapping, obtain a sufficiently large humane box trap. (You can often borrow one from your local animal shelter or rescue group.) Plan ahead: what will you do with the cat once he's trapped? If you plan to take him to a shelter, don't set the trap on a night before a day when the shelter is closed. Closely supervise and monitor your trap. Pay attention to the weather. Never expose a trapped cat to extreme heat, cold, wind, or rain. And remember: a trapped cat is highly stressed and should be considered dangerous. Cover the trap with a blanket to lessen his fright and stress (allow for air circulation, and don't let the cat get overheated), and keep him trapped for as little time as possible.

If you do plan to keep the cat or place him yourself, your first priority is a complete veterinary examination, including tests for feline leukemia (FeLV) and other diseases, followed by sterilization. *No stray cat should ever be rehomed before this all-important procedure is done.* If you bring the cat to a shelter, tell shelter personnel as much as possible about the cat and where and when you found him. If you know who the former owner was, tell the shelter personnel.

Another Cat for You?

Should you adopt the cat yourself? Be honest, realistic, and sensitive to the needs of your human and feline family. Each household has a "feline-carrying capacity" beyond which it may be unwise or unhealthy—for humans and cats alike—to go. Review chapter 5 before making your decision.

No matter how much you love cats, and how badly this one needs a home, don't make the mistake of adopting too many cats.

If you can't keep the cat yourself, try to place him in a secure home with someone you know—someone who's willing to take responsibility and make a commitment to the cat's permanent well-being. Never place a "Free to Good Home" advertisement. Work through a responsible shelter or rescue organization or people you know and trust.

THE TRAGEDY OF QUASI-OWNERSHIP OF CATS

The "not really my cats" of the United States live in a twilight world of quasi-ownership. They're fed, given names and nicknames, perhaps even let into homes some of the time, maybe even taken to the veterinarian when they're very sick or obviously injured. "But they're better off than if no one was feeding them," say their well-meaning food providers. Perhaps.

Feeding Strays—Should You or Shouldn't You?

At least 15 percent of American households regularly feed stray cats. Is this a good idea? From the cat's perspective, it probably seems like it. And folks who put out those bowls of discount cat chow likely feel they're doing a good deed. But by feeding—without accepting full responsibility for—one or more stray cats, you can cause inadvertent harm to the cats.

The tragedy of overpopulation

The cats you're feeding may not be sterilized. The extra nutrition you're providing them allows them to have more, and healthier, litters of unwanted kittens more often, adding greatly to the tragedy of feline overpopulation.

An ever-growing problem

As your quasi-owned cats multiply and continue to live around your home because of the stable food source, you might find yourself with a full-fledged colony of stray, feral, semiferal—and reproducing—cats. Unless you take positive steps to manage the colony and curtail its growth, this could become not only a financial burden, but a neighborhood nuisance and even a public health menace.

It's important to know whether "part-time" cats you're feeding are strays or true ferals. If they're reasonably friendly and approachable, and seem friendly (if cautious) around people, they're probably *strays*—cats who were once owned but have been abandoned or become lost. But if the cats are extremely wary and even unapproachable, seeming to melt away into invisibility when people are about, they're more likely *feral cats*—cats who were never owned, and who were born to either stray or feral mothers. The problems of handling and managing groups of truly feral cats are much more complicated and difficult than the problems of handling strays.

Threat of illness and death to your "owned" pets

If quasi-owned cats don't receive regular veterinary care and vaccinations, they could catch and spread contagious diseases rapidly among the group, causing tremendous suffering and painful death. If you have cats of your own (that is, cats for whom you acknowledge full responsibility and ownership), ill strays could pass disease on to your own cats.

A Whole Colony?

If you've been feeding a large group of mostly feral, unhandleable cats, don't try to resolve the problem alone. Help is available! Seek advice from humane organizations and cat-rescue groups. They'll advise you on the pros and cons of feral cat colony siting, handling, care, and long-term management. Above all, make sure the colony stabilizes in size and that every cat is sterilized, safe, and healthy.

Food Is Not Enough

Quasi-ownership is a breach of the Feline Covenant. It's a failure of responsibility. You're failing every cat you feed but don't claim as your own. Take the plunge. Cat food is not enough. Love is not enough. An on-again, off-again friendship is not enough. Every cat deserves a loving, safe, permanent home and a committed, caring owner—not just the occasional bowl of chow and a cute nickname. Give that stray a chance to place his paw print on your heart.

BRINGING A CAT INDOORS TO STAY

OK, you've taken a deep breath and made the big decision: this cat—a former stray or your own indoor-outdoor cat—is coming indoors to stay! How will you convince your big, active, roaming guy, after years of wandering unsupervised, or of twenty-four-hour access to his cat flap, to make the big switch? How will you help him shift his focus from his old outdoor haunts and pursuits to his new safe, enriched indoor environment—and his deepening relationship with you and your family?

Attitude Adjustment and Strategic Planning— Essential First Steps

Your *attitude* is critical to your—and his—success. For cats, just as for people, habits, even unhealthy ones, can be hard to break. Believe that what you're doing is best for your cat, and your love and concern for him will help smooth over any rough spots in the transition.

Enlist the support and cooperation of everyone in your household. Discuss your plans, invite everyone to suggest and help implement cat-proofing and environment-enrichment ideas, and go shopping for new cat toys together. Discuss and practice door discipline—particularly important with children. (See chapter 6.)

What will your cat rules be? Decide together. Will he have the run of the entire house? Or will some rooms be cat-free zones? Where will litter boxes be located? Who's responsible for daily cleaning? Where will the cat eat? Where will he sleep? Will he be allowed in bedrooms at night?

Ready, Set, Charge It!

Is the cat you're bringing in from the cold your own cat (not a former stray)? If he's been spending any time indoors, chances are you already have a climbing-and-scratching post, a selection of toys, and other feline necessities. But if you don't, go shopping. Review chapter 6 for cat-proofing strategies and supplies.

Cold Turkey—or the Gradual Approach?

Whether you plan an all-at-once transition or a more gradual approach, start right away. Looming bad weather may be to your advantage, as spending time outdoors will seem less attractive to your cat than usual. By the time fair skies return, your cat—with planning and a little luck—will have happily settled into his new life and can enjoy the lovely weather in his cat-safe screened enclosure. (See chapter 9 for ideas!) If there's an imminent threat to your cat's life or well-being as long as he retains unsupervised outdoor access, you don't have the luxury of a gradual approach.

Some cats adjust instantly and happily to an indoors-only lifestyle. Many cat experts recommend the all-at-once approach as the easiest way to get through the hardest part of the transition quickly. If you choose this cold-turkey approach, be aware that any backsliding can make the transition much lengthier and tougher. Cats respect and respond well to consistency. Once you declare the outdoors off-limits, and your cat escapes even once, he'll be less likely to take your determination seriously.

If the situation permits, and your cat is accustomed to twenty-four-hour freedom to come and go, it might be best to try a gradual transition. If your cat uses a cat flap, start to close it off before dusk and reopen it well after daybreak. Veterinarians maintain that much of the trouble cats meet, whether in animal, automotive, or other form, comes by dark. By keeping your cat indoors during his most instinctively active hunting times—dawn and dusk—you'll lessen one of his major motivations for being outdoors.

During these dusk and dawn hours when the hunting urge is strongest, engage your cat in vigorous, interactive play. A rousing pounce-and-capture session just before breakfast and dinner will help him associate his new indoor environment with pleasant company, exhilarating fun, and anticipation and enjoyment of a tasty meal. This is most important during the first critical few weeks of the transition—but don't neglect playtime once your cat is settled indoors. These new rituals and routines will become very important to him, and he'll look forward to them with eager anticipation.

The Transition—Patience, Positive Feelings, Persistence

As your cat gradually adjusts to his new environment and routines, expect a certain amount of grumbling. Commiserate—cheerfully and with a positive, loving, sympathetic attitude. Extra attention, love, and playtime will help keep his mind off the call of the moonlit streets. If he seems unusually restless, especially at night, confine him to an interior room (with everything he needs, of course) where he'll be less likely to be aroused by scents, sounds, and sights of the outdoors.

Every cat is an individual. In making this big transition, your cat's experience will vary depending upon his temperament, age, gender, activity level, and personality. Use your own judgment, and let your cat's reactions guide you.

During the transition process, observe your cat carefully—especially for signs of stress or undue unhappiness. By catching potential problems early, you'll not only make the transition easier, but also prevent more serious potential problems, like inadvertently established misbehavior patterns.

Unfortunately, a few cats—determined wanderers who've spent years outdoors—seem to have a great deal of trouble adjusting to an indoors-only life. If he starts spraying, urinating, defecating away from his litter box; endlessly scratching at the door; howling, becomes unusually aggressive, or refuses to eat, take your cat to the veterinarian. If medical causes for the problem are ruled out, your veterinarian can prescribe a short course of certain types of mild tranquilizers or other drugs. Along with a sensitively designed behavior-modification program, these drugs can help smooth the transition for "problem adjusters."

Never attempt to diagnose and medicate your cat yourself. Your veterinarian has the skill and experience to evaluate the situation and select the correct medication, dose, and duration of treatment. No medication will provide a magic quick fix, though. Your cat will still need your understanding, support, and patience—and you'll need to offer extra attention and playtime, and fine-tune his environment to maximize his comfort and sense of well-being.

CHAPTER 20

Humane Education:
Be an Everyday Activist for Cats

THE PROBLEMS

Relaxing in your easy chair, your own dear cat purring in your lap, it's easy to forget that not every cat enjoys a life as safe, happy, and healthy as the one you provide him. But part of the Feline Covenant is reaching out, beyond your own cat and your own home, and making a difference in the lives of felines everywhere. The problems are huge, serious, and pressing. But you *can* make a difference: one day, one person, one life, one cat at a time. Start right now. Do it for your own cat and for all the noble feline tribe.

Feline Overpopulation

When there are millions more domestic cats born each year than homes—any homes—can be found for, when thousands of cats owners forget to have their cats sterilized ("Oops!") or "want him to have a little fun first," or "want her to have just one litter" because she's so special, or to make her a "better pet," or so the kids can see the miracle of birth—it's the cats and kittens who suffer. But think also of the legions of shelter workers—caring people who love cats yet must spend endless days killing them. They do the dirty work behind closed doors for a society that can't or won't be bothered to prevent feline overpopulation. When life is so cheap, we all suffer. We all lose.

Whose fault is it? Every cat owner who fails to get his cat sterilized before that cat fathers or bears kittens is at fault. What can you do? First, set a good example: make sure your own cat is spayed or neutered. Talk to friends, neighbors, and relatives who own cats. Find out if their cats have been sterilized. If not, ask why. Perhaps a bit of gentle myth-busting, or a timely reminder from you, is all it will take. For tips on what to say, review chapter 3.

Support and promote free and low-cost spay and neuter services in your community. Support the annual "Spay Day U.S.A." sponsored each February by the Doris Day Animal Foundation (227 Massachusetts Avenue, NE, Ste. 100, Washington, D.C. 20002-4963; www.ddaf.org/DDAF/SpayDay). Ask your own veterinarian to participate in spay and neuter clinics, if she doesn't already. Looking for a unique gift for a friend or relative? How about a gift certificate for spay or neuter surgery for their cat?

The Tragedy of Feral Cats

It's estimated that there are over 60 million never-owned, or feral, cats in the United States. Often gathering in colonies around a persistent food source (such as a city Dumpster or college cafeteria), these cats, for the most part, live short, miserable lives and die tragically, leaving behind only the next generation of kittens to continue the cycle of tragedy.

In some places, though, caring folks have banded together to try to improve the lives of these all-but-forgotten felines. Once a colony is identified, the cats are humanely trapped, one at a time. Each cat is given a complete veterinary checkup, including tests for diseases. Cats who are very ill or who carry transmissible diseases such as feline leukemia (FeLV) are euthanized. Healthy cats are vaccinated and sterilized. Kittens still young enough to be socialized to humans, and older cats who seem approachable and tameable, are sheltered and prepared for adoption.

The others—the true ferals who will never be tame enough to be adoptable—have their ears "tipped" or tagged for easy identification later and are released at the original colony site. The colony is then managed by a team of permanent guardians who provide daily food and water, stay alert for injuries and needed veterinary care, insure that the colony doesn't grow larger, monitor and correct any problems that arise, and remove kittens for adoption before they become unapproachably feral.

Proponents of this approach to feral-cat-colony management (called TTVARM, for "trap, test, vaccinate, alter, release, and manage") can point to many successes and thousands of feline lives saved and improved. TTVARM and similar approaches should never be thought of as a desirable permanent strategy, though, but only as a means to an end. The ultimate goal is for every kitten birth to be intentional and for each kitten to have a safe, loving home waiting for him or her.

The TTVARM approach is controversial for a number of reasons. Some observers feel that letting the cats remain at large, even fed and monitored, leaves them open to too many perils and diseases. Others look at the dangers to small wildlife and birds in the colony area; even well-fed cats stalk and hunt prey. Some observers see feral colonies as providing a safety valve, endlessly absorbing cats that are born without homes and cats who continue to be abandoned, thus offering tacit societal approval to this irresponsible and inhumane approach to animal life. Still others see these groups of outdoor cats as a possible public-health menace, especially in rabies-endemic areas. To curb the dangers to wildlife, some colony managers have experimented with enclosing the entire colony in a large, screened or fenced-in area.

Many feral colonies start out as groups of strays—cats who have wandered away from home and become lost, or who've been dumped or abandoned by their owners. A few generations later, the colony is truly feral, made up of cats who have never been socialized to humans. Ultimately, preventing this kind of tragedy through responsible ownership is the only humane solution.

Commercial Exploitation and Abuse of Felines

Even in this so-called enlightened modern age, our society still not only condones but often celebrates entertainment and recreational activities and events that exploit cats—especially big cats such as lions, tigers, cougars, and leopards. Taking advantage of the public's fascination with felines, promoters of circuses, roadside menageries, animal-performance events, and bogus "cat sanctuaries" keep cats large and small on display, or make them perform, for paying customers. Too often, the owners of these cats have little or no knowledge of the special needs of the animals in their care. And too often, when the cats become ill, difficult to handle, or unable to perform, they're dumped on one of the few real cat sanctuaries that have the knowledge and expertise to care for these exploited and abandoned animals. The dumped ex-performers are often plagued with severe medical and behavioral problems.

How can you help? Refuse to patronize such establishments and events. If you become aware of a roadside zoo or performing animal show that may be exploiting cats (or other animals), bring it to the attention of humane authorities.

You can also help cats being exploited in other ways. Did you know, for example, that products made from the fur of cats (and dogs) have found their way into the United States in the past? The Humane Society of the United States found that millions of dogs and cats are raised and killed annually for their fur, primarily in China and other Asian nations, by inhumane methods. The fur from these animals has even been used to manufacture fur cat toys and figurines, among other items. Recently, a federal law was passed to prohibit the import, export, or sale in the United States of dog and cat fur that had infiltrated the U.S. market in garments and animal figurines. Become an educated consumer. The Humane Society of the United States urges consumers not to buy fur of any kind other than synthetic, or faux, fur.

Ailurophobia; Cat Hatred and Abuse

Some people have a deep-seated, pathological fear of cats. Called *ailurophobia*, this fear is not the direct threat to cats it might seem at first glance, as most ailurophobes will do almost anything to avoid encountering cats or having anything to do with them. Unwanted by the sufferer, ailurophobia can be very disabling and greatly diminish the quality of life. Ailurophobia can sometimes be largely mitigated, if not totally cured, through a program of gradual desensitization.

A much more serious threat is people who simply hate cats. These people not only wish cats harm, but often go out of their way to hurt and kill cats. Domestic cats are small, vulnerable, and ubiquitous—easy targets for torture, abuse, and cruelty. Too often, society, parents, law-enforcement authorities, and others who should know better still see abuse of cats (and other animals) by children as a normal part of growing up—taking a boys-will-be-boys approach.

What can you do? Insist on strict, unshakable, zero tolerance for even the mildest abuse of cats and other animals. If you have children, or are responsible for teaching children, set a good example every day through your own gentle, respectful treatment of all animals. Intervene at the first sign of even "playful" abuse—poking with sticks, throwing toys at a cat, tail pulling, yelling in the cat's ear—anything at all except gentle, kind, respectful interactions.

Teach children from an early age how to approach a strange cat, how to safely pick up and hold kittens and cats, and how to recognize the warning signs a cat sends when he's had enough. Above all, teach, through your example, actions, interactions, words, and attitude that cats are valuable living beings to be cherished and protected, not toys, ornaments, or momentary diversions to be cast aside when the novelty wears off.

The Humane Society of the United States offers a variety of print materials for activists and others concerned about animal protection.
(HSUS)

THE SOLUTIONS

The problem are vast, and the feline suffering is great. It can feel overwhelming. How can you—just one person—even start to make a difference?

1. Join The Humane Society of the United States. The Humane Society of the United States is the nation's largest animal-protection organization, with almost 7 million members and constituents. The Humane Society of the United States works, through legislative, educational, and investigative means, to improve the lives of all animals here and abroad. Many of The Humane Society of the United States's most active members subscribe to *Humane Activist*, a bimonthly activist newsletter that's free upon request, and monitor HUMANElines, a free, weekly electronic alert presenting succinct information on timely animal issues. Contact The Humane Society of the United States (2100 L Street, NW, Washington, D.C. 20037) or go to the Web site (www.hsus.org) for more information on The Humane Society of the United States's membership and programs.

The National Association for Humane and Environmental Education, a division of The Humane Society of the United States, publishes *Kind News* for children throughout the school year.

(NAHEE)

2. Write letters to the editor of your local, regional, or metropolitan newspapers encouraging cat owners to have their cats spayed and neutered without delay. Include the names and addresses of local veterinarians, shelters, or organizations that sponsor low-cost spay and neuter clinics.

3. Support your local animal shelter—both financially and with your time. Volunteer to work in a local shelter. Shelters need and appreciate all kinds of skills: everything from writing and office work to cage cleaning and cat socializing.

Support your local animal shelter—both financially and with your time.

(FRANTZ DANTZLER)

4. Call a local politician and find out what he or she is doing to protect animals, especially cats, in your area. Start with the board of selectmen, board of aldermen, or mayor's office or a state-assembly member, state legislator, or city council member. Then, move up to your congressman, governor, and senator. Remember, as a constituent, you're their boss.

5. Have you noticed a group of cats hanging around a Dumpster, alley, or parking lot? Perhaps it's a feral colony that has lost its guardian or monitor—or never had one. Alert your local shelter or cat-rescue group to the presence of the cats.

Be an Everyday Advocate

Wherever you go, whatever you do, whomever you speak to, communicate the message of responsible cat ownership. Having read this book, you now know much more about cat care and cat behavior than most cat owners. Share your knowledge! Know someone who's planning on getting his son a "Christmas kitten"? Explain why it's such a bad idea, and suggest alternatives. Know someone who's just adopted a kitten or cat? Suggest some books to read (like this one). Has a coworker been talking about buying a baby bobcat or cougar cub? Tell him why ownership of wild cats is such a bad idea. And remember, you're not alone. Many resources can offer assistance as you spread these responsible, humane messages.

Be creative! There are numerous ways you can get across your message of responsible cat ownership at work, at school, at your place of worship, in the cat-food aisle of the local supermarket, at the pediatrician's office, at the park. Practice on your own family and good friends.

Best of all, you'll find you can celebrate and promote the value of feline life without being a pest or a nag. Emphasize the joy and wonder inherent in a close, loving, lifelong relationship with a cat. Demonstrate how treating your beloved cat to an indoors-only lifestyle helps you to maintain and enhance your special interspecies bond every day, in a million ways, large and small. You'll find that most people, especially cat owners, really want to do the right thing. Too often, they just don't know what the right thing is, or they've been misled by one of those old myths we demolished in chapter 3. Approach them gently, and with the good of their cat—and all cats—firmly in mind. They'll likely end up thanking you for your concern and for the information you offer.

Making a Difference, One Cat at a Time

Loren Eiseley (1907–77) was a naturalist, poet, paleontologist, and essayist who deeply understood the human-animal bond. In his classic essay, "The Star Thrower," (Harvest), Eiseley speaks of how one person can make a difference, even against tremendous odds.

A man wanders, feeling hopeless and overwhelmed by the tragedy of life. On a lonely seashore, he encounters a solitary figure plucking starfish from high on the beach where the tide has abandoned them, and hurling them, one by one, back into the sea.

Feeling even more powerless and dejected then before, the man leaves, telling himself, "The star thrower is a man, and death is running more fleet than he along every seabeach in the world."

But something—the star thrower's quiet dedication and persistence, perhaps—haunts him. He realizes he's been challenged—called upon to make a choice. Returning to the lonely shore, he finds the thrower still returning stars, one by one, to the sea. "I understand," he finally says. "Call me another thrower." And as he hurls a star far beyond the breakers, he muses, "He is not alone any longer. After us there will be others."

Faced with tides of death and oceans of indifference, the Star Thrower made a difference—one star at a time. By living the Feline Covenant, you, too, can make a difference: one person, one life, one cat at a time.

(FRANTZ DANTZLER)

INDEX

body language (*continued*)
  fur and coat, 143
  kneading, 144
  licking, 143
  posture, 143
  rolling on his back, 143–44
  rubbing and head bunting, 143
  tail talk, 142
  whiskers, 142
Body Language and Emotions of Cats, The (Milani), 214
Bordetella bronchiseptica
  vaccinations for, 251
boredom, 141
Britain (and domestic cats), 13
  Victorian age, 16
breeding cats for looks, 33, 35–36
broken bones
  medical emergency and, 270

"carpet scooting," 241
cat beds, 97
cat food. *See* food
cat-safe plants. *See* under plants
cat secrets reveled, 60-61
cat-urine wars, 105–7
cats (choosing and being chosen), 39–57
  adults cats, 48–49
  giving cat away, 56–57
  health and personality, checking, 51–52, 52
  incompatibility, 56–57
  kitten or cat, 47–48
  longhair or shorthair, 50-51
  male or female, 50
  neglected or mistreated cats, adopting, 56
  nose-to-toes once-over, 52–54
  one cat or two, 47, 49–50
  selecting, 39–56
  shelter cats, 45–47
  pedigreed cats, 42, 42–43, 43–44
Catholicism and cats, 14
catnip, 96
cats-only clinics, 182–83
CFA (Cat Fancier's Association), 42

change (feline fear of), 279–96
  babies, 280-82
  death and grief, 284–85
  moving, 285–87
  new spouse, partner, or housemate, 283–84
  senior cats, 288–96
  as a threat, 139–40
  when children leave home, 282–83
chattering, 145
cheap pets, cats as, 27
children (and cats), 159–68, 282–83
  cats as surprise gift, 165–66
  as a child-training aid, 166–67
  introducing cat to, 79–80
  as a reason for ownership, 4–5
  toddlers, 163–65
  "using" a cat, 167–68
  See also babies
China and domestic cats, 13
Chlamydia, vaccinations for, 250
circulation problems
  medical emergency and, 269
claws, body language of, 142–53
clay litter, 100-101
climbing, 89–90
  climbing trees, 92–93
  declawing, 156–57
  height, 93
  See also scratching
clumping litter, 101
coat, checking, 54
coccidia, 203
cold noses and health, 241
Colette, 37, 45
collars, necessity of, 26
common cat courtesy, 82
companionship, 88
  as a reason for ownership, 5
constipation, 234
Cornell Book of Cats, 2nd Edition, The, 214
CPR, medical emergency and, 269
crystal or silica litters, 101

death and cats, 284–85
declawing, 156–57
dental care, 221–22
devil, cats associated with, 14

diarrhea, 233–34
digestive problems, 233–35
Dinictis (Eocene ancestor of cats), 10
disasters, preparing for, 272–75
diseases of age, 290-91
disposable convenience pets
  cats as, 27
dogs
  cats as low-maintenance alternative to, 23
  introducing cats to, 77–78
  versus cats, 30
domestic cats (health and care of), 17–18
domestic cats (origin of), 9–18
  Catholicism and, 14
  Egypt and, 11–13
  feline-human relationship, history of, 11–16
  Great Plague, 15–16
  modern, 16–18
  prehistoric, 9–10
  religious abuse of, 15
  Victorian age, 16
  domestication, 173–74
  domineering cats, 176–77
  Doris Day Animal Foundation, 41, 310

ear medications, 238
ear mites, 226
ears
  checking, 53
  cleaning, 223
  body language of, 142
Egypt
  domestication of cats and, 11, 12
  worship of, 12–13
Eiseley, Loren, 315–16
environment and cat ownership, 6
environmental irritants, 231
euthanasia, 292–94
evacuations and pets, 273–74
evil behavior
  myths concerning, 22
exploitation and abuse, 311–12
eye medications, 239
eyes
  body language of, 142
  checking, 53

INDEX

routine, importance of, 141
rubbing and head bunting
    as body language, 143

safe retreats, 71, 72
scratching, 89–90
    declawing, 156–57
    inappropriate & destructive,
      156–57
    scratch posts, 90-92
    See also climbing
senior cats, 288–96
    baseline blood tests, 288
    diseases of age, 290-91
    euthanasia, 292–94
    grieving, 295–96
    letting nature take its course,
      292
    medical life-prolonging
      interventions, 291–92
    senior changes, 288–90
shelter cats, 45–47
shock, as medical emergency, 268
shy cats, 177–78
size, importance of, 54
sleep, 138–39
Smilodon californicus (saber-tooth
    cat), 10
snacks, 205
sneaky behavior
    myths concerning, 22
socialization, 169–80
    adaptation and, 174
    domestication, 173–74
    domineering cats, 176–77
    fearfulness, 176
    household, acclimating cat to,
      178–80
    of kittens, 171–73
    overdependent, 175
    shy and retiring, 177–78
    uniqueness, dealing with,
      174–75
solitary behavior, 20-21, 116

space bubble, 80-81, 140
"Spay Day U.S.A.," 310
spaying
    affecting size and energy, 24–25
    description of, 245
    importance of, 37, 41
    pediatric, 246
    sterilization, benefits of,
      243–44, 244, 245
    See also neutering; population
spider bites, 230
spouse, cats accepting, 283–84
"Star Thrower, The" (Eiseley),
    315–16
status, as reason for ownership, 4
stray and lost cats, 41, 297–307
    adopting, 304–7
    identifying, 299–300, 300, 301
    protecting yourself and your
      cat, 299
    quasi-ownership of cats, 302–4
    stays, feeding, 303–4
    trapping, 301–2
stress, 140-41
supplements in cat foods, 205
survival ability
    myths concerning, 21

tags, necessity of, 26
tail, checking under, 53
tail talk as body language, 142
tapeworms, 229
temperature, taking a cat's, 239
*Think like a Cat: How to Raise a
    Well-Adjusted Cat* (Johnson-
    Bennett), 213
Thomas, Elizabeth Marshall, 137
Thoreau, Henry David, 31
ticks, 228
training cats, 23
trapping stray cats, 301–2
traveling with cat, 255–61
treats, 205
TV and cats, 107–8

underhanded behavior
    myths concerning, 22
unfriendly behavior, 116
    myths concerning, 20-21
uniqueness of cats
    dealing with, 174–75
urination
    cat-urine wars, 105–7
    cleanup, 105–6, 106–7
    inappropriate, 152, 152–53

vaccinations, 75, 248–51, 251–52
vegetarian diets, 198
veterinarians, 181–96
    alternative health care, 194–96
    attitude, 186
    billing and financial
      considerations, 191–92, 192
    cats-only clinics, 182–83
    evaluating, 185–86
    feline health insurance, 193–94
    importance of, 75–76
    leaving the cat, 191
    prevention, 183
    second opinions, 189–90
    selecting, 183–84
    waiting-room etiquette, 187–89
    when to call, 265–66
Victoria, Queen, 16
vocalization, 144–45, 145–47
vomiting, 233

Wain, Louis, 16
waiting-room etiquette, 187–89
water, 206–7
whiskers, body language of, 142
wildness, 30-31
window seats, 107
Winn Feline Foundation, 17
wool and fabric chewing, 156
worms and bad food, 241

yarn as ideal toy, 25
yowling, 145